Violent Affect

violent affect

affect literature, cinema, and critique after representation

marco abel

University of Nebraska Press
Lincoln and London

Chapter 2 is based on the author's critical essay
"Judgment Is Not an Exit: Toward an Affective
Criticism of Violence with *American Psycho*," which
appeared in *Angelaki* 6.3 (2001): 137–54. A Taylor &
Francis publication, http://www.tandf.co.uk/journals.

Chapter 6 is based on the author's critical essay "Don
DeLillo's 'In the Ruins of the Future': Literature,
Images, and the Rhetoric of *Seeing 9/11*," which ap-
peared in *PMLA* 118.5 (2003): 1236–50.

Library of Congress Cataloging-in-Publication Data
Abel, Marco.
Violent affect : literature, cinema, and critique after
representation / Marco Abel.
p.   cm.
Includes bibliographical references (p.   ) and index.
ISBN-13: 978-0-8032-1118-6 (alk. cloth)
ISBN-10: 0-8032-1118-X (alk. cloth)
1. American fiction—20th century—History and
criticism.   2. Violence in literature.   3. Violence in
motion pictures. I.Title.
PS374.V58A63   2007
813'.509355—dc22   2006103289

Set in Chaparral Pro by Bob Reitz.
Designed by Ashley Johnston.

For Magda and Richard Abel

In memory of Magda Löhr (1909–2006)

Contents

Preface

The violence of sensation is opposed to the violence of the represented (the sensational, the cliché). The former is inseparable from its direct action on the nervous system, the levels through which it passes, the domains it traverses: being itself a Figure, it must have nothing of the nature of the represented object. [Violence] is not what one believes it to be, and depends less and less on what is represented.
—Gilles Deleuze, *Francis Bacon*

I can't help but dream about a kind of criticism that would not try to judge.
—Michel Foucault, "The Masked Philosopher"

Any project that lays claim to the attribute of novelty, let alone "radical" novelty, deserves to be received with immediate suspicion. More often than not, such works turn out to be merely minor (albeit at times important) modifications of familiar arguments (how many more "radical" social constructivist arguments does one have to endure?). Despite my awareness of the danger inherent to what is at least in part a marketing trap—the seductive force of novelty, however superficial, has long functioned as the sales engine of capitalism—I nonetheless proceed by submitting that the following study has indeed something new to offer with regard to its chosen subject matter, images of violence in literature and film. Specifically, what differentiates this book from existing studies of imaged violence such as, for instance, the generally illuminating monographs or collections by Stephen Prince (1998, 2000), Christopher Scharrett (1999), J. David Slocum (2001), Stephen Jay Schneider (2004), or James R. Giles (2006) pertains to its basic methodological—indeed ontological—assumption, namely, that signaletic materials of any kind are not representations *of* something but, instead, constitute the *reality* of representations (or the real forces at work in what are often deemed representations). Put differently, unlike other critical studies of violence in literature and film, mine does not frame the encounter with violent images in terms of signification and meaning (mediation) but, instead, in terms of affects and force—that is, asignifying intensities.

Why does this methodological—and ontological—difference make a difference? To evoke Baruch Spinoza's well-known claim that we do not even know what bodies can do, the conceptual gambit of this project is that we do not even know what violent images are, let alone how they work and thus what they can do—and this despite the ever-growing body of intellectual labor expended on the subject matter (albeit with greater frequency and systematicity in film and media studies than in literary studies, as evidenced by the fields' respective bibliographies on this subject). In contrast to this Spinozist provocation, the existing body of scholarship on violent images tends to assume that it already knows what an (violent) image is and how it works. It simply assumes that violent images, just like any other image, *represent*. Operating on the representationalist assumption that (violent) images are representations—reflections of something prior to their emergence, that is, immaterial traces of absent presences—these studies sooner rather than later turn their attention away from their alleged focus (the violence of images) in favor of analyses of what they "represent" or "mean."

As a result, however, these studies neglect important aspects of these violent images—aspects so crucial that they may at least partially negate the very conclusions representationally based studies of violent images tend to promote. If, for instance, we indeed do not yet know what violent images are and how they work because they are not first and foremost representations, then we may have to question the "post-theorist" assertion that the social sciences and their "hard findings" are superior to the "mere interpretations" of traditional film (or literary or cultural) studies, since the social sciences undoubtedly operate their investigations of violent media images by assuming that those images are indeed representational (see Prince, "Film Scholars"). In what I take to be a rather typical social scientific approach to violent images in Hollywood films, Nick Browne and Theresa Webb, for instance, study the extent to which bodies in Hollywood films can sustain the violence with which they are confronted. Their data shows that fictional cinematic characters' ability to experience pain far exceeds the violence any real human body could possibly endure. Clearly, so the researchers conclude, Hollywood violence is just not realistic. Who would have thought? Any fan of the great British Invasion group The Kinks would have certainly known this without counting instances of violence in these films. As they sing in their hit "Celluloid Heroes," heroes of the big screen never feel lasting pain and certainly never die. Not even differentiating between instances of violence in animated films and photographic realist films, studies such as the one by Browne and Webb end up not only producing rather underwhelming results but also promoting conclusions that are questionable precisely because of their neglect to theorize their object of study: images and how they work and what they do.

In general, then, it seems to me that the results produced by social scientific research can be assumed to be valid *only* if the basic assumption underlying their approach to the object they study is actually valid—and I suggest it may not be. And yet, social policy is made—and institutional relevance established—on the basis of such findings. Thus, throwing into relief how problematic the basic assumptions of such studies are may, in the end, not be a small matter.

In turn, my Spinozist provocation that we do not yet know

what violent images are and how they work also troubles more traditional "interpretative" studies (humanist or not) of (violent) images. Like those of the social sciences, these studies ultimately tend to skirt the real issue (how violent images operate and what they do) in order to get to the level of what such images "represent." The difference between the social sciences and interpretative studies is that the former accept the representational hypothesis and make claims about these representations' social (behavioral) effects, whereas the latter are more interested in debating the political (ideological) effects of such representations. But in so doing, they may undermine the very conclusions they offer in the name of an identity politics–driven version of justice. According to these studies, (violent) images are good or bad depending on how accurately they reflect the world they are supposed to represent, as well as on the context within which the depicted violence occurs. But if these images do not primarily represent anything to begin with—or, in any case, if these images' work is not primarily representational—then whatever political advocacy is offered, no matter how admirable, faces the problem of irrelevancy, since it grounds its political stance in something that simply does not exist as such.

Indeed, here lies the crux of my intervention. Because of the assumption of established studies—social scientific and interpretative alike—that (violent) images are *representations* of something else, critical practice ends up, in one form or another, laying claim to what they believe to be a well-founded position of *judgment*. That these existing studies of (violent) images ultimately are about judgment is, however, no accident, for the purpose of such representational studies is ultimately always Platonic in nature. Their goal is precisely to distinguish between good (just) and bad (unjust) copies and to maintain the ability to judge bad images (of violence) as a necessary and effective means to curb them and their alleged negative effects (behavioral or ideological). That is, such judgment always serves the implied purpose of drawing a line between the judging subject (the critic) and the judged object (the image, violent or otherwise), even if the language of judgment is not explicitly used. (I.e., the distancing, analytic language characteristic of representationally based academic discourse functions as a rhetorical device to direct attention away from the very moralizing judgments that actually are at work but, today, are often deemed too unfashionable for them to be expressed directly.) The very ability to judge images based on their representational quality is considered a necessary (though perhaps not sufficient) tool in the fight against violence. Representational studies of violence always insinuate the existence of a nonviolent space, suggesting that a nonviolated phenomenological whole exists prior to the onset of violence. To (re)establish this state of affairs is the (implied) hope of representational criticism and characterizes its politics and moral view.

My hypothesis, however, is that representationally based critical encounters with violent images are based on a potential conceptual error and that this error directly derives from commonly accepted assumptions about (violent) images—to wit, that they are reflections of something else. In fact, I will argue that the very recourse to images qua representations *is* itself a form of violence, rather than constituting the assumed antidote. Moreover, the following study of violent images offers the view that the hope to escape violence as such is an impossible one—because ontologically violences are everywhere and inescapable.

I purposefully offer this proposition with some polemical force in hopes that it will ultimately be welcomed as my attempt to provoke a different trajectory of thought about the subject at hand. If taken seriously, however, this claim demands that the questions we ask of violent images are not what they mean and whether they are justified but *how* they configure our ability to respond to, and do things with, them. The plane of encounter with these images is, in other words, not that of judgment but that of ethics (response-ability). I will call what is ultimately a thoroughly subjunctive encounter with violence "masocriticism." Such a mode of engagement with violent images begins, and continues to pursue, its inquiry by asking, what would happen *if* we began with the ontological assumption that violences are everywhere and understood it as the engine of an *experimental* endeavor rather than a dubious claim to truth?

Though this study limits itself to a discussion of violent images, its implications transcend the primary subject matter, for it is very much concerned with the *practice* and *pedagogical force* of literary, film, and cultural criticism. Specifically, although my study is not designed to function as an extended engagement with the critical reception and de facto application of post-structuralist thought to the study of literary and cinematic images, it can nevertheless be read as proposing that post-structuralist critical practice has not yet been post-structural enough. Notwithstanding the many excellent engagements with post-structural thinkers such as Jacques Derrida, Michel Foucault, or Gilles Deleuze, I, for one, tend to think that most of the time these encounters do not go far enough precisely because they continue to conceive of signaletic material in representational terms. Hence, Derrida becomes the high priest of undecidability, Foucault the sage of subversion, and Deleuze the guru of minoritarianism. While it is understandable that these thinkers are often received in such ways—after all, Derrida *is* concerned with undecidability, Foucault with resistance, and Deleuze with the minor—what often gets crucially omitted from their thought is that all three conceptualize language and images in terms of *force*, that is, arepresentationally. Hence, to my mind, as long as critical practice continues to produce work in the name of post-structuralist thought without heeding what I take to be its key provocation, it will continue to perpetuate claims about its object of study that, to use Theodor Adorno's phrase, do not heed the primacy of the object.

In addition to this book's relevance for the general discourse on (violent) images and its attempt to put a specific understanding of theory (especially Deleuze but also Foucault, Adorno, and Michael Hardt and Antonio Negri) to work, this study also brings together a number of key texts in Deleuze's oeuvre that have thus far received relatively little attention in literary, film, and cultural studies: *Masochism: Coldness and Cruelty* and *Francis Bacon: The Logic of Sensation*. In fact, in conjunction with Deleuze's (and Deleuze and Félix Guattari's) work in general, much of my conceptual toolbox will be developed from these two key monographs—both of which specifically engage violent subject matters. Thus, as a potentially added benefit, the present book invites the reader to (re)consider Deleuze's work in light of the (new) connections I forge through considering these books together.

Given the above, I therefore ask the reader to read the following study as an attempt to do otherwise—that is, as an *experiment*. This book should not be read as a history of violent images, and although all of my primary sites come from post–World War II American fiction and cinema, this book makes no claims about the particular nationality of these violent images. Of course, in the age of "post-theory," one of the central tenets of scholarship is that one must contextualize a work of art if one wants to understand it. In response to this historicist commonplace, I agree with Slavoj Žižek that the proper Deleuzean counterclaim is to suggest that "too much of a historical context can blur the proper contact with a work of art (i.e., that to enact this contact one should abstract from the work's context), but also that it is, rather, the work of art itself that provides a context enabling us to understand properly a given historical situation" (*Organs without Bodies* 15).

Or, as Derrida has taught us long ago, while context—social, historical, psychic, political, and so on—matters, "il n'y a pas de hors-texte." However, I take Derrida's statement less as a directive for critics to fetishize textuality than as an articulation of a sense of a network of exteriority within which no one term is privileged. Just as no meaning can be determined out of context, so no context allows for the total saturation of a text's meaning. In fact, one of the more crucial lessons offered to us by post-structuralism is that context is never really "outside" the text precisely because context and text are the result of the *same* network of forces, or, to use Deleuze and Guattari's key concept, plane of immanence. That is, it is impossible both to escape context by turning to a more or less hermetically sealed-off hermeneutic conception of the text (close analysis) and to escape excessive textuality by pointing to the outside of a text, the context. Either move is impossible because it necessarily would occur merely in response to the engendering play of asignifying forces (what Derrida, for instance, calls, among other terms, "différance") without which there would be neither text nor context.

While historical and contextual approaches undoubtedly have much to offer, they are nevertheless specific examples of the very representational approach to violent images that this book wants to put into suspension, at least momentarily. Hence, articulating in greater detail the *costs* of such representational approaches to violent images and offering, alternatively, an encounter with such images as asignifying intensities or affects, this study will gradually work itself through a number of literary and filmic sites—a few moments in the films of the Coen Brothers, the discursive relationship between Bret Easton Ellis's novel *American Psycho* and its film adaptation by feminist director Mary Harron, Patricia Highsmith's fiction, the acting work of Robert DeNiro, and Don DeLillo's essay on 9/11. This choice of primary sites, while undoubtedly based on personal preferences, actually embodies a two-fold logic: on one hand, it articulates a specific instantiation of an affective smearing of violence across a sliding scale of intensities; on the other, it reflects this work's process of generation as such. Each encounter with one specific site ended up provoking a new question with which the site itself was not concerned as such and thus necessitated my turning elsewhere as a means to find a site that tackles the very question the previous site provoked but did not address.

Thus, the argumentative logic of this book performatively offers a pedagogical engagement with violent images that derives its ethical impetus directly from the sites themselves, from *how* the imaged violence itself calls forth critical response-ability—not "for" these objects but *before* them. In the end, I will suggest that while such response-ability can never escape the moment of judgment, suspending its occurrence is a question of habit(uation)— of pedagogical repetition embodied by a masochistic practice of inhabiting the moment *before* subjective interpretation, that is, the moment of the event of violence itself.

Acknowledgments

In the summer of 1995, I read for the first time Bret Easton Ellis's *American Psycho*. For better or for worse, the physical experience of reading this novel had a profound impact on me. At various moments in my encounter with this text, I felt the urge to set the book aside to go out for a walk in the unbearable summer heat of Atlanta, Georgia. Exposing myself to temperatures around one hundred degrees Fahrenheit and near 100 percent humidity seemed a more sensible thing to do than sitting in silence in my chair pondering some of the most nausea-inducing passages in Ellis's infamous novel. Being less morally outraged by the book's content than physically affected by the experience of reading this text, I could not help but sense my fascination with this novel and what it was capable of doing to me. In hindsight I think it was this capacity of Ellis's novel to affect me that initially pointed me in a direction of research of which this book is the end result. For this reason alone, my first expression of gratitude must go out to Bret Easton Ellis.

But for ultimately channeling what was initially not much more than a feeling of being intrigued (and confused) into what I hope is now an intellectually coherent and stimulating argument, I am indebted to many others whom I encountered over the years, be it in person or through their work. It would be impossible to provide a complete list of all the names of those who inspired my own thinking. I am grateful to all of you. Still, I must single out some people whose intellectual labor left indelible marks on the shape this project has taken. First of all, I am particularly grateful to Kathryn Hume, Jeffrey T. Nealon, and John Muckelbauer, without whose invaluable advice and astonishing intellectual generosity I could never have finished this book. My countless discussions with them allowed me to generate and test out a sustained theoretical version of what started out as merely a vaguely sensed theoretical inclination toward my object of research. So thank you for never tiring of reading what were at times excruciatingly long rough drafts of individual chapters!

As well, I feel blessed to have been able to profit from a series of incredibly smart and sharing interlocutors: Richard Doyle, Evan Watkins, Steven Shaviro, Charles Stivale, Philip Jenkins, Dan Smith, Jeffrey Karnicky, Jim Roberts, Ryan Netzley, Megan Brown, Christine Harold, Kevin DeLuca, Pat Gehrke, Gina Ercolini, Debbie Hawhee, and Elizabeth Mazzolini all offered me friendship and good counsel over the years that sustained my interest in this project and gave me energy to bring it to a finish. I also want to thank my colleagues in the Department of English at the University of Nebraska, which serves as my institutional home: the warm, welcoming atmosphere that awaited me upon my arrival in Lincoln in 2004 enabled me to finish my book in a relaxed and intellectually stimulating environment. I want to express my gratitude especially to Wheeler Winston Dixon and Gwendolyn Audrey Foster, who have been more than forthcoming in sharing their knowledge of academic publishing. Likewise, thank you to Linda Ray Pratt, who gave me my first tenure-track job here at UNL, for putting such faith in me, as well as Joy Ritchie, who in her capacity as my department chair showed continuing support of my work. Furthermore, I must thank Nick Spencer, not merely for reading parts of the manuscript, but also for the countless discussions of all things theory and, importantly, football! Let's go Reds! And, of course, many thanks to Ladette Randolph and everyone else at the University of Nebraska Press who worked so diligently on the final production of this book, as well as to Alexandra Jenkins for her swift and diligent fact checking. I am also grateful to Rainer Smolinski and Thomas McHaney, who both counseled me to consider going to graduate school and, in the case of the latter, helped me get my first publication, without which I probably would not be in this country right now.

But such a book is not written without also receiving much support from people who belong to a different, nonacademic part of one's life. Having moved from Germany to the United States in 1992, I feel especially grateful for the enduring friendship of some of my oldest friends from Germany, including but not limited to Marc Donay, Christian Weisz, Joachim Milkowski, Daniela Heirich, Utz Farber, and, from Atlanta, my first "home away from home," T. Scott Barrett. Whenever I hit a rough spot during the writing of this book over the years, I felt comforted by the knowledge of your friendship. Last, but certainly not least, my warmest gratitude goes to Robyn Gay for her support, kindness, and integrity.

In the end, however, this book would have simply been impossible for me to write without the never-ending support of my parents, Richard and Magda Abel. Though they will not be able to read this book (barring the case of a future translation into German), I nevertheless take great pleasure in knowing that they will be able to have this book at home on a bookshelf as a material trace of my intellectual labor that they supported so generously over the years.

The Violence
of Sensation

Miller's Crossing, Affect, and Masocriticism

Violence. Most would be happy if they never had to experience it, and many are convinced of the existence of nonviolent spaces, whether they existed only in the past and elsewhere, are actually available in the here and now, or, perhaps, are only going to emerge in a yet to come time and space. And yet, notwithstanding the all-pervasive privileging of the nonviolent over the violent, violence surrounds us, has surrounded us, and it is hard to see how it will not surround us in the future. Violent images are the lifeblood of TV and abound in the history of cinema; the history of literature and the arts in general would be unthinkable without them. And what about the perversely luring image of violence in form of a car crash on the New Jersey turnpike? This event of real violence inevitably produces traffic jams—in the *other* direction, caused by voyeuristic drivers seduced by the image of others' pain. But violence is not just everywhere in imaged form. Can anyone remember a single moment when there was not some violent conflict somewhere around the world or a day without murder, rape, battery, or other acts of violence? Or what about the war on terror, subsequently renamed "global struggle against violent extremism": does anyone really believe that this specific violence can ever be completely eliminated? What about the violence of hate speech or all-pervasive economic exploitation? What about the violence entailed by the demand that passengers take off their shoes when going through airport security, not to mention that they submit themselves to random body searches? The violence of the attacks of 9/11 has now mutated—permanently, irrevocably, it seems—into a multiplicity of practices whose violence is admittedly less recognizable than that of a plane explosion. But why assume that violence exists, and is real, only when its occurrence is easily recognizable?

Of course, the violence involved in another person entering my private space, even if I believe that he has no other motive than ensuring the safety of all passengers (but how exactly do I know this?), is not the same as the spectacular violence involved in blowing up the World Trade Center. The violence that is part of the routine practices of U.S. airport security personnel getting too close for my personal comfort at least partially derives from the fact that I simply have no way to prevent this violation of personal space from happening: if I objected in any way, I would instantaneously undergo an incorporeal transformation, from private citizen of another country to suspect, and consequently would be violated even more. This violence is not of the same kind as the violence of the bombs in Madrid, London, Egypt, or Iraq, though this does not make it any less real or significant. Nor is the violence of 9/11 of the same kind as the violence perpetrated against the millions who died in German concentration camps, Soviet gulags, or civil wars that have been and still are fought all over the world—and are often more or less covertly sponsored by the very countries that are the staunchest practitioners of a rhetoric of democratic nonviolence.

Indeed, to say that these examples of real and imaged violence are not the same, that they are *different*, and that there is a problem with considering them as examples of Violence instead of regarding them as a series of different violences—this is the first gambit of the present study.[1] In fact, part of my argument throughout this book will be that one of the drawbacks of representational criticism of violence is that it tends to eradicate this very difference by configuring the *event* of violence as always being about something other than its constitutive forces, intensities, or rhythms.

But let us slow down, as we are getting ahead of ourselves. One thing that I think is uncontroversial—unlike, perhaps, some of my statements in the previous paragraphs—is that violent images tend to be controversial.[2] To some, they are maddeningly repulsive and responsible for the decline of Western civilization; to others, they are excitingly subversive, responsible for provoking uncomfortable questions and powerful truths about "normative" society. And to others still, violence just "rules," to evoke the brilliantly limited rhetorical capacities of those two great practitioners of all things un-PC: Beavis and Butt-Head. Whatever differences critics may display in their critical engagement with violent images in film and literature, however, the one thing everyone (okay, maybe not Beavis) seems to agree on is that a key attribute of such images is their ability to raise the question of their *ethical* value. Indeed, we may argue that violent images' provocation of the ethical moment is neither limited to nor randomly mobilized by institutionalized habits of critical reflection. Instead, violent images *themselves* constitutively raise the question of ethics, as the remainder of this chapter will argue in greater detail. That is, in this introductory chapter I hope to build a conceptual toolbox that may be productive for a critical engagement with violent images that desires to encounter them on the level of their own *reality* rather than on the level of their "meaning."

The Violence of Sensation

Take, for instance, *Miller's Crossing* (1990), an American independent film by the Coen Brothers that explicitly foregrounds the question of ethics as the central driving engine of the film's violent narrative. The film opens with a remarkable scene that cinematically dramatizes the focus of the study ahead. As we see ice cubes being dropped into an empty glass of whiskey, we hear an Italian American voice declare: "I'm talkin' about friendship. I'm talkin' about character. I'm talkin' about—hell, Leo, I'm not embarrassed to use the word—I'm talkin' about ethics." Just before the final declaration, the camera cuts to a long shot of the speaker, showing us a pudgy, round-faced man sitting in a chair on the guest side of a desk. The man sports a thin mustache that concurrently indicates the care he puts into his physical appearance and the rather ridiculous character of what he believes to be the look of a sophisticated gangster of the late 1920s. Viewers familiar with the violent gangster film cycles of the late 1920s and early 1930s that led to the implementation of the Hayes Code will immediately sense that this guy is no "Little Caesar" (as played by Edgar G. Robinson in Mervyn LeRoy's *Little Caesar* [1930]), "Public Enemy" (as played by James Cagney in William Wellman's 1931 film of the same name), or "Scarface" (as played by Paul Muni in Howard Hawks's 1932 film). As the camera slowly zooms in onto the speaker's face, the man who will later be identified as Johnny Caspar (Jon Polito) continues his speech:

> You know I'm a sporting man. I like to lay an occasional bet. But I ain't that sporting. When I fix a fight, say I pay a 3 to 1 to throw a goddamn fight, I figure I got the right to expect that fight to go off on 3 to 1. But every time I lay a bet with that son of a bitch Bernie Bernbaum, before I know it the odds is even up, or worse, I'm betting on the short money. The sheeny knows I like sure things. He's selling the info that I fixed a fight.

After a brief silence, a close-up of Caspar highlights his mouth making smacking noises, again indicating that he is anything but a man of sophistication. Then he forces the issue: "So, it's clear what I'm saying?" Cut back to Leo (Albert Finney), sitting in his chair behind an impressive desk, coldly responding: "As mud."

Believing that Leo not only has understood but also agrees with his position, Caspar, again shown in a close-up, carries on: "It's getting so a business man can't expect no return from a fixed fight. Now, you can't trust no fix, what can you trust? For a good return you gotta go betting on chance." In Caspar's view, then, ethics means first and foremost the elimination of chance. With chance in play, so he argues as the camera intercuts his lines with shots of Leo and two other gangsters present in the room—Tom

(Gabriel Byrne), the man we initially saw only in a blurred image, and Caspar's hit man, "the Dane" (J. E. Freeman)—"you're back with anarchy. Right back in the jungle. That's why ethics is important. What separates us from the animals, beasts of burden, beasts of prey—ethics. Whereas Bernie Bernbaum is a horse of a different color, ethics-wise. As in 'he ain't got any.'" After a moment, Leo asks Caspar, "So you want him killed?" to which the Dane, rather than Caspar, answers, "For starters."

On one level, the film's exposition seems traditional and predictable enough. Viewers are allowed to observe the wheelings and dealings of underworld characters and are led to expect violent conflict to emerge before the film is over. We expect this not only because of any potential prior exposure to the filmmakers' work, other gangster films, or pulp fiction/crime novels but also because the film's narrative itself is constructed in linear fashion: we are privy to a present conversation in which we learn why past grievances demand future resolution.[3] In other words, the film provides us with the cause for the violence that is yet to come. Violence on this level is a function of narrative, or of probability: given the narrative information, it is extremely likely that at least one of the characters will be dead before the end credits roll across the big screen.

Yet, on another level this scene also confronts viewers with a different kind of violence. It is a violence rendered visible through the intensities of the coloration of the mise-en-scène. This violence confronts spectators on the level of affect *before* it is made available to them on the level of narrative or symbolism, that is, representation. It is the violence of sensation rather than the violence of representation, to use the distinction that Gilles Deleuze introduces in his study of the violent works of British painter Francis Bacon. According to Deleuze, Bacon's creative—indeed ethical—formula is "to paint the scream more than the horror" (*Francis Bacon* 34). That is, Bacon is more interested in painting an affect that sustains the intensity of violence than the cause (the horror) that produced the effect (the scream).

Painting the cause would be analogous to the depicted violence in films such as Oliver Stone's *Natural Born Killers* (1994) or Robert Rodriguez' *Sin City* (2005) in which the causes of violence and their effects tend to be copresent through traditional two-shot or shot-reverse-shot figures. No matter how brutal and aesthetically compelling the images, they remain thoroughly narrativized (logical) and thus rational, regardless of our level of (moral) disgust with them. Remaining on the level of familiar images of violence that have long become clichés in the history of cinema, they tell us very little in the end about the violence of sensation or the sensation of violence precisely because "sensation is that which is transmitted directly, and avoids the detour and boredom of conveying a story" (Deleuze, *Francis Bacon* 32). As such, sensation has nothing to do with a viewing subject's feelings: "there are no feelings in Bacon: there are nothing but affects, that is 'sensations' and 'instincts'" (35). Accounting for affect, or the "rhythmic unity of the senses" (39), in phenomenological terms would simply be "insufficient because [phenomenology] merely invokes the lived body. But the lived body is still a paltry thing in comparison with a more profound and almost unlivable Power" (39). Sensation—affect—is presubjective: it is what constitutes the subject rather than being a synonym for an already constituted subject's emotions or feelings. Whereas phenomenology's conception of sensation or affect is tied too much to the living organism (affect qua emotion), the affect Deleuze has in mind is the affect of the body without organs whose enemy is organization, that is, the reductive force of representation.[4]

Differently put, "to paint the scream" is a matter of "capturing forces" (Deleuze, *Francis Bacon* 48) rather than representing them. As Deleuze writes, the "task of painting is defined as the attempt to render visible forces that are not themselves visible" (48).[5] If we replace "cinema" for "painting" we have here an articulation of an artistic imperative that the Coens put into practice in the opening sequence of *Miller's Crossing*. While they do not get rid of narrative (or what Deleuze also calls "figuration"), they *intensify* the level of figuration through their color scheme to the point where the equivalent of Bacon's "Figure" emerges in the form of Caspar.

In Bacon's work, the Figure is an icon or image that emerges out of a painterly process of isolating it from the field, "the round area or parallelepiped" (6) within which it exists. As Deleuze puts it, the "relation of the Figure to its isolating place defines a 'fact': 'the fact is . . .,' 'what takes place is . . .'" (6). The Figure, in other words, does not signify: being isolated, it avoids "the *figurative, illustrative,* and *narrative* character the Figure would necessarily have if it were not isolated" (6). In the Coen Brothers' film, Jon Polito's character appears isolated by the intensity of the brown mise-en-scène, all doom and gloom and claustrophobically suffocating, as indicated by the sweat on Caspar's bald head and upper lip and further emphasized visually through Polito's brilliant portrayal, with his mouth, almost like a fish out of water, gasping for air, lips pursed side to side. Like Bacon, the Coens do not appear to oppose figuration but, rather, intensify figuration to produce the Figure; they go through narrative in order to get to the level of pure affect, that is, sensation. This immanent strategy crucially differs from standard avant-garde filmmaking practices that reject figuration/narrative *wholesale*—thus immediately reintroducing narrative through their very act of dialectical rejection.

What we witness in this scene, however, is not the actual force that is exerted upon Caspar's body. For although force may be the "condition of sensation, it is nonetheless not the force that is sensed, since the sensation 'gives' something completely different from the forces that condition it" (Deleuze, *Francis Bacon* 48). Why is this important from an artist's, as well as critical, point of view? Simply put, the problem is that we, as spectators, are not privy to the actual, but to us invisible, forces that impinge on the body, be it that of one of Bacon's screaming popes or that of *Miller's Crossing*'s seething Caspar. Hence, the question for Bacon, and the Coens, is how to make *us* sense these invisible forces, or how to actualize what is merely virtual in the frame? Merely depicting these forces will not do, as that would at best position viewers in a representational framework in which we would be able to perceive these forces while nevertheless remaining unable to sense their intensity. This is why "Bacon creates the painting of the scream [in which] he establishes a relationship between the visibility of the scream (the open mouth as a shadowy abyss) and invisible forces, which are nothing other than the *forces of the future*" (51, my emphasis). As a result, we are exposed to the scream as an assemblage of intensities, allowing us to sense the sensation of the scream and thus to be affected by the affect inhering in the scream. By keeping the cause of the horrific scream "off-screen," Bacon manages to paint the violence of sensation—as embodied *in* the scream—rather than the violence of representation, as would be the case if he represented whatever is just to the side of the frame.

What is to the side? We do not know—and only a *future* moment could reveal this as of yet invisible force. By withholding this future moment, however—by *suspending* it—we are confronted with the future qua future, made sensible to us rather than represented for us in "the unity of the sensing and the sensed" (Deleuze, *Francis Bacon* 31). What we see is a "living" body, horrified by invisible forces—which are nothing else but the forces of the future. As a result, Deleuze argues that a reversal of Heideggerian phenomenology occurs: "Death is judged from the point of view of life, and not the reverse, as we like to believe" (52–53). According to Deleuze, when "Bacon distinguishes between two violences, that of the spectacle and that of sensation, and declares that the first must be renounced to reach the second, it is a kind of declaration of faith in life" (52). The violence of sensation—embodied in the Figure (as opposed to the violence of the spectacle, narrative, symbolism, that is, representation)—is an affirmation of the encounter with futurity in the present, in life. For Martin Heidegger, life is to be judged from the horizon of possibility—that is, death. For Deleuze, in contrast, the ethical task is once again to be able to believe "in this world, this life, [which] becomes our most difficult task, or the task of a mode of existence still to be discovered," as he and Félix Guattari put it in their final collaboration, *What Is Philosophy?* (75). It is, of course, the time-image theorized in Deleuze's second book on the cinema that is responsible for making this belief once again available to us; in *Francis Bacon*, it is the concept of the Figure that accomplishes the same task.

Either way, what matters is that in art "it is not a matter of reproducing or inventing forms, but of *capturing forces*. For this reason no art is figurative. Paul Klee's famous formula—'Not to render the visible, but to render visible'—means nothing else" (Deleuze, *Francis Bacon* 48, my emphasis). Indeed, this is what happens in *Miller's Crossing*. Of course, representational (figurative) violence eventually ensues, and it could not be any other way. As Deleuze argues, "the first figuration [representation, narrative] cannot completely be eliminated; something of it is always conserved" (79). After all, "it is easy to oppose the figural to the figurative in an abstract manner, [for] we never cease to trip over the objection of fact: the Figure is still figurative; it still represents someone (a screaming man, a smiling man, a seated man), it still narrates something" (79)—even if it is a typically quirky tale so characteristic of the Coen Brothers' oeuvre. Yet, there is "a second figuration," which "the painter obtains, this time as a result of the Figure, as an effect of the pictorial act" (79)—or as a result of the mise-en-scène, the cinematic staging of the scene, the "how" that gives rise to a representational "what."

So, *before* the inevitable figuration of violence occurs in *Miller's Crossing*, we are already exposed to the Figure of violence, the violence of sensation. As spectators, however, we "experience the sensation only by entering the painting" (Deleuze, *Francis Bacon* 31), by reaching the unity of the sensing and the sensed. How does this happen? How do spectators enter a painting, a film, or any (art) object in general? Or, more precisely, how are spectators *made to* enter the object? Continuing his explanation of Bacon's use of color, Deleuze argues, "Color is the body, sensation is in the body, and not in the air. Sensation is what is painted. What is painted on the canvas is the body, not insofar as it is represented as an object, but insofar as it is experienced as sustaining *this* sensation" (32). I suggest that if we replace "filmed" for "painted" and "screen" for "canvas" then we have a pretty accurate description of what goes on in the Coen Brothers' film: sensation is what they film, and what they film and is subsequently projected on screen is the body—not insofar as it is represented as an object, but insofar as it is experienced as sustaining *this* sensation.[6] And, importantly, as for Bacon, this sensation is frequently violent, as is the case, for instance, at the precise moment when Caspar proselytizes about his sense of ethics.

The Violence of Ethics

In fact, that the question of ethics is raised at and through the very moment when the audience can sense the violence of sensation is no coincidence, for ethics is a question of responsibility, or better yet, response-ability, that does not depend on rational choice. Theorizing ethics qua performative subjectivity, literary theorist Jeffrey Nealon posits that "responsibility is not merely *choosing* to respond, at least if this responsibility is to be an *affirmation* of alterity. [. . .] Rather, the ethics of performative subjectivity is enacted precisely in and as a *response* to the always already exterior, to the other that is the ground of the same. The point is not that I need always to remember to act '*as if* I was already responsible'; rather, 'I' am nothing but this responsibility" (*Alterity Politics* 169). The affective or intensive forces inhering in the violence of sensation constitute such an exteriority, something that impinges on the body from outside. These forces produce effects *prior* to their inevitable narrativization, their eventual territorialization onto the plane of representation—and because these forces affect me before the narrative apparatus of capture organizes them for me, I am already response-able. With my responsibility always already being response-ability—my constitutive ability to respond *before* these images represent—what counts in such a conception of performative ethics is to examine "the production of effects, not the zero-sum game of deciding what an identity or movement really or authentically 'means'" (170).

A critical encounter with violent images would therefore have to attend to these images' *affective* intensities—their *effects* rather than their representational "meanings." Attending to the effects provoked by the reality of violent images in film and literature is the aim of this study. To do so, it is indeed necessary to think of these images in affective terms rather than addressing them on the level of their representational quality, as is commonly done in the major studies of the subject matter.[7] By "affect," however, I do not mean what a given subject is phenomenologically made to feel (feeling is merely affect territorialized onto the subject) but, to use Brian Massumi's words, "a suspension of action-reaction circuits" (28). Affect, in other words, is not so much a matter of cause and effect resulting from action or movement; rather, affect is a "state of passional suspension in which [the body] exists more outside of itself, more in the abstracted action of the impinging thing and the abstracted context of that action, than within itself" (31).

This, I suggest, is indeed what *Miller's Crossing* provokes us to consider in greater detail, as it wages the question of ethics precisely at the moment when it confronts us with the violence of sensation that occurs before any figuration of violence results. The question of the ethics of violence, in other words, emerges prior to any representation of violence. Hence, as long as we engage the imaging process of violence based on representationalist assumptions, we essentially remain oblivious to their constitutive intensities—notwithstanding that such accounts cannot help but be affected by them. If nothing else, attending to the violence of sensation would require us at least partially to redirect our attention away from films by Quentin Tarantino, Sam Peckinpah, or any shoot-'em-up blockbuster, that is, any film that merely renders violence visible (as opposed to rendering visible the invisible forces—intensities, affects—of violence). Or, rather, we might want to think about films such as *The Wild Bunch* (dir. Sam Peckinpah, 1969) or *Pulp Fiction* (dir. Quentin Tarantino, 1994) not so much in terms of their represented violence but in terms of the intensities that percolate *within* the clichéd violence of representation.

But let us be even more precise with regard to *Miller's Crossing* and what it offers us with regard to the intersection of violence and ethics, or response-ability, for the film playfully engages two different conceptions of ethics. In the film's opening scene, we witness how a (violent) character desires to sidestep chance, or, perhaps better, we witness his inability to deal with chance.[8] This inability makes Caspar insist that "ethics" are supposed to be a safe and sound contract written in stone that he can trust so that he will not have to worry about any unwelcome surprises. To him, ethics is a matter of keeping the outside—exteriority, chance—at bay. On the level of narrative, the problem with Caspar's suggestion that violence can be avoided as long as everyone heeds the contract's terms, however, is simply that he cannot fathom that his sense of ethics is not only unconventional and questionable in and of itself (since when does fixing games count as ethical behavior?) but also contrary to that of the other characters in the film who do not share his enthusiasm for "ethics."[9] Indeed, for them Caspar's ethics are not a means to prevent violence but instead an inspiration—however unintentional—for becoming-violent. Or, as Leo explains his refusal to grant Caspar's request to kill Bernie, he sees no reason to get rid of Bernie, a dues-paying customer and hence protected wise guy. Differently put, Leo suggests that his contract with Bernie is as good as Caspar's, and who is to say that one is more ethical than the other? As long as his set of rules are being adhered to, Leo has no cause to take action; and since he is the ultimate boss, Caspar's rules simply carry less force than his. Of course, in upholding his contract with Bernie, Leo violates his contract with Caspar, as Tom repeatedly reminds Leo throughout the film. Caspar pays Leo so that Leo will protect him against his enemies. From Caspar's point of view, then, Leo's refusal to help is yet another example of a lack of ethics that demands, in his view, drastic response: to wit, he tries to kill Leo and take over his position as the underworld leader.

However, as viewers we are not invited just to accept Caspar's definition of ethics and wait for the kill-'em-all type of violence to occur. Rather, we have *already* been made privy to the experience of violence in the very absence of this "excessive" type of violence. The film's cinematography has rendered visible a body—not Caspar's but the brown filling every frame—that sustains the sensation of violence through its purely affective force, its intensity. Even though nothing is happening (yet), we nevertheless *sense* Caspar's (body) time literally expiring; that it will take another ninety minutes of screen time or so before he will actually be killed is in this regard rather incidental. That is, at the moment of Caspar's static exposition of ethics, he is cinematically made to subsist in, while being isolated from, the brown mise-en-scène, which renders visible Caspar's ultimate ineptitude as both an ethicist and a gangster. Concurrently, this moment of violence already calls forth our response, our response-ability. Regardless of whether we recognize the violence inhering this moment, we are made to respond. Response, and thus ethics, simply cannot be reduced to a moment of representational recognition and, in fact, is always already constitutive of it.

While Caspar's sense of ethics as a static, unmoving contract permeates many of the Coens' films including *Blood Simple* and *Fargo*, their *style* of filming provides us with a different *sense* of violence and thus ethics. Challenging the audience with an absurd definition of ethics out of the mouth of what would appear to be a rather unethical man, *Miller's Crossing*'s discourse on ethics nevertheless fascinates because of the way it affectively lends Caspar's proprietary definition of ethics an ominous sense of violence.[10] So saturated is the scene with brown overtones that the goings-on can hardly be taken as naturalistic or realistic. The overbearing, claustrophobic, intense presence of the thick layers of brown that fill every frame lends Caspar's sweating a different force: more than just perceiving it, we, as spectators, sense Caspar's sensation. As such, we are indeed not meant to take seriously Caspar's sense of ethics as an acceptable justification for violence; instead, *we are meant to sense the violence of ethics* itself. And since sensing is a matter of style, the audience is asked viscerally to immerse itself in the mise-en-scène, like the characters bathed in the surreal brown light. By entering the thickness of the mise-en-scène, the viewer encounters the violence of sensation. But this violence is not simply sensational, although the

Coens' films are not free of a certain level of sensationalism. Recall, for instance, the ending of *Blood Simple* or the parking garage and woodchipper scenes in *Fargo*. Likewise, Caspar's ethical declarations make all too obvious where the film is heading, and, sure enough, we do not have to wait too long for a sensationally violent shoot-out to transpire. Yet this occurrence itself must be considered the logical working out of Caspar's definition of ethics—that is, ethics as a static contract. But what we see in the scene at hand is a direct image of violence, not one that is mediated through movement as in *Natural Born Killers*, where the kinetic aspect of the film dominates our sense of violence to such a degree that we cannot help but feel violated by it. Whereas in the latter film violence occurs in the (visual) presence of the action causing the violation of bodies (people are killed by gun shooting, e.g.), in *Miller's Crossing* the "body infolds the *effect* of the [violent] impingement—it conserves the impingement minus the impinging thing, the impingement abstracted from the actual action that caused it and actual context of that action" (Massumi 31–32). In the very absence of what we commonsensically think of as violence, violence occurs to the film's bodies in front of our eyes and thus affects us.

The film makes clear that when it comes to violent images the question is never whether or not one *should* respond to them (by criticizing or affirming them according to their representational value); rather, *Miller's Crossing* clarifies with admirable rigor that we are always already response-able, not "for" these images or their consequences but *before* them. How, then, do these images call forth our response-ability? And importantly for the present study, how can a critical encounter with such images articulate this response-ability in such a manner that it does not abdicate its response-ability by territorializing this ethical question onto the representational plane of judgment? In other words, what critical and conceptual tools are available to us that might accomplish the task given us by *Miller's Crossing*: to heed the singularity (ethics) of violence, to respond to it—and thus be response-able before it—by heeding the primacy of the event?

The Violence of Masochism

In *Francis Bacon*, Deleuze emphasizes how difficult it is for the painter not to relapse into the cliché. In fact, Deleuze suggests that one "can only fight against the cliché with much ruse, perseverance, and prudence: it is a task perpetually renewed with every painting, with every moment of every painting" (79). Note that Deleuze is far from advocating an "anything goes" relativist ethics, as opponents of post-structuralism in general often allege. Fighting the cliché is not a matter of random subversion but of carefully planned, thought-through, and repeated practice that *in* its repetitiveness varies to itself. Just recall, for instance, Deleuze's reading of Nietzsche's concept of the Eternal Return. In contrast to the traditional (existentialist) understanding of the Eternal Return, Deleuze proposes in *Nietzsche and Philosophy* that the Eternal Return ought not be understood as an infinite returning of the same but as an eternal recurrence of that which has the capacity to differ from itself. *Only* that which has this capacity is capable of returning. What returns, thus, is difference itself or, rather, the force of differentiation. Furthermore, in *Difference and Repetition*, perhaps the key text for any understanding of Deleuze's oeuvre, the philosopher brings this understanding to bear on medieval theologian Duns Scotus's univocity of being thesis, which operates as the driving force of Deleuze's work. Unlike many of his post-structuralist fellow travelers who labored over the problem of metaphysical presence, Deleuze was never really too bothered by this problem because to him Being can always be said *only* of becoming. If Being "is" always already becoming, Being, or presence, is not quite the problem as, say, Derrida's work suggests it is.

In the case of Francis Bacon's painterly practice, being confronted with a canvas that is always already filled with (cliché) images, he invents a technique of manually produced, accidental, free marks that helps him to "extract the improbable Figure from the set of figurative probabilities" (Deleuze, *Francis Bacon* 77), that is, from narrativization that is a priori inscribed into the canvas. Bacon uses this technique as a means to hack into the already existing (clichéd) order of the canvas.[11] He creates what Deleuze calls a "diagram" that can be called "'nonrepresentative,' precisely because [it] depends on the act of chance and [expresses] nothing regarding the visual image" (77). Making these chance-dependent marks is a prepictorial act, a practice that is intended to allow the painter himself to enter the painting before beginning the act of painting as such.

Crucially, this encounter with the canvas allows Bacon to enter "into the cliché, into probability. He enters into it precisely because he *knows what he wants to do*, but what saves him is the fact that *he does not know how to get there*, he does not know how to do what to do" (Deleuze, *Francis Bacon* 78). And is this not the very problem we encounter when confronting the question of violent images: that we simply do not know *how* to do it and because of this uncertainty end up having immediate recourse to the clichés of representation? That is, even though we cannot but respond to (violent) images, this response is all too quickly articulated on the plane of representation, thus immediately transcending the *event* of response as such.

Continuing his description of Bacon's strategies for combating the cliché, Deleuze suggests that the painter will only get to where he wants to be "by getting out of the canvas. The painter's problem is not how to enter into the canvas, since he is already there (the prepictorial task), but how to get out of it, thereby getting out of the cliché, getting out of probability (the pictorial task). It is the chance manual marks that will give him a chance, though not a certitude" (*Francis Bacon* 78). Again, is this not what we are faced with when dealing with violent images: finding means that afford us a chance to escape the cliché? But in order to have any chance of escaping the cliché we need to affirm, well, chance as such—something that is easier said than done. That is, we have to affirm the roll of the dice, which is opposed to the doubling up practice of the "bad" gambler. The latter encounters chance and futurity in terms of probability, whereas a Nietzschean affirmation of a *single* roll of the dice treats chance as independent of probability. The ethical task is to affirm the multiplicity immanent to this single throw: "It is not a matter of several dicethrows which, because of their number, finally reproduce the same combination. On the contrary, it is a matter of a single dicethrow which, due to the number of the combination produced, comes to reproduce itself" (Deleuze, *Nietzsche and Philosophy* 25). What I am suggesting here is, simply, that Deleuze's description of Bacon's painterly practice offers us a specific set of tools that may allow us to develop a criticism of violence that escapes the critical clichés precisely because it works by affirming chance. The tools I have in mind pertain to the formal practice of masochism that underlies Deleuze's analysis of Bacon's paintings as well as his subsequent work on the cinema.[12]

Consider, for instance, the Coen Brothers' *Fargo*, a film of interest here because it cinematically establishes, and dramatizes, a "masochistic contract." Such a contract, as Deleuze explains in his study of Leopold von Sacher-Masoch's writings, "implies in principle certain conditions like the free acceptance of the parties, a limited duration and the preservation of inalienable rights" (*Masochism* 91–92). Yet, the ultimate purpose of this contract is to derive a law from it: "the masochist aims not to mitigate the law but on the contrary to emphasize its extreme severity" (91). To emphasize this severity (and to derive the law from the contract), the masochistic contract is written in a very precise language, rhetorically constructed as tightly as the bounds that the masochist's mistress will apply to his body.[13] This tight construction of the contract might, however, result in the problem that "the law it generates always tends to forget its own origins and annul these restrictive conditions" (92). That is, the law that might emerge from the contract, once in place, begins to violate "the contract in that it can apply to a third party, is valid for an indeterminate period and recognizes no inalienable rights" (92). Whereas the contract stipulated, indeed presupposed and depended on, the specific relation between the masochist and his mistress—with *this* mistress rather than another—the ensuing transformation of the contractual exigency into a legal apparatus issues forth an incorporeal transformation of the mistress herself: she is now other to her contracted self, assuming a different, "legal," subject position. This new subject position places new demands on her that exceed those of the original contract. In fact, the nature of these demands is such that others can accomplish them as well. Consequently, the law, because it *is* the law, allows someone else to be substituted for the mistress. With this replacement, however, the singularity of the initial *ethical* commitment of the mistress to the masochist vanishes. In other words, the transformation from contract into law is a transformation from singularity (ethics) into generality (morality). Yet, as Deleuze points out, "as a general rule, [. . .] in masochism the contract is caricatured in order to emphasize its ambiguous destination. [It implicitly challenges], by excess of zeal, a humorous acceleration of the clauses and a complete reversal of the respective contractual status of [the signatories]" (92).

This is precisely what happens in *Fargo*. In the first twenty seconds of the film, an epigraph scrolls across the screen, asserting that the story we are about to see is based on true incidents. It is here where the film first sets up a rigid contract with its audience—a contract that is characterized by a humorous acceleration of clauses. Subsequently, it plays out this contract's logic in the rest of the film, gradually undermining this very contract precisely so that it will not ever be applied as a generality to all films.[14] *Fargo* sets up a masochistic contract as a means to affect viewers so that they become and remain response-able to the film's violent subject matter, regardless of how absurd or unrealistic the violent events may appear. Yet, this response-ability is one of singularity, since it does not require that I must recall that I am responsible as a viewer "for" these images when I watch them but that I am always nothing but this response-ability *before* the singularity of an event (of violence). In other words, contrary to Caspar's sense of ethics as a static, written in stone contract, the Coens' cold and clinical cinematic style repeatedly invokes a contractual relationship between film and audience in which the implied signatories of the contract agree to a mode of engagement that sets specific rules for the encounter without determining its outcome. Chance, or the future, remains necessarily an integral part of the game.

Rather than viewing *Fargo*'s cinematic rendering of the masochistic contract as an occurrence limited to this film, however, I want to suggest that a critical affirmation of this contract might serve as a productive *methodological* algorithm for a critical engagement with violent images—an algorithm that is grounded in Deleuze's ontological view of images. This pedagogical algorithm is not, however, a transcendental critical law; instead, it is "grounded" in the singularity of the encounter with an event as such—an encounter that, being initiated from within the event itself, heeds the irreducible specificity of that which calls forth response and thus response-ability. Such singularity ethically requires that one heed the event's primacy—that is, the affective intensities constitutive of (violent) images—which is precisely what blocks the application of the outcome of one encounter to the context of a different event. One could say that this kind of pedagogical algorithm is in no small way affected by a certain kind of forgetting—the forgetting of the (illusory) sense that one already knows what the object with which one is confronted is. Whereas the application of transcendental critical laws necessarily presupposes a priori knowledge of the object that allows one to apply a law with certainty, the masochistic pedagogy I am describing here is, as such, not applicable precisely because it is characterized by a *style* of encounter rather than a set of rules constituting a law. Whereas the latter is always a generality, the question of style is always one of singularity.

In this context, I should point to the masochist's desire to educate, a desire that might appear to be counterintuitive, given that one might be inclined to argue that the repeated pain to which the masochist exposes himself suggests that he does not learn at all (how else to explain the essentially incomprehensible repetition of pain?). However, rather than conceiving of forgetting as that which allows for the return of pain and memory as that which would prevent pain from occurring, Deleuze suggests that "forgetting is the impossibility of return, and memory is the necessity of renewal" (*Foucault* 108). Hence, the masochist's "forgetting" of his prior pain should not be read as negative—as his failure to learn. The masochist is not a Hegelian subject who somehow fails to learn from his failures. Rather, forgetting is the enabling mechanism that, in conjunction with memory (configured as memory of the future), enables the masochist to become-otherwise. Education, in the masochistic economy, is therefore not based on imitation but on the concept of alliance, of response or encounter. Or, as Deleuze writes, "we learn nothing from those who say: 'Do as I do.' Our only teachers are those who tell us to 'do with me,' and are able to emit signs to be developed in heterogeneity rather than propose gestures for us to reproduce" (*Difference and Repetition* 23).

Crucially, the formal practice of masochism might be useful for a criticism of violent images not just because masochism is a pedagogical practice but especially because it is a *pedagogy of violence*—a practice of response to violence that insists on an encounter with violence on its own terms. Masochism carefully regulates its economy of violence. Masochism is a critical and clinical pedagogy that creatively establishes a belief in this world through disavowal. As Deleuze explains, "Disavowal should perhaps be understood as the point of departure of an operation that consists neither in negating nor even destroying, but rather in radically contesting the validity of that which is: it suspends belief in and neutralizes the given in such a way that a new horizon opens up beyond the given and in place of it" (*Masochism* 31). Contesting the validity of that which is—is not this Nietzschean provocation precisely what must be affirmed if one wants to escape the cliché, if one wants to avoid an immediate reduction of the event inhering the violence of sensation to the clichés embodied in the violence of representation?

How, then, does the masochist manage to contest the status quo? First and foremost, he contests the validity of that which is by having recourse to the fetish, but, as Deleuze insists against psychoanalytic dogma, the fetish is "not a symbol at all, but as it were a frozen, arrested, two-dimensional image, a photograph to which one returns repeatedly to exorcise the dangerous consequences of movement, the harmful discoveries that result from exploration; it represents the last point at which it was still possible to believe" (*Masochism* 31). This freezing of movement—the production of the time-image—is akin to slowing down, indeed arresting, the movement inherent to representation that proceeds always with too much speed from that which is (the reality of an image) to that which is characterized by the logic of lack (the representation of reality). Just as the time-image slows down the logic of the movement-image, which, according to Deleuze, largely dominated cinema history before the end of World War II, so the masochistic act of fetishizing (or obsessively lingering on and returning to) the same image is a critical and clinical practice mobilized to open up the given—what is—to the future. Indeed, this is a practice that traverses all of the central personae of this study: the Coen Brothers, Bret Easton Ellis, Patricia Highsmith, Robert DeNiro, Don DeLillo, and, indeed, Gilles Deleuze.

Obsessively lingering with the object—and thus forging an alliance, indeed a friendship, with it—allows that existence to become other to itself; through this specific practice of encountering the other, existence becomes available to the masochist as a moment of pure differentiation, of futurity. Or, to put this same argument in formal terms, masochism is, according to Deleuze, "a state of waiting; the masochist experiences waiting in its pure form. Pure waiting divides naturally into two simultaneous currents, the first representing what is awaited, something essentially tardy, always late and always postponed, the second representing something that is expected and on which depends the speeding up of the awaited object" (*Masochism* 71).

The masochist, however, creates this state *actively* with the help of the masochistic contract. It is the contract that stipulates the precise rules by which the masochistic economy—consisting of the mistress and the masochist—is to proceed. Doing so, the carefully regulated masochistic practice actualizes varying configurations of image forces that allow something new—namely, the future—to emerge. Through this actualization of virtual forces resulting from a process of giving oneself over to the other by suspending movement, the masochistic contract positions the masochist in such a way that he encounters himself as different from himself: "I is another" (Deleuze, *Cinema 2* 133). This is why the masochist literally suspends his body with the help of his mistress: to engage in a practice that continually alters the parameters of his body and thus his subjectivity. He expands his capacity to be affected by difference. Bound in chains, stretched to the limits of what the body can take, frozen in a moment of time, the masochist becomes the one who takes seriously and responds to Spinoza's contention that we do not even know what a body can do (finding out is by definition a question of experimentation and thus the future).[15] And the masochist affirms this experience precisely as a means to encounter difference, the new—the future. He is both the subject of and the audience for violence. He bears witness to it while he is also being cast as the person presumed guilty.

But it is only in the practice itself that the masochist enters this double-becoming. He is thus never in the present but always of the future—a yet to come, a subject yet to be produced through and in the practice itself, in and through its performative force. As Deleuze writes, the masochist "waits for pleasure as something that is bound to be late, and expects pain as the condition that will finally ensure (both physically and morally) the advent of pleasure. He therefore postpones pleasure in expectation of the pain which will make gratification possible. The anxiety of the masochist divides therefore into an indefinite awaiting of pleasure and an intense expectation of pain" (*Masochism* 71). Actualized as a pedagogical algorithm for a critical engagement with violence, the task would then be to defer the advent of pleasure that criticism clearly derives from the arrival of the moment at which the critic gets to articulate his judgment of violence, or certainty (even if it comes in form of the assertion that the representational meaning remains undecidable). This is possible only if the critic gives him- or herself over to the expectation of pain resulting from the intensity of the encounter with violent images.

Ethics, configured masochistically as response-ability, is, therefore, a matter of speed modulation, of slowing down the speed of judgment, or representation. The attraction of representation, of judgment, is precisely the intensity of this speed, the rush felt by quickly arriving at the meaning, the significance, of violent images, which is affirmed all the more precisely because it allows us to escape the speed inhering the violence of sensation, one that moves intensively rather than extensively, slowly rather than quickly, remaining momentarily frozen rather than instantaneously moving elsewhere. I submit that this masochistic pedagogy—itself a practice of violence—would be productive for an encounter with *all* images; yet, violent images, because of their special discursive status, present us with a limit case for this masochistic pedagogy that the following chapters intend to hold up to the test of actual critical practice.

Masocriticism

Given the masochistic practice of the yet to come, the register of re-presentation becomes meaningless—or in any case its usefulness is put into question—as the yet to come is a question of *production*. Conceptualized this way, a criticism of violence must engage in a rigorous practice of deferrals, of diagnosing instead of judging images, of producing a symptomatology instead of a history of syndromes, of responding through the affective, visceral side of language and images rather than through their second order level—representation.[16]

Clearly, masochistic practice can never be based on prediction, on prior knowledge; rather, the masochist is forced to give himself over to the yet to come, the future, as his body will be reconfigured only through his engagement with his mistress that is regulated through their contract. In other words, the masochistic—read, critical—body is inevitably altered by the encounter with the future rather than with the past or present. The masochist is thus engaged in a perpetual production of subjectivity, one that shifts and permeates as it comes into contact with specific machines or gets disconnected from others. Rather than either pleasure or pain, the masochist is interested in the affective experience of the moment, the in-between, the suspense and what it does. And the question of what it does necessarily belongs to the future, for the masochist must experiment—"do it"—before he can find out.[17]

Masochism—and its critical practice, what I propose to call "masocriticism"—is thus not an epistemology but a pragmatics. I borrow the term "masocriticism" from Paul Mann's essay of the same title. However, even though his essay provides an interesting metacommentary on the practice of criticism, I strongly disagree with his view of masochism as being about lack and representation: "The Hegelian system is masochism writ large (or masochism is shrunken Hegelianism). Masochism is a theater in which one submits to enslavement and thereby hopes to overcome enslavement" (43–44). Via Deleuze (and Guattari), I hold against Mann's reading that masochism is not a theater but a factory, not about representation but about production. Masochism is a practice—one that is not about the hope to overcome enslavement but about *regulating* the moment of enslavement. The masochist needs someone else and must thus act with the other rather than imitate a preexisting set of actions or states. The masochist *needs* his mistress. This relation is a priori configured in terms of an ethical alliance that is characterized by a double movement: just as the mistress must heed her contracted obligation to the other (the masochist), so the latter seeks out his subjection to the other (the contracted mistress). This double movement describes a double-becoming, a becoming-otherwise that is specific to, since generated by, the relation itself.

And the same characterizes the critical practice of masocriticism: just as the text to be responded to, through its sheer existence as a specifically configured object, arrives before me with a set of expectations derived from its process of generation (which is irreducible to the concept of intentionality and exceeds the explanatory force of context), so the critical act seeks out, through subjection, an encounter with this other (the text) in such fashion that the singularity of this other, of its process of generation and the inhering affective force, is aided in its effectivity, in realizing itself, rather than being reterritorialized onto a plane where its virtual potential is weakened or simply blocked. In short, maso-criticism—conceived of as the immanent condition of possibility for an encounter with violence—necessitates response, and the latter requires a giving over of oneself to the Other, to becoming-other, to the process of being affected and effectuated by and from the future—to the experiment.

Consequently, a masochistic practice strongly resonates with Deleuze's notion of storytelling. As he writes in his analysis of cinema, "story-telling is not an impersonal myth, but neither is it a personal fiction: it is a word in act, a speech-act through which the character continually crosses the boundary which would separate his private business from politics, and which *itself produces collective utterances.* [. . .] Not the myth of a past people, but the story-telling of a people to come. The speech-act must create itself as a foreign language in a dominant language, precisely in order to express an impossibility of living under domination" (*Cinema* 2 222–23). A critical speech act must produce itself as foreign to the clichés of a critical discourse steeped in representationalism. Importantly, however, doing so is not a matter of subversion, which is a thoroughly representational concept and practice. Nor is storytelling a question of self-expression, just as the masochist is not interested in expressing himself. Rather, both storytelling and masochism are practices of collective production, machines for the production of the future. They both work as a means to articulate the impossibility of living under domination or to contest what exists. And this strikes me as the task of masocritical practice as well: being in the business of producing speech acts, masocritical practice is a priori configured as a *collective* utterance. Being engendered only by an affirmation of an alliance with the other qua the other's engendering force and thus its mutability, masocriticism participates in the collective production of futurity as an event that is always to come; *in* this production, *in* this immanent reconfiguration, the forces of that which "exists" (representation) are intensified and redirected for them to become-otherwise.

Masochistic practice, of course, entails more than just speech acts, but it is nonetheless crucially governed by one specific speech act—the contract. Through this contract, the masochistic practice is tightly regulated, yet it is through this regulation that the future arrives in the form of pure difference. With the help of the contract, the masochist gives himself over to his mistress under the precise regulations upon which they agreed, thus setting in motion their mutual process of becoming-otherwise (a process that Caspar's definition of ethics blocks—with fatal consequences for his ability to exist).

Again, this practice of giving over introduces the moment of the future, the creation of future stories, of people yet to come, as the masochist has merely provided parameters of and for his experiences, but by no means has he determined the action, its time, or location. Instead, he enters an alliance with the other, a life in domination, but this domination simultaneously consists of a refusal to be dominated by dominant culture. The masochist tweaks domination into something else, an encounter with the violence of sensation in which the future, alterity, emerges, becomes actualized—but only with the help of the other.

Importantly, masochism as a practice/pragmatics of violence violently pushes the concept of alterity to its own limit. If an encounter with alterity is taken seriously in ethical terms, violence seems to constitute the extreme limit: do I give myself over to the other even though I will be violated? The masochist answers this question in the affirmative, even though the affirmation necessitates, and is thus limited by, the masochistic contract. Nonetheless, the masochist's response to alterity reveals the liberal humanist rhetoric of communicative reason and its desire for consent ("let us acknowledge our difference and agree to disagree, so we all can get along") for what it is: an obliteration of difference (and as such violence writ large) rather than an affirmation of difference.

In short, masochism—masocriticism—is a rigorous practice of experimentation that, to borrow from Deleuze's description of the time-image, "carries out a *suspension of the world* or affects the visible with a *disturbance*, which, far from making thought visible [is] on the contrary directed to what does not let itself be thought in thought, and equally to what does not let itself be seen in vision" (*Cinema 2* 168). The masochist suspends the world by creating a new one with the help of the other (a person, an object, an image). Being (literally) suspended, the masochist becomes-other, just as the other is affected by the masochist and becomes-masochist (*pace* an entire tradition of criticism influenced by Sigmund Freud who considered masochism and sadism as one coherent entity: sadomasochism). Together, they create a world, stories, and thought that do not refer to systems of judgment. Their world, stories, and thought, though real, are more akin to what Deleuze calls falsifying narration, which "frees itself from [and] shatters the system of judgment because the power of the false (not error or doubt) affects the investigator and the witness as much as the person presumed guilty" (*Cinema 2* 133).

The following chapters aim at developing and performing this shattering of judgment in their repeated encounters with violence. Chapter 2 focuses on the novel and film *American Psycho* in order to delineate more carefully what it may cost critical practice to approach violent images through the lens of representation; chapter 3 provides a theoretical genealogy that explains why representation is always already a question of judgment; chapter 4 engages the fiction of Patricia Highsmith—especially her Ripley novels—in order to investigate how a fiction writer creatively works through the problem of representation as a problem of judgment in the context of violence; chapter 5 focuses on the acting work of Robert DeNiro in order to complicate the key distinction of working through and acting out that structures much of the moral discourse on (media) violence; and chapter 6 turns to Don DeLillo's essay on 9/11 in order to show in conclusion what the payoff of masocriticism may be for the so-called real world.

Throughout this book, I will pursue a double focus: on one

2 Judgment Is Not an Exit

Representation, Affect, and *American Psycho*

Comparison, Representation, Judgment

Mary Harron opens her generally well received film adaptation of Bret Easton Ellis's infamous 1991 novel *American Psycho* as if she consciously wanted to heed Jean-Luc Godard's well-known anti-representational adage "not blood, red," with which he matter-of-factly responded to a *Cahiers du Cinéma* interviewer who suggested that Godard's *Pierrot Le Fou* was banned for children under eighteen because "there is a good deal of blood in *Pierrot*" (Godard, "Let's Talk about Pierrot" 217). Against a sterile backdrop of pure white, small red blotches slowly drip down the screen, one by one, without further (contextual) commentary or explanation except for the nondiegetic, eerie violin sounds that accentuate the dripping. Conditioned by numerous horror movies, countless articles on the making of the film, prerelease reviews evaluating Harron's adaptation, and, potentially, the memory evoked by the book itself and the public controversy it spawned, the audience probably expects Harron to cut to the chase right from the outset and show Patrick Bateman—psychotic Wall Street broker extraordinaire—committing one of his grisly deeds. Given that Ellis's novel has gained the questionable reputation of being one of the most scandalously gory American novels ever to be published by a mainstream publishing house, it makes only sense for Harron to mark from the first scene what the novel is all about: violence.[1]

The slow dripping of the red gradually mutates into a slow drizzle, perhaps suggesting a gaping wound waiting off-screen to be revealed by one of the next shots. The audience readies itself for some potentially discomforting images—perhaps a close-up of a slain woman with her breasts cut off, a homeless beggar with his eyes gouged out, or a well-dressed yuppie put out of his misery by one swift blow to the head with a designer ax.[2] After all, we have seen many horror flicks before, and thus we know that the red we see must be blood. Yet, to our surprise—articulated by audible sighs of relief conveyed through chuckling or outright laughter by the audiences with whom I watched the film the day of its theatrical release—the next shot reveals the red running down the white screen as nothing more ghastly than a decorative condiment being drizzled around the circumference of an expensive looking nouvelle cuisine dessert. What once was blood now appears to be raspberry sauce.

With this wonderfully Godardian opening moment, the film performatively introduces the novel's singular asignifying, affective force. Or so it seems, for almost instantaneously Harron abandons her attempt at rendering cinematically Ellis's violent text as a question of affects and forces rather than significations and meanings. As this chapter will argue in greater detail, the film substitutes the latter question for the former by extracting and reshaping the novel's forces in such a manner that the film quickly turns into a relatively traditional satire—in this case of Wall Street capitalism in the 1980s as exemplified by Patrick Bateman, the psychotically violent yuppie protagonist of Ellis's novel. In cinematically instantiating the critical reception of *American Psycho* that obsessively judged Ellis's alleged satirical representation of Reaganomics, Harron's film symptomatically embodies the tendency of cultural criticism to conceive of violence as a matter of representation and, in turn, to mark as *judgment* the inevitable violence it does to a (violent) text.[3]

Remarkably, Harron's film received considerably more praise than scorn, and none of the negative critical responses have even come close to approaching the level of hostility launched against

Ellis's novel.[4] Even when the film is reviewed unfavorably, it is still seen as an improvement over the book. In fact, those who consider the film a failure blame the book for it. For instance, Tony Rayns claims in *Sight and Sound* that overall "the film doesn't work" (42). He goes on to argue, however, that, "against the odds, Mary Harron and Guinivere Turner have succeeded in extracting a viable narrative screenplay from this plotless blank. [. . .] [T]hey have sensibly junked a huge amount" (42). How, then, can we explain that the film has generally been well received when the textual basis for it has been so widely and forcefully reviled? Why has Harron's film adaptation avoided the anger and outrage that Ellis has been fighting off since the book's publication? This question emerges as being even more pertinent if we consider that many critics (from both the left and the right) who are concerned about the effects that art might have on a given audience maintain that film tends to be a medium that through its visceral immediacy has the power to affect an audience more violently than a book. To begin answering these questions, I suggest that we have to attend to one of the film's main effects, namely, its indexing the practice of critiquing both Bret Easton Ellis's novel and (violent) texts in general. This indexing occurs, however, precisely because the film deploys (a response to) the critical discourse surrounding what I call the event "American Psycho" as one of its key narrative engines.

Taking seriously this suggestion results in an important methodological consequence for this chapter, namely, that it does not provide a sustained interpretation of either the novel or the film. This chapter is not interested in uncovering the meaning of either text but rather in mapping out the relationship between them as it manifests itself on and through the surface level of critical practices and discourse. Unlike most instances of cinematic adaptations of literary blueprints, I maintain that *American Psycho* is a special case because of the role played by the critical discourse surrounding the novel. This is not simply turning a poorly written book into a respectable film, as may have been the case, for instance, with many noir films of the 1940s and 1950s (especially those not based on the works by Dashiell Hammett, Raymond Chandler, or James M. Cain).

What, then, does criticism of violence do? One answer is that it compares. Just consider that one of the most repeated statements about media violence is that, supposedly, today we have more mediated violence (TV, movies, video games) than ever before. In fact, this comparative statement has achieved the false wisdom of "common sense," as it has been produced by having been repeated ad nauseum for the last three decades.[5] An example of performativity in the Derridean sense, such a cliché is part of the target of my project. It is because such "common sense" wisdom has coagulated to a stale dogma that our critical and ethical task is to abstract clichés from the existing mise-en-scène of critical discourse in order to articulate what violence does and how it works. In doing so we will begin to develop a different pedagogical network that offers a mode of response to violence that, while always constituting a form of violence itself, commits its violence immanently, always heeding the primacy of a specific articulation of violence as a multiplicity of forces.

Again, then, criticism compares, whether themes and styles, authors, or directors, across decades or within a given year.[6] And, perhaps most importantly, criticism's ultimate interest tends to be a comparison of a different yet related kind: that between the text and the reality it is said to represent. Notwithstanding the theoretical interventions of post-structuralist philosophers (or artistic practices such a L-A-N-G-U-A-G-E poetry), one of the most dominant habits of cultural criticism from Plato to the present has been to compare a work of art to reality; further, at least since Plato, this comparison has been inscribed with the tendency to judge the work of art in terms of its truth value.[7] The closer art resembles life, the higher its value; the less accurate its representation—the more dissimilar the copy is from the original—the more questionable its merit.[8] Obviously, it would be overly simplistic to claim that today's critics are exclusively, or at least predominantly, Platonists, and it would be equally problematic to suggest that cultural criticism has not moved beyond Matthew Arnold's practice of moral criticism. However, by diagnosing the discourse spawned by *American Psycho*, I want to show that the particular *style* of contemporary engagement with violent cultural texts continues to perpetuate that which has emerged with Platonism's denunciation of simulacra as dangerously inferior artifacts compared to "true" copies: that is, the critical habit to respond to violent art as a matter of representation that inevitably, however subtly, demands a judgment of it.

Focusing on the event "American Psycho," of course, is not a neutral choice. Rather, I am interested in it precisely because the novel, its critical reception, and the film as part of the latter violently articulate the problematic at hand: the way critical discourse habitually translates the asignifying forces of (literary and cinematic) images—affective intensities—into a signifying regime of judgment. This regime consistently questions the value of violence as if we already knew what violence in the realm of aesthetics is or can do, all the while ignoring in its sheer self-assurance the Nietzschean provocation to investigate the value of value itself. Attending to the event "American Psycho," then, will hopefully help us work out what is at stake in the question of imaged violence, thus allowing us to formulate a series of problems that subsequent chapters will reframe, develop, and respond to.[9]

Given that criticism is about comparing, the question emerges whether we can imagine ways of comparison that do not rely on, or have recourse to, the mode of judgment as a crucial component of critical practice. Or, to put a different spin on this question, given the inevitability of violence that criticism does to that which it encounters (i.e., *any* criticism is selective and thus omits, paraphrases and thus changes, translates and thus alters, cuts into the object and thus extracts), is it possible for criticism to mark its violence not immediately as judgment?[10] The task here is neither to get rid of comparison as a critical tool nor to deny the inevitable violence of one's critical practice. Rather, it is to ask why this violence tends to be marked as judgment and what the cost of this is, as well as whether we possess alternative tools that might allow us to engage in comparative criticism without accepting its invitation to judge.

Deleuze's Symptomatology

What, then, might be the problem with judgment? Considering criticism's potential to be something other than critique—which, from Kant on, has been the most venerated way of reacting to an (artistic) event—Gilles Deleuze provides one answer to this question and, in turn, offers us a way of responding to events without judgment or, in any case, without immediately having recourse to it. Evoking Friedrich Nietzsche, Baruch Spinoza, and Antonin Artaud, Deleuze argues in "To Have Done with Judgment" that the problem with judgment is a pragmatic one: "Judgment prevents the emergence of any new mode of existence. For the latter creates itself through its own forces, that is, through the forces it is able to harness, and is valid in and of itself inasmuch as it brings the new combination into existence. Herein, perhaps, lies the secret: *to bring into existence and not to judge*. If it is so disgusting to judge, it is not because everything is of equal value, but on the contrary because what has value can be made or distinguished only by defying judgment" (135, my emphasis). It is important to stress Deleuze's assertion that "not everything is of equal value." In other words, neither Deleuze nor fellow post-structuralists such as Jacques Derrida or Michel Foucault are relativists or nihilists, as the antitheory crowd often alleges. Given the genealogical connection to Nietzsche, to whom the nihilist was the enemy, this can be news only to those who falsely believe that the German philosopher holds mass at the altar of nihilism. I see my argument in friendship with this nonnihilistic, nonrelativist, Nietzschean genealogy, for which value has to be produced, not reproduced. In contrast, judgment reproduces value based on a preexisting (moral) ground, thus perpetuating the same modes of existence rather than helping the new/difference to emerge.[11]

Deleuze suggests we take Spinoza's claim that we do not even know what a body can do more seriously. For Deleuze the crucial question is not how to judge a body but to find out what else a body is capable of and how it can exist differently: how else can a body enter relationships with other bodies whose operative engine is *affective* force—with the vector of this force (its weight and direction, that is, its intensity) determining the capacity of a body both to be affected by and affect other bodies? Hence, for Deleuze, whose critical eye always searches for that which has the capacity to produce new lines of flight productive of new modes of existence, it is love and hate—forces, affects—instead of judgment that provide the impetus for writing critically on literature or film, for diagnosing which responses work and which do not.

Love and hate, I should stress, are fundamentally different modes of intensity than judgment, notwithstanding the important fact that all three affective modalities are part of the same sliding scale of responsiveness and thus response-ability. Seen in this light, the critical task of comparing is *not* a question of judging any given term of the comparison as superior or inferior, good or evil. From Deleuze's point of view for whom "the only true criticism is comparative [. . .] because any work in a field is itself imbricated within other fields" ("Brain Is the Screen" 367), the judgmental mode of comparison seems only to perpetuate the status quo, as this chapter will show in the next sections. It continues to affirm a given moral ground based on which judgment is passed, thus remaining incapable of inventing a new mode of response or line of flight. Against this, Deleuze engages in comparative criticism because it allows connections to be drawn, linkages to be foregrounded, differences to be articulated—in short, it allows for the production of new modes of existence, of becoming-affected otherwise.

Perhaps most importantly, comparative criticism as conceived and practiced by Deleuze is capable of diagnosing art in terms of symptoms rather than syndromes. He does not ask what the disease (syndrome) "is" in order to cure it but investigates the symptomatic forces (in Nietzschean terms, active and reactive forces) that make up the syndrome: he asks what symptoms do, how they work, rather than debating whether something is bad or not. Instead of blaming a virus and trying to get rid of it because of what it *is*, for instance, Deleuzean symptomatology diagnoses which forces of the virus's makeup can be harnessed productively. The question is always, how can these forces be deployed *differently*? As Paul Patton, one of Deleuze's most lucid commentators, explains, "While [illness] is clearly a reactive force, its value depends on the nature of the subject and how it responds to the illness which acts upon it. The same physiological state may weaken some powers but also open new possibilities of feeling or bring about new capacities for acting and being acted upon" (63).

Rather than conflating syndromes with symptoms and thus overlooking the way illness is always multiple, symptomatology harnesses the varying forces immanent to modes of existence as a way into human relationships, into multiplicity. Hence, symptomatology fights and experiments with the multiplicity of forces immanent to something like cancer (or, as will be seen throughout, violence), not because of some moral understanding of what the syndrome *is*, but because of what the symptoms *do*—that is, because of their effects.

Put differently, comparison is always a sort of classification, something Deleuze was particularly fond of throughout his life.[12] He argues that a "classification always involves bringing together things with very different appearances and separating those that are very similar. [. . .] A classification is always a symptomatology" ("Brain Is the Screen" 368). Deleuze's use of symptoms, however, ought not to be confused with hermeneutic psychoanalytic practices where symptoms are ultimately something to be uncovered and cured. Of course, not all psychoanalysis is hung up on uncovering symptoms. For example, Slavoj Žižek proposes for psychoanalysis to focus on the fetish rather than symptoms because today "ideology functions in a way that is much closer to the notion of [the former]" ("Philosopher" 8). His notion of symptom, however, crucially differs from Deleuze's in that for Žižek everything begins and ends with the Lacanian notion of constitutive Lack—the impossible nonobject of desire that, for

Lacanian psychoanalysis in its best form, defines the process of subject, and thus social, formation. In contrast, Lack—representation—plays no such role in Deleuze's thought. It is precisely this conceptual aporia between Deleuze and Jacques Lacan that, despite their thoughts' many seeming convergences, marks the irreducible difference between them.[13]

For Deleuze, then, symptomatology diagnoses the differences between objects in order to emphasize the differences without eradicating them, without reducing them to some prior original identity, including the central Lacanian concept of Lack that is supposed to govern the entirety of our sociopsychic economy. Further, it describes these differences as being produced on the same plane of immanence—that is, objects' differences result from the same field of surface forces at work in the same cultural-historical matrix. To compare something with something else, therefore, is always a matter of diagnosing one object *through* the other, as a response to it, in an attempt to describe what the differences are, where they come from, what their intensities are, and what they suggest about the forces that have produced the difference.

Immanence, as Alain Badiou puts it, "requires that you place yourself where thought has already started, as close as possible to a singular case and to the movement of thought" (14). Hence, immanent criticism does not desire an (unattainable and thus always lacking) outside from which to judge safely the morality of the event. Commenting on the political and ethical inefficacy of cultural and political criticism's desire for an outside, prominent Marxist cultural theorists Michael Hardt and Antonio Negri concur with Deleuze's philosophy of immanence and contend that "we should be done once and for all with the search for an outside, a standpoint that imagines a purity for our politics. It is better both theoretically and practically to enter the terrain [. . .] and confront its homogenizing and heterogenizing flows in all their complexity, grounding our analysis in the power of the [. . .] multitude" (46). In other words, the only way out is through.

Taking the basic tenets of symptomatological comparative

criticism—intensity, immanence, and a Bartlebyesque attitude toward judgment, the exhausted "I would prefer not to" instead of the sadistic desire to transgress as a performative means to pass judgment—as the arrow of thought to be caught and redirected, let us turn to the comparison at hand: feminist director Mary Harron's cinematic response to Ellis's much-loathed *American Psycho*. Responding to both Deleuze's attitude toward comparative criticism and the objects of comparison, I want to diagnose the differences between the novel and its movie adaptation as symptoms of the larger discourse that the novel has produced and, in turn, been affected by since the prepublication of selected passages of Ellis's text in *Time* and *Spy* that introduced the public to the novel's title character, Patrick Bateman, as he engages in extreme acts of violence. All too often, critics argue that Harron's film captures the essence of Ellis's novel but is better because it condensed the excesses of the book. It is against this eradication of difference between two works of artistic production—the elision of specificity in favor of ultimately collapsing the two texts as one—that I want to deploy Deleuze's concept of "symptomatology," which he first introduced in *Masochism*: "Symptomatology is always a question of art" and is offered against dialectical sublimation in order to foster "a critical and clinical appraisal able to reveal the truly differential mechanisms as well as the artistic originalities" (14). By symptomatologically engaging Harron's film as a response to the event "American Psycho"—that is, to the novel *and* its discursive history—I ultimately conceive of the rest of this chapter as an attempt at articulating what it costs critical discourse consistently to read Ellis's novel representationally, that is, as a satire of the immoral materialist excesses of Reaganomics or, as Gavin Smith puts it in his review, as "a mordantly funny and agreeably blatant satire with genuine subversive bite" (72).

More specifically, I want to examine what it costs us in terms of our capacity to respond to a violently boring as well as boringly violent text such as *American Psycho* when critical discourse continues to affirm—indeed celebrate—Harron's decision to remove the novel's "excess fat in a kind of cinematic liposuction" (Holden B1). As a result of Harron's flattening out of Ellis's text, the film ends up eradicating the novel's varying intensities as embodied by its compositional cornerstones (repetition, boredom, and violence) in order to repeat the critical order-word "satire" that has dominated the popular and critical reception of Ellis's novel from the very beginning.[14] I want to foreground what happens with a type of criticism that "continually relies on and returns to older aesthetic categories [such as satire], even in its engagement with radically different forms of cultural production"—namely, that it remains incapable of heeding these works' "call for new terms for describing our responses to innovative works, new directions to be used in the work of critically commenting on them" (Ngai 16). In other words, while I will specifically compare admittedly selective moments from Ellis's novel and Harron's film adaptation, I am not so much interested in simply asserting that these two texts are different, let alone that one is better than the other. Precisely because the real question violent images raise is not whether violence is good or bad but what it does, I instead want to examine what the texts' differences consists of, from what practices these differences emerge, and why the differences indeed make a difference for cultural criticism's capacity to respond to both *American Psycho* in particular and aesthetic violence in general.

Harron's Film as a Double Response

From the beginning, critics have concentrated on three related questions about Ellis's novel: whether the text's violence is immoral or not, whether *American Psycho* is a successful satire or not, and whether the incessant repetitiveness and flatness of the book's prose indicates a satirical purpose or mere lack of authorial skill. Those who condemn the novel as immoral consistently reject its satirical component and deny Ellis any skill whatsoever. Christopher Hudson, for example, argues, "If there had been some anguished purpose behind [the novel's] obscenities—for instance, to reflect upon man or his society in extremis—they might, just possibly, have been defensible. *American Psycho* appears to be empty of any purpose whatsoever, other than to get its author back in the news after the critical and commercial failure of his second novel, *Rules of Attraction*" (qtd. in Lebeau 127). Terry Teachout concurs: "It's ineptly written. It's sophomoric. It is, in the truest sense of the word, obscene" (45). And, most infamously, Roger Rosenblatt encourages *New York Times* readers to snuff Ellis's book because of its "moronic and sadistic contents," because it is "so pointless, so themeless, so everythingless," and because the novel's main character "has no motivation for his madness [and] is never brought to justice."

Those who are willing to entertain the idea that the novel might have a moral purpose attempt to rescue the novel from its detractors by making as good of a case as possible for the text's satirical intentions and effects.[15] Critics' attitude toward Ellis's style, in turn, tends to be determined by how they judge the overall effect of the novel: those who judge it as conservative reject his style as artless; those who judge the novel as a more or less good satire think of the style as at least not entirely pointless.[16] Regardless of the outcome of the critics' judgment, however, the novel's violence itself is never conceptualized; it never constitutes the focus for response in and of itself. Indicative of the general difficulties surfacing when critical discourse encounters the issue of violence, the reception of *American Psycho* always configures the novel's violence as allegorical or metaphorical, as being about something other than violence itself—and the success of the violence's representational status determines the critical judgment of it. In other words, the critical violence done to Ellis's text—itself further highlighted by the passionate, often vitriolic rhetoric deployed by the critics—marks itself in terms of "judgment," as being concerned with whether violence is good or bad rather than with what it does.

Now, this critical violence done to the novel—one which consistently marks itself as "judgment"—does not so much constitute a problem because any of these critics are "wrong"; rather, it raises the more interesting questions of what judgment does, of what its effects are. Among the many effects this specific critical judgment had, one of the most remarkable was to have established the conditions of possibility for future responses to Ellis's *American Psycho*—in this case Mary Harron's film. In other words, Harron hardly could ignore the vicious and well-publicized character of the critical response to Ellis's novel, for the specificities of the reception's terms constituted the discursive formation by which any articulation of future responses was bound.[17] Whatever her personal response to Ellis's text might have been, by the time of shooting her film, Harron's response was inevitably bound to be a response to Ellis *through* the critical response that circulated in the public for the previous decade. Given the frequent attacks on the novel as dangerously immoral garbage, the possibilities for Harron to respond to the text without immediately setting herself up for the same kind of response that Ellis received were limited. To avoid the potential critical outrage looming at the horizon, Harron—who in her first feature-length film, *I Shot Andy Warhol* (1996), revisited the biography of Valerie Salonas, the infamous author of the SCUM (Society for Cutting Up Men) manifesto and wannabe assassin of Andy Warhol—was essentially forced to respond to the critical discourse by amplifying the element that was thought to be the solely redeeming factor of Ellis's violent novel: namely, its satire.

Of course, films are subject to rating systems and thus cannot always show what novels can, lest they receive an X rating. (Incidentally, we can easily imagine Oliver Stone, who had been interested in directing the film, greatly amplifying the violence and getting away with it.) However, I argue precisely that focusing on the representational *quantity* of cinematic gore constitutes, in a sense, the problem with much of cultural criticism of violence. Harron's film would not necessarily have been more affectively charged had she included more violence. Affect is not simply a matter of "more" in the purely quantitative sense of the word; rather, it is a matter of more or less in the sense of intensity. For instance, an example of the former would be to get drunk by consuming a bottle of Scotch; an example of the latter would be to get drunk on water (see Deleuze and Guattari, *Thousand Plateaus* 166). The question, thus, is how and to what effect cinema could render *American Psycho*'s violence nonrepresentationally, rather than whether more lenient codes would lead to more truthful representations. Can we, for example, imagine a Godardian encounter that does not depend for its affective force on representing Ellis's violence by trying to push the boundaries of industry limits to their utmost? That is, Godard's questions—"But are these the words and images to use? Are there no others?" (*Two or Three Things*, 1966)—remain as relevant as ever when it comes to any attempt to image an event.

In other words, by magnifying the novel's satirical aspects, Harron's film emphasizes that Ellis's violent novel *really* represents a critique of the social rather than constituting mindless glorification of violence, as has frequently been alleged.[18] From this symptomatological view of the event "American Psycho," then, it does not come as a surprise that the film embodies the critical debate that preceded it. The film does indeed mark its main interest in satirizing the shallowness and cruelty of 1980s American capitalism, a fact almost unanimously attested to by the film's critical reception. (In fact, one hardly finds any positive review of the film that does not use the word "satire." Even the reviews expressing dissatisfaction with the film discuss it in these terms.)[19] Without question, according to the film, Ellis's novel negatively judges its representation of Wall Street America; in turn, the film positively judges what it perceives to be the novel's satirical representation and does its best to clarify this purpose. The novel's violence, in all of this, functions merely as a metaphor for capitalism's cannibalistic cruelty—one that can be accepted precisely because it merely allegorizes the larger point of the novel.

Four relatively brief examples suffice to illustrate how exactly the film modifies the novel in order to amplify and elucidate its satirical—and thus representational—quality. First, Harron splices different scenes from the book together as a means of clarifying Bateman's motivation and psychology. She thus neu-

the novel's intense violence by turning it into a rather comforting and familiar slapsticklike violence that is easily recognizable to the audience from, say, the Scream franchise. Violence in Harron's film is, by and large, a matter of laughter, albeit at times uneasy laughter, whereas in the novel, to many critics' consternation, the violence inspired nothing but pure incomprehension. In short, all of these stylistic devices serve Harron to take the wind out of those critics' sails who might otherwise have been inclined to crush her film for the same reasons that they lambasted Ellis's book. Crucially, Harron succeeds at this task precisely by transforming the critical discourse on the book into the engine for the production and structuring of her cinematic images.[23]

Spending any more time than I have already on mapping out the satirical trajectory of Harron's film would go against the point of this chapter, namely, that Harron's film is a symptomatic *effect* of the novel and its reception, an effect that has already manifested itself rather obviously in the film's reviews. The fact is, Harron's film constitutes a response to Ellis's novel that has solicited a critical reception almost completely the reverse of that provoked by the original text: to wit, critical discourse affirms Harron's satirical strategies and praises her decisions to alter the novel so that just about everything offensive about it has disappeared. Here, I just want to demarcate the *cost* involved in allowing the order-word "satire"—which tends to be merely another name for the even older order-word "Truth" and the regime of representation within which it functions—to dominate one's (institutionalized) response to a text such as Ellis's. After all, what do we know once we have determined that the novel is satirical? What do we know about the force of the text—the force of language and images as such—once we know that *American Psycho* is a (un)successful satire? What exactly do we know about even sympathetic readers' extreme difficulty in dealing with the novel once we have endlessly repeated and obeyed the order to confine the text on the level of satire? What precisely do we know about the obsession that effectuated and affected the writing of the text and, in turn, the reading of it once we have concluded that the text was meant to be satirical or once we have decided whether or not Bateman really did the violent deeds just depicted (even if we decide that we cannot decide)?[24] And, finally, what do we know about that which upsets so many readers of *American Psycho*—the "excessive," unexplained, "incomprehensible" violence—once we agree that the novel satirizes the capitalist excesses of the past?

We have to ask ourselves, therefore, what other effects Harron's strategic modifications of Ellis's novel (might have) had: what does Harron's strategy and its wholehearted embrace by critical discourse cost us with regard to our capacity to respond not only to Ellis's extremely violent text but also to violent images in general? To find some answers, let us examine Harron's handling of what arguably constitutes the novel's most important dynamic: the interaction between its boringly slow passages of endlessly repeated details of Bateman's life and the speeded-up interruptions of violent outbursts.

The Boredom of Violence, the Violence of Boredom

The main difference between Harron's film and Ellis's book is marked by the extent to which boredom is deployed as a major stylistic strategy. Remember that one of the most annoying parts of the novel is the endless repetition of brand names, workout routines, restaurant menus, clothing advice, television programs, music criticism, misogynist comments, and non sequitur chitchat. Arguably, what happens in reading the novel is that (faithful, or perhaps better, patient) readers become bored by Ellis's narrative—despite its occasionally undeniable humor—and eventually begin to long for some action. (Remember too that the first scene of graphic violence does not even occur before about one-third of the way into the book.) The action, of course, arrives—as a surprise to those readers who paid little attention to a number of hints indicating that something may be amiss with Bateman and perhaps less surprising to those who have put those hints together and at the very least were aware of Bateman's penchant for violent actions. But, as shocking as the torturing of a homeless man and his dog surely is, it is only the gradual increase in repetition of exceedingly brutal mutilations of business acquaintances and former or current sex partners that through a speeded-up cumulative effect begins to affect the readers in such a manner that they find themselves in a position they have not occupied before, that they have not desired—a position that calls for a response for which, evidently, the "tools" are not (yet) immediately available.[25]

Hence, as evinced by the book's reception, most readers sooner or later begin to long precisely for that from which they have wanted to escape: the boring itineration of consumer goods, shallow observations, and senseless activities. In other words, Ellis's abandonment of any pretense to characterization, psychology, or motivation paradoxically lures readers into longing for the very violence Ellis does to English prose. Readers prefer the affective quality of prosaic, though often comical, boredom to that of heightened graphic aggression, yet it is, of course, the exposure to the former that affects and effectuates the response to the latter. Clearly, then, the repulsiveness of the text decidedly exists on both levels, as evidenced by the *force*fulness of the critical responses to it: that of the actual physical violence committed by Bateman and that of the prose itself. What readers discover is that, in the end, there indeed exists "no exit" (Ellis 399), no way out from the endless onslaught of the different but mutually resonating affective registers of violence.

Contrary to the novel, the film's emphasis on the "realness" of Bateman's actions—heightened by its explicit reliance on detection as a main plotting device—provides the audience with an exit by translating the question of violence and affect into that of truth and representation, without ever hinting that truth itself is an affectively charged product and practice of violence as well. However, it is hard to believe that readers struggling just to get through the novel are all that concerned with the question of whether or not Bateman actually committed the violent deeds. If nothing else, this question—the question of truth—arrives afterward, but whatever arrives then has already been affected and effectuated by the particular level of intensity of the encounter with the style and content of the narrative. To hate or to love as a response occurs prior to the analytic mode, prior to the potential concern with questions about truth. That the question of truth, satire, or representation indeed arrives, almost inevitably, speaks more to the institutional power to order and train readers in "adequate" or "moral" reading habits than to what the book itself does.

Yet, asking representational questions constitutes perhaps the main mechanism by which criticism has held at bay questions of affect, of asignification.[26] But since it is impossible to reject ad hoc, and thus claim a stance outside of, representational language, it is only by going *through* this diagram of reading ("representation") that critical language has any chance of providing readers with new tools to encounter a book such as *American Psycho*. Jeffrey Nealon eloquently argues this point: "Simply to assume such an 'outside' place would be to treat as the object of my discourse that which, in fact, constitutes the very conditions of possibility for discourse in general: a representative metaphysical structure characteristic of the epoch of modern subjectivity that sets up the parameters for what can be said and the ways in which it can be said. The only way to begin speaking about this system, then, is from within" (*Double Reading* 86–87). I am not claiming that masocriticism somehow miraculously transcends the logic of representation; rather, as I hope to show throughout, the matter is one of *slowing down* this logic or condition of possibility.

Whatever these new critical tools will be, then, for them to be different from the existing ones they would have to allow the affective quality of language or images intensively used by texts such as *American Psycho* to subsist without reducing them to the level of any other text. Instead of eradicating that which is different about the intensity of the affective component inherent to these texts, critical language would have to affirm affect as a means of articulating the new modes of existence invented in and by these artistic practices.[27] Perhaps the legendary American New Wave band Talking Heads was right in provoking us to "stop making sense." The problematic of violence simply cannot be "resolved" by ascribing meaning to something that, as Nealon argues vis-à-vis the unspeakable violent horror of Auschwitz, "is an irreducible event in that it cannot be reassuringly reduced to a logic that can be said to have brought it about" (*Double Reading* 77–78). Violence, in this sense, is not to be "understood" or reduced to theories of signification. Deleuze's symptomatology, therefore, emerges as a valuable tool for analysis because it productively cuts into what Brian Massumi astutely locates as the central problem of cultural discourse today, namely, "that there is no cultural-theoretical vocabulary specific to affect" (27).[28]

So, it is precisely the novel's "excessive" violence that overwhelms, frustrates, annoys, upsets, and even sickens; it is this overkill that provokes readers to throw away the book, to tear it apart, to spit at it, and, potentially, to talk or write about it. In other words, if nothing else, the value of the book is that it forces its audience to encounter the undeniably visceral response they have. The novel solicits a pure affective response from the audience, even though most critics who wrote about it have been unwilling—perhaps incapable—of acknowledging this, thus ironically emulating all those characters populating *American Psycho* who have proven to be incapable of seeing that their "boy next door," as Bateman's fiancé fondly calls him, is also the killer from hell. After all, how does one write about affect—asignifying forces—if one has been trained to respond to literature (and film) on the level of representation, meaning, and truth? How does one respond affectively—or, better, how does one heed one's affective response without immediately territorializing it onto a different level—when one of the most insistent sets of order-words has commanded us to care about whether or not a work of art accomplishes goals that are valued by critics or society, whatever that may entail?

But I immediately need to qualify the preceding paragraph's topical claim. For it is not so much the "excessive" violence of Ellis's *American Psycho* that creates its affect overload; instead, the

contesting one of the most widespread clichés about so-called postmodernism—to wit, that its artistic expressions are supposed to be affectless, a critical notion that was probably first articulated by Fredric Jameson in his landmark study in which he discusses the "waning of affect in postmodern culture" (10). It seems to me, however, that the extremely violent yet flatly narrated fiction of writers such as Dennis Cooper or Brian Evenson, to name but two additional examples, is anything but affectless. Or rather, such works can be deemed without affect only if we reductively conceive of affect in terms of a subject's emotions and feelings. Instead, what appears to be without affect—due to the narrative voice's seemingly monotonous flatness or the overall absence of psychological depth—instantiates nothing but a different degree of affective intensity. These fictions have their own affective force—one that is not defined by any lack in relation to the humanist privileging of psychological depth. By describing fictions such as Dennis Cooper's *Frisk* (1991) or *The Sluts* (2004), as well as Brian Evenson's "The Polygamy of Language" (2000) or *The Brotherhood of Mutilation* (2003), as affectless, literary criticism automatically territorializes these works onto the level of judgment (since generally, a lack of affect qua subjective emoting is deemed "bad" in one way or another) and neglects to diagnose how the violence in these texts actually works.

To return to the event "American Psycho," it seems to me that whereas Ellis's novel solicits its readers to diagnose what the textual violence does and how it works, the opposite occurs in Harron's adaptation. Arguably, the minutes leading up to the first scene of explicit violence—Bateman's killing of a homeless black man and his dog—are able to create effects similar to the book. Harron strings together a series of comedic events: serious looking waiters enumerating dinner menus; Bateman partying dressed in power suits; Bateman's obsessive cleansing routine; his vapid office routine; his shallow interaction with his fiancé; his love for cash machines; his troubles with the suspicious dry cleaner; his inability to get a table at Dorsia, his restaurant du jour; his crowd-pleasing sweating over other yuppies' better looking business cards; and his lecture on the state of the nation, consisting of a seemingly comprehensive string of catch phrases used by politicians on the campaign trail. All of this is quite funny. Then, almost out of nowhere, Bateman passes a homeless person. He stops, cynically teases him with a twenty-dollar bill, and then stabs him to death. At this moment, most of the audience with whom I watched the film went audibly quiet, sensing that they had been tricked by the preceding repetition of agreeable though mundane comedy. The violence on the screen seemed now to affect our response not only to that scene but also to the humorous moments before. Perhaps we felt betrayed by the narrative strategy, perhaps not, but it is clear that the film manages to solicit a rather visceral response at this stage.

However, whereas this sequence of scenes works well, the rest of the film does not—*if* the idea was to tap into the affective force of Ellis's novel. Harron's strategy was to condense the repetition of the book so that she could get it out of the way, not having her narrative weighed down by the repetition of the novel. As Harron tellingly comments on her technical problems to render the book cinematically, "I had to kind of give it more the façade of a plot" (Harron, Ellis, and Bale). Hence, in the first twenty minutes we essentially get the book in a nutshell. *Harron speeds up precisely that which is all about slowness in the book* in order to get on with her goal of creating a swiftly moving satire. This frontloading of the repetition prevents her from ever retuning to it, thus never slowing down the narrative so that no affects can emerge other than those solicited by standard Hollywood narratives in which chases and cheap thrills are the highpoints of affective production. Further, because Harron gets rid of any modulation of intensities, the violent scenes in the film become predictable, as they are never again set up as a surprise moment. Now we just move from one scene of violence to the next, evenly paced, whether it is a scene merely suggested or actually shown.

Finally, the film tames the affective force of violence through a twofold trick. First, it turns the violence into slapstick. (Bateman, naked, chasing a prostitute with a running chainsaw through the staircase of his Upper East Side apartment home must constitute one of the weirdest images of the film. Yet, one senses that this scene's over-the-topness might actually provide a key to a different cinematic response to the novel. Perhaps the film is not slapstick enough.) And second, the film renders identical the novel's radically different affective series of music criticism and violence. The book carefully juxtaposes the music criticism chapters not only to the violent chapters but to all other events in the book, thus severing the music chapters from the plot, casting them as pure interruption, as narrative breakdowns, as a form of narrative violence, dramatizing that narration works by breakdowns—by violence. By contrast, the film has Bateman rhapsodize about Genesis, Whitney Houston, and Huey Lewis and the News as a prelude to—indeed almost simultaneous with—his torturing of his victims, thus eradicating precisely that which gives rise to the specific affective encounters provoked by the reading of the novel: Do we feel more sickened by Bateman's assessment of the music or by his outrageously violent torture devices? And what does the answer to this question say about the reader? The film's strategy of having Bale read parts of the music chapters as farcical lead-ins to the ensuing violence—absurdly suggesting that the badness of the music almost inevitably leads to violence, which is akin to claiming that reading *American Psycho* leads to committing homicide—not only turns different series of events that intersect with each other into one and the same moment but it also results in the audience mostly laughing at the combination of ludicrous music criticism and slapstick violence. (Bale's performing a funny dance while pronouncing the greatness of Huey Lewis's "Hip to Be Square" merely accentuates the absurdity of the scene.) The fact that Harron sets all killings of prostitutes and acquaintances to Bateman's music lectures merely heightens the comedy, thus turning the potential for revolting, intensively sensed affects into one of comforting humor.

We should note that the book does not really clarify who is speaking in the music chapters. Although we (perhaps correctly) assume that it is Bateman, the matter remains somewhat ambiguous. In any case, it is unclear at what moment, in what form, and to whom the music criticism is narrated. The film, on the other hand, eradicates the narrative breakdown by unambiguously equating the narrative voice with Bateman. Whereas the book configures the question of breakdown—violence—as a question of (dis)embodied voice, the film posits voice, the satirist's point of view, as an exit, an escape route leading away from the allegedly immoral toward a moral place of judgment. Ellis's novel configures point of views as an effect of narrative violence; the film presupposes the untarnished existence of one point of view.[31]

The film is evenly paced, with very few up and downs. Indeed, it is oddly boring. But this boredom is of a different *kind* than the one produced by Ellis's novel. Whereas the latter is upsetting precisely because we have no capacity to respond to it in any meaningful or comforting way—because Ellis insists that boredom works as boredom only when disrupted by violence as violence, and vice versa, that is, as two series that exist parallel to, and yet affect, each other as well—the former is reassuring because we are led to affirm the satirical component (and the position of judgment such a narrative mode affords us). Ultimately, then, we can enjoy the film for its humor, its ridiculing of its characters and their world, and all the while remain convinced that we are living in a better world, that we have progressed, and that we are neither the perpetrators nor the victims of violence in any form. Hence, one might say that the movie is not boring enough. For if it had been boring in the sense of the novel, we would be forced to come to terms with the affects created by this boredom—with the potential to face violence qua violence rather than as a mediated form of satirical critique—regardless of whether or not the medium of film possesses a more immediate affective quality than literature.

But that the film is perhaps not boring enough is not so much a lack inherent to the film or an expression of a desire for the film to "represent" more accurately. (Affect is a matter of doing, not signification.) Rather, the diminished level of boredom present in the film constitutes Harron's symptomatic cinematic response to the critical discourse on *American Psycho*, for one of the two main complaints against the novel was precisely that it was too boring and thus could not sustain any readerly interest. (It was, of course, also the perception that the novel's boredom accentuates the novel's violence that, in turn, formed the basis for the most violent reactions to Ellis's text.) The agreeable pace of the film caters to our existing capacity to read or watch—react to—a text. It furthers that which we are trained in throughout high school and college, through film (and literary) criticism, academic and popular alike, as well as through an endless exposure to the majority of Hollywood narratives that thrive on at times outrageous but mostly tame, cliché-ridden solicitations of affective viewer responses. That is, in such narratives affect itself turns into a cliché at the very moment it is territorialized onto merely visceral, physical emotions. This is not to deny that such emotions are important (see Shaviro or Sobchack for excellent arguments in this direction), but if affect is configured as nothing but emotion, or is made to do nothing but appeal to emotions, then the (position of the) subject itself is never put at stake, thus inviting him or her to activate judgment as the primary mode of response.

In the process of "humanizing" Ellis's work along the lines configured by the critical language used in response to his novel—that is, by creating a way out that depends on the individual, fully psychologized, truthful human agent—everything that the novel is almost too self-evidently about is eliminated: affective intensity. In the novel, affect is configured and produced by the text's simultaneous potential for boring and horrifying its readers, a potential that the novel achieves precisely because it proves that horror and boredom are *not* contradictory terms but instead exist as affects next to each other on the same plane of immanence, mutually producing and thus modifying each other. Boredom violates expectations, standards, bodies, and violence, in turn, is boring. (Note that the clinical rendering of it in *American Psycho* merely repeats the same violent scene with the similarly repeated addition of some extra spice. Harron—maybe out of recognition of the violent scenes' inherent boredom that nonetheless so forcefully affect readers—resists this narrative strategy by slapstick-ing all but the first violent scene.) The differences between these two forms of violence can only be determined in their effects, not in their intrinsic meaningfulness. The simultaneity, even in-discernibility, of shock and boredom so obviously missing from Harron's response to Ellis's text, affects our capacity to respond. As Sianne Ngai writes in a different context, the "sudden excita-tion of 'shock,' and the desensitizing we associate with 'boredom,' though diametrically opposed and seemingly mutually exclusive, are both responses that confront us with the limitations of our capacity for responding in general" (10).

Harron's representational reading of Ellis's novel turns a text that so obviously has affected readers on a visceral level through its alternating speeds—the boring slowness of the endless lists and so on and the fast-paced action of the often surprising violence—into a text that wants its audience to have a mostly cerebral response that is encouraged precisely by a rather even-keeled, predictable narrative pace that has rid itself of the novel's differentiating engine: repetition and violence. Like the critical reception that preceded it, the film focuses on what the book al-legedly means—a critique of the capitalist excesses of the eight-ies—and thus somehow never gets around to articulate what the book does, namely, that it produces readers apparently incapable of responding to the text's affective force in any way other than judging it.

To put the last point in Nietzschean terms, the novel produces untimely readers, readers who are yet to come, who are of the future that must be produced, readers who first have to develop the capacity to be affected without desiring to turn their affec-tive response immediately into a question of logos, rationality, cognition, and representation.[32] The film explains, delimits, and justifies to the audience the few moments it affords them of truly affective encounters with the images in front of them. It coerces them to respond judgmentally rather than affectively, or, in any case, privileges judgment as a particular modulation of affect. Harron's film, thus, is symptomatic of the common critical practice to pass judgment based on the representational quality of images and words. It solicits responses that reproduce the very regime of pedagogical discipline that has instilled in audiences the tendency to read and view texts representationally. Consequently, the film, as a continuation—indeed, an instantiation— of the critical discourse on Ellis's novel, eradicates those forces of the novel that have the capacity for producing difference, that which is unknown. But, as Deleuze argues about the possibility of and for writing, "How else can one write but of those things which one doesn't know, or knows badly? It is precisely there that we imagine having something to say. We write only at the frontiers of our knowledge, at the border which separates our knowledge from our ignorance and transforms the one into the other" (*Difference and Repetition* xxi).

It seems to me that violence is precisely such a frontier. Although we claim that we know violence when we see or experience it, violence has remained one of the great incomprehensible events of life—even more so in light of the fact that countless explanatory apparatuses have been mobilized to explain its causes.[33] Hence, *pace* just about all responses to Ellis's novel, including Harron's, *American Psycho*'s value appears to be precisely in presenting us with a practice of writing at this frontier, in experimenting with that which is "unknown" to us. (And this value might very well not have emerged as forcefully had it not been for Harron's film and the differences it symptomatically indexes.) In refusing to provide a premade explanation, the novel invents a new, albeit horrifying, knowledge, one that does not make sense of the frontier but inhabits it without reducing it to something other than what it is: the ultimate other. Responding to the other (violence) *as* other, as that which does not signify anything, as that which can be encountered merely through its forces that produce specific affective effects, however, would require criticism to heed Deleuze's encouragement to defer judgment, to do away with it: "Affect as immanent evaluation, instead of judgment as transcendent value: 'I love or I hate' instead of 'I judge'" (*Cinema 2* 141).

periment with, and articulate something about, affect in regard to a text so clearly productive of affective responses.[35] Criticism will continue to Other the capacity and knowledge provided by, and immanent to, affect as long as it persists to rely almost exclusively on an Enlightenment discourse of rationality, understanding, logos, and judgment (the possibility of which depending on a clear-cut distinction between a subject's preexisting point of view and the perceived object). By perpetuating the order-word "representation" (a syndrome), criticism continues to ignore that representations are made up of forces (symptoms), just as subjects are constituted by their point of views rather than the other way around. (Not coincidentally, the novel relentlessly shows us that identity is nothing but a series of masks, which are not defined by originary Lack but by their specific, nonlacking, *effective* reality. In contrast, the film insists that underneath the [beauty] mask we see Bateman peel off in front of his bathroom mirror there exists a "true," stable identity—even if this identity is described as nothingness, as Bateman's recognition that "There is no real me. [. . .] I simply am not there.") I want to suggest that cultural criticism must heed these surface forces if it wants to explain anything about language or images. Accordingly, any political project formulated in response to occurrences of violence in film or literature that might be interested in the question of resistance or subversion is, I think, trapped as soon as it focuses on the question of representation and judgment. It has no tools to account for the *emergence* of representations and is thus bound to ignore that representations are simply not "about" representations but always about forces—about doing, not meaning. Judgment—a critical practice immanent to the concept of representation in that the latter conceives of signs as reproductive and thus encourages a judgment of them in terms of their more or less accurate resemblance to reality and truth (the twin pillars for our conception of morality)—turns out to be part of the problem, *not* the solution, as I will argue in more detail in chapter 3.

Critically insisting on the superiority of the film costs us a lot, namely, a serious attempt to provoke questions about affect, to think about what affect can tell us about art, to ponder what happens to the alleged rarity of resistance once we give affect a bit more credit. To paraphrase Deleuze, once we focus on affect, the question is no more how we can resist (answer: by critique) but how we can tap into the affective forces—lines of flight—that constitute the social.[36] The social is always already in flight, according to Deleuze and Guattari; if fleeing constitutes an immanent component of the social, then affect does as well, as fleeing is a form of affect. Flight, then, is a question of intensities or affects: How fast or slow is this fleeing? In what direction and with what force does it proceed? And with what acceleration and pressure does it move? Hence, the political and pedagogical question to ask—one that, I think, Ellis's novel provokes but perhaps could be actualized only through Harron's cinematic response—is how we can become capable of becoming-affected by forces without immediately turning their affect into a critical discourse of logos. Masochism and its economy of boredom and contractual violence might have to say some interesting things in response, as I suggested in chapter 1. In terms of cinema, we might want to think about how film—as one of the more privileged affect producing machines thanks to the viscerally immediate quality of visuality—could teach us how to respond on the level of affect to a text such as *American Psycho*.[37]

But perhaps the preceding chapter has moved too quickly. In claiming that the practice of contemporary criticism continually expresses its desire to judge, I might have given the impression that all of contemporary criticism merely consists of an extension of Matthew Arnold, that well-known figure of Victorianism whose critical project is, rightly or wrongly, often understood to be synonymous with exercising value judgments. Well-known reference books such as C. Hugh Holman and William Harmon's *A Handbook to Literature* describe Arnold's project as "seeking to judge literature by high standards" (117), a sentiment seconded by the *Norton Anthology*'s introduction to Arnold ("culture represents for Arnold the most effective way of curing the ills of a sick society" [1348]), manifesting the reception and subsequent canonization of his thought as a moral, judgmental endeavor. Although the case may be more complicated than the entries on Arnold make it out to be, his own words lend much support to the idea that literary or, more generally, cultural criticism ought to contribute to the production of a civilized—read, moral—society. So he tirelessly went to bat for the critical study of the humanities—especially literature—to cure culture from its ills. In what can be considered his critical manifesto, the widely anthologized essay "The Function of Criticism" (1865), for instance, Arnold writes of the purpose of criticism that its business is "to see the object as in itself it really is [. . .] to make the best ideas prevail" (*Norton* 1391). Positioning himself against the popular belief in utilitarianism, Arnold instead advocated a criticism that remains "disinterested" (1397), by which he meant an independence and objectivity of the critical consciousness rather than a lack of interest as such. Hence, he writes in one of his best-known formulas, "By steadily refusing to lend itself to any of those ulterior, political, practical considerations about ideas [the task of criticism is] to know the best that is known and thought in the world, and by in its turn making this known, to create a current of true and fresh ideas" (1397).

Arnold never tired of repeating this formula—his basic definition of critical practice. He therefore tries to distinguish this description—or, rather, prescription—of critical practice from that of passing "mere" judgment. Arguing that "mere judgment and application of principles is, in itself, not the most satisfactory work to the critic" (*Norton* 1402), he promotes a more nuanced deployment of critical judgment: "it is by communicating fresh knowledge, and letting his own judgment pass along with it—but insensibly and in the second place, not the first, as a sort of companion and clue, not as an abstract lawgiver—that the critic will generally do most good to his readers" (1401). Yet, despite his reticence to come across as too much of a moralizer, it is quite clear that Arnold is indeed invested in the ability of literary criticism to better its readers' "sense of conduct." Arnold believes that the education in proper conduct makes the study of literature superior to that of the natural sciences, as he argues in "Literature and Science," his response to Thomas Henry Huxley's claim that the study of literary works does not provide sufficient knowledge of the world in light of the enormous developments in the natural sciences since the medieval ages. Arnold counters Huxley's claims by arguing that science produces "knowledge [that is] not put for us into relation with our sense of conduct" (1436)—that is, scientific knowledge, while undeniably important, has nothing to say about the moral questions faced by individual and society. In short, despite Arnold's complicating his view of criticism as not being directly a judgmental discourse, he ultimately conceives of his practice as precisely that—and thus confirms his subsequent reception in the field of literary studies.

Are contemporary critics, then, still Arnoldians? Yes and no. Clearly, as illustrated in the previous chapter, public criticism as published in popular culture magazines or daily newspapers knows almost no other mode of operation—particularly when it encounters the issue of violence. In that sense, magazines such as *Entertainment Weekly*, newspapers such as the *New York Times*, or TV shows such as *Ebert and Roper at the Movies* do not so much function as objective distributors of information than as filter mechanisms that regulate what their audience will read, listen to, and watch. The sheer abundance of information is thus channeled in certain directions. The frequent occurrence of moral judgment passed by these sites operates simply as one of the most powerful tools to direct, indeed produce, cultural knowledge.

Cultural studies scholar Lawrence Grossberg calls this mechanism a "regulatory regime" (*We Gotta Get Out* 164). The same regime has, of course, been operating on many other registers for a long time. For instance, the production code of the Motion Picture Producers and Distributors of America (MPPDA), "written in 1930 but not effectively enforced until 1934" (Schatz 2), regulated Hollywood's film productions until it was replaced by the MPAA rating system in 1968, which introduced the letter rating system that, in modified form, is still in place today. Likewise, the TV ratings mandated by the Telecommunications Act of 1996 codify images for the small screen based on the same "niche market" principle that Hollywood uses. What both the "wholesale" and "retail" principles of governing images have in common, however, is the media corporations' desire to keep the government at arm's length. Lest the government enforce a law that would regulate the entire industry from outside, media companies have always been savvy enough to avoid such external regulations by couching their internal regulating mechanisms in moral terms. For instance, the production code was dominated by a rhetoric to protect the "uneducated"; likewise, contemporary rating systems are justified as a means to preserve the innocence of children, who may be corrupted by being exposed to violent or sexually explicit images.

Conveniently for media corporations, this moral justification goes perfectly in hand with a larger transformation of capitalism. It is not a coincidence that the rating system emerged at the very moment Hollywood was in serious financial difficulties. One of the solutions to its insolvency was to heed a lesson learned from Madison Avenue two decades earlier. As Thomas Frank persuasively shows in *The Conquest of Cool*, corporations discovered niche marketing in the 1950s. A sales principle based on a retail rather than wholesale approach, niche marketing targets only a small segment of the population. As a result of this key shift in corporate sales strategy, American capitalism began to work much more efficiently: instead of worrying about producing a product that appeals to the largest common denominator, corporations can produce many products targeted at specific, different consumer groups. Even better, corporations are now capable of selling lifestyles rather than mere products; as a result, many more products can be sold, as long as they are all marketed to a certain niche group desiring to participate in a certain lifestyle. With this transformation, the speed of capital began to accelerate, just as it did with the invention of Taylorism before and then again with the shift to stock market–driven capitalism some decades later.

In the case of Hollywood in the post-1968 era, it became possible for studios to produce films made for certain age groups. Consequently, it managed to regain some of the relevancy it had lost since the end of World War II. With images of real violence broadcast live on TV (i.e., Vietnam, the assassination of JFK, or the murder of Lee Harvey Oswald) and the sexual revolution in full bloom, the rating system allowed Hollywood films to provide viewers with images that expressed more closely the zeitgeist than the overly generic images that it was condemned to make due to the regulations of the code (notwithstanding that Hollywood had already been pushing hard to expand the code's boundaries). Though Hollywood never regained the power and popularity it enjoyed in its golden age, it began to recover financially in the early 1970s and remains a more or less potent and healthy industry to this day, notwithstanding the cyclic complaints heard

judgment constitutes a serious problem for literary criticism, de Man's "solution" ultimately remains within the gravitational pull of the very problem he diagnoses.

Paul de Man: Debunking Meaning

De Man responds in "Semiology and Rhetoric"—a paradigmatic essay illustrating American deconstruction in a nutshell—to what he perceives as the disciplinary rejection of formalist and intrinsic criticism (New Criticism) in favor of a critical practice that is interested in the "nonverbal 'outside' to which language refers" (3).[3] He quickly arrives at the heart of his concern, which is worth quoting at length:

> With the internal law and order of literature well policed, we can now confidently devote ourselves to the foreign affairs, the external politics of literature. Not only do we feel able to do so, but we owe it to ourselves to take this step: our *moral conscience* would not allow us to do otherwise. Behind the assurance that valid interpretation is possible, behind the recent interest in writing and reading as potentially effective public speech acts, stands a highly respectable *moral imperative* that strives to reconcile the internal, formal, private structures of literary language with their external, referential, and public effects. (3, emphases mine)

In other words, de Man begins his seminal deconstructive endeavor as a response to a moral imperative that he perceives to be permeating contemporary critical practice, namely, that criticism must heed the positive and negative effects literature may or may not have on the external world. This moral imperative is simultaneously produced and perpetuated by a fundamental binary relation that, in by now familiar deconstructive practice, de Man sets out to undo: to wit, the inside/outside opposition that ultimately allows for judgments to be made about the text from a place outside of it.

Clearly, then, de Man begins his deconstructive investigation of critical practice by claiming that, contrary to what many may have thought, criticism has *not* moved outside the realm of judgment. In fact, this could not occur precisely because the inside/outside binary continued to affect various modes of criticism as a constitutive force. Whereas New Criticism, for example, reduced "meaning" to the formal structures of the text, subsequent developments in criticism posited form to be merely a trapping of literary meaning and content and then found the text's meaning in its referential quality. As de Man writes, the "polarities of inside and outside have been reversed, but they are still the same polarities that are at play: internal meaning has become outside reference, and the outer form has become intrinsic structure" (4). Hence, one of the responses to a New Critical hermeneutic was reader response criticism that relocated the nexus for textual meaning from the author or text to that of the reader's, or discourse community's, activity.[4]

The rest of de Man's essay deconstructs the "inside/outside metaphor that is never being seriously questioned" (5) by first flipping the binary to emphasize the deprivileged term and then replacing it with a new conceptual pair as a means to examine relations such as rhetoric/grammar, theory/practice, reading/understanding, and metaphor/metonymy. Deploying insights gained from semiology that shift the question from what something means to *how* it means, de Man counters the dominant assumption that literary language is metaphorical by delineating how it is metonymical. In the process, he shows that the understanding of literary language as metaphorical leads to a referential criticism that wants to have it both ways: "of being, to paraphrase Marx in the German Ideology, a formalist critic in the morning and a communal moralist in the afternoon" (6).

For our purposes, we do not have to discuss in detail how, specifically, de Man discusses Archie Bunker, William Butler Yeats, and Marcel Proust to establish that literary language is governed by a metonymical rather than metaphorical logic (i.e., by contiguity and chance rather than analogy and identity). What de Man concludes, however, is important. He finds that precisely when the highest claims are being made for the unifying power of metaphor, these very images rely in fact on the deceptive use of semi-automatic grammatical patterns. The deconstruction of metaphor and of all rhetorical patterns such as mimesis, paronomasia, or personification that use resemblance as a way to disguise differences, takes us back to the impersonal precision of grammar and of a semiology derived from grammatical patterns. Such a reading puts into question a whole series of concepts that underlie the *value judgments* of our critical discourse: the metaphors of primacy, of genetic history, and, most notably, of the autonomous power to will of the self. (16, emphasis mine)

Metaphors, in other words, are always already metonymies. The upshot of de Man's argument is that a "rhetorization of grammar (as in the rhetorical question)" based on a metaphorical understanding of language leads to "indetermination, in a suspended uncertainty that was unable to choose between two modes of reading," whereas what he calls a "grammatization of rhetoric [. . .] seems to reach a truth" (16). Whereas a metaphorical encounter with literary language merely leads to more interpretations that are ultimately unable to determine any meaning of the text, de Man suggests that (metonymically governed) deconstruction as exemplified in his essay arrives at a decision, at a truth, albeit a negative one (16).

Yet, in "true" Nietzschean fashion, de Man hastens to assert that at the moment of staking a claim for deconstruction as a superior textual engagement ("deconstruction is not something we have added to the text but it constituted the text in the first place" [17]) it is also necessary to debunk the "critic-philosopher" (17) as the owner of truth. As de Man argues, "if truth is the recognition of the systemic character of a certain kind of error [the poetic belief in the primacy of metaphor over metonymy], then it would be fully dependent on the prior existence of this error" (17). The implications of this claim are at least twofold. First, deconstruction is a form of antihumanism, for "the distinction between author and reader is one of the false distinctions that reading makes evident" (17). Neither readers nor authors control "meaning." Second, and for our purposes more important, deconstruction is ethically obliged to deconstruct the very truth it finds; it has to deconstruct itself. This, however, means nothing less than that deconstruction, as popularized by de Man's critical writings, practices a mode of criticism characterized by a "state of suspended ignorance" (19). That is, because "one reading is precisely the error denounced by the other and has to be undone by it [we cannot] in any way make a valid decision as to which of the readings can be given priority over the other; none can exist in the other's absence" (12).

Here de Man has arrived at a peculiar place—one that, due to the influence of his work, had enormous consequences for the way criticism was practiced throughout much of the 1970s and 1980s. He has indeed drastically complicated some of the basic assumptions of contemporary literary practice that continue to produce a criticism not all that far away from Arnold's. Yet, symptomatic of American deconstruction—and, indeed, the dominant tendency of literary criticism at large—de Man's approach ultimately does not escape the economy of judgment either. For if we follow his own logic that began with his deconstructing the inside/outside binary, then we have to be suspicious of what he posits as the necessary "state of suspended ignorance"—or, in Jeffrey Nealon's terms, "the demonstrable necessity of totalization's failure" (*Alterity Politics* 78)—constituting literary practice, critical and poetic alike. At the very moment he pulls the rug from underneath the inside/outside distinction that gives critics a purchase on a critical position outside the text that allows for the production of moral value judgments, de Man's logic also reaffirms judgment in itself. After all, if the truth of criticism is its ignorance or inevitable failure and, thus, its necessary deferral of judgment, then its truth exists only in relation to a prior error—that of judgment itself. If this is the case, however, then it is not at all clear what de Man's elaborate procedure has gained him in the end, other than further complicating the concept of judgment and how it operates (by necessity?) in criticism. Whereas criticism used to find meaning in a text that it then proceeded to judge, de Man delineates the necessary failure of this project (it fails precisely because representations are never present as such; they are governed by constitutive absences) and instead posits impossibility itself as the meaning of a text: the very fact that we can never conclusively decide what a text really means *is* the text's meaning. In this sense, de Man's efforts do not provide a way out of the economy of judgment, even though they clearly and helpfully display how the dominant practice of literary criticism (referential criticism) continues to function in a neo-Arnoldian fashion.

Lawrence Grossberg: Affecting Cultural Studies

But if even de Man's enormously sophisticated critical response to literature does not and cannot escape judgment, then we may have to ask why this is the case: why is it that, when all is said and done, American deconstruction "merely" intensifies the logic of judgment without reaching a breaking point at which a fundamental transformation might occur? It seems that one way of answering this question is hinted at by Lawrence Grossberg in his critique of cultural studies, the very discipline he helped shape in significant ways. Cultural studies, just like New Historicism and New Materialism, the two most popular theoretical paradigms before it, casts itself in opposition to deconstruction, perceiving it to be too textual and too ahistorical.[5] Regardless of the validity of this critique, these newer critical paradigms tried to shift critical attention to history, material practices, and sites altogether different from what was perceived as the privileged location of literature.[6] Yet, in all that, so Grossberg seems to think, a new dead end has been produced, one, I might add, that is hardly new at all, for it is the same dead end that traps de Man's project in the realm of judgment: to wit, *the economy of representation itself now emerges as the problem.* Just like de Man's efforts remain intricately tied to a representational economy (the never-ending flipping of the binary undoes taken for granted hierarchies but does not displace the system of signification and meaning itself), so Grossberg argues that cultural studies—that which supposedly negates deconstruction and its emphasis on reading texts—also remains within the familiar confines of representation.[7] If Grossberg is right, it appears that the allegedly new paradigm, which has remained dominant to this day, might not be able to provide the impetus that it promises.

In "The Victory of Culture," Grossberg's main target consists of the *logic* of mediation (as opposed to the existence of mediating processes). Directing his prolegomenon—a genre that "defines a project and the conditions which make such a project both necessary and possible"—specifically at the discipline of cultural studies, he asks whether "it is reasonable to continue following the same path" of identity politics that has obsessed cultural studies (3). Specifically, given that identity politics is a politics of mediation and representation, Grossberg argues, "cultural studies has to respond to the increasing importance, both theoretically and politically, of the asignifying, whether understood as the material, the body or affect" (4). Of course, Grossberg is not the first to recognize the importance of the asignifying; Friedrich Nietzsche, for one, theorized the asignifying throughout his oeuvre (see, e.g., "On Truth and Lying in the Extra-Moral Sense"), thus producing a thought arrow that was later picked up and redirected by the likes of Gilles Deleuze and Michel Foucault. Yet, I think it is worth quoting Grossberg at length on this issue, for he succinctly expresses a historical point that affects contemporary thought precisely because it has largely gone uncontested, especially in cultural studies:

> North Atlantic Modernity has always recognized that there is something else to human existence beyond the epistemological but it always assigns this excess to the domain of the irrational, the unstructured, the unmappable (e.g., as desire or creativity). Thus when they are talked about,

> they are either immediately reconfigured into the realm of
> representation, or they are treated as the concrete, the par-
> ticular, the atheoretical. As a result, much of contemporary
> cultural theory and criticism assumes a binary opposition
> between affect, the body, materiality and the concrete on
> the one side, and ideology, subjectivity, consciousness and
> theory on the other. (4)

Nietzsche explained the human desire for truth by linking it to
moral and rational reasons that subsequently turned the constitutive force of language—which for him is the power of the false,
or lying—into the sphere of the irrational and, thus, immoral.
Similarly, Grossberg suggests that contemporary thought continually bypasses forces of asignification, whether by denigrating
them as irrational and personalized experiences or by translating
them into a different regime that it is more familiar and comfortable with: that of representation. In the previous chapter I showed
one of the consequences of this latter operation—namely, that
the asignifying forces of violence in *American Psycho* are turned
into a question of representation that in turn allows and, indeed,
necessitates a moral judgment of these forces. The point to mark
here is that Grossberg locates the same operation that I located
in a rather textual manner to be operating at the heart of the very
discipline that casts itself *against* textual "readings."

The main part of Grossberg's essay attempts to map out how
the logic of mediation emerged, how it functioned, and what it
produced. One of the key concepts emerging in relation to the
logic of mediation is that of culture as a "descriptive and normative" concept (10). Crucially, so Grossberg argues, "the very act of
producing the concept of culture involves the construction of a
place which allows one to both describe and *judge* the changes in
everyday life" (10, emphasis mine). That is, culture as a concept
produces the possibility—or, better, necessity—for judgment:
"art as morality" (10). Referring to Arnold's belief that "culture is
the best that has been thought and said" (qtd. in Grossberg 10),
Grossberg shows how cultural studies and its concerns are not

far at all from a seemingly outmoded operation of criticism.[8] The fact that the concept of culture—so crucial to the field of cultural studies that more or less opposes literature and its apparent fetishizing of the text—is intricately linked to an Arnoldian sense of morality helps explain why, for instance, the cultural response (and I take this term in its largest sense) to Bret Easton Ellis occurred in the manner it did. After all, Ellis was clearly marked and marketed as "culture" ever since his first novel *Less Than Zero* (1985) turned him into the *nom du jour* in the mid-eighties, allowing him to frequent circles otherwise reserved for the cultural elite of the East and West Coast establishment. Precisely because there was scant questioning of Ellis's high cultural position, the shock of *American Psycho* was all the more intense: if art/culture embodies the best of mankind and if Ellis is somehow part of culture in this sense, then criticism has no problem to justify commenting on him; but this very ease with which it could embrace Ellis also made it singularly unprepared for dealing with *American Psycho*, and its attendant event, as such. That is, because cultural criticism assumed itself to be capable of addressing one of its own, it found itself unable to encounter a text that marks itself in terms radically unfamiliar to it—hence the need to address Ellis's text in terms of "satire" for those who wanted to defend it. Satire, at least, constitutes a familiar concept and can in turn be mobilized to articulate a judgment about the text and what it is said to satirize—thus perpetuating the idea that culture is the best that has been thought and said by mankind.[9]

So, precisely because Ellis had been marke(te)d as "culture," judgment was demanded, even in light of the fact that *American Psycho* itself was hardly perceived as deserving of this attribution. This ought to be noted simply because of the existence of many other texts that arguably did what Ellis's did long before. The difference, though, is that many of these brutal, "immoral" texts are marke(te)d not as fiction or literature but as mystery, suspense, horror, and so on. The reality of this distinction should be clear to anyone who frequents bookstores, where fiction is separated from all of the other categories, thus faintly resembling the moral segregation between "immoral" pornographic material and allegedly morally uplifting or instructive ones.[10] But it is this constitutive operation that allows criticism—literary, film, and cultural studies—to judge a specific set of texts; in fact, it becomes the moral imperative to do so.

In contrast, the same operation of criticism appears to become impossible at the very moment it is confronted with texts not marke(te)d as culture. So, for instance, Patricia Highsmith or Jim Thompson's fictions do not lend themselves to the same critical operation precisely because it is far from clear that the critical apparatus of high culture *should* be brought to them. It is not at all established that, say, Highsmith's *The Talented Mr. Ripley* (1955) or Thompson's *Killer Inside Me* (1952) is worthy of our collective critical efforts. In fact, both Highsmith and Thompson have received barely more critical attention in scholarly outlets than Ellis has—despite the fact that the latter has written only six books to date, whereas both Highsmith and Thompson, cult authors categorized as crime/mystery/suspense writers, authored more than thirty. The same holds true for the great African American crime writer Chester Himes. Literary studies "proper" prefers the canonized, and often rather bourgeois literary practices of African American writers such as Ralph Ellison, James Baldwin, or Toni Morrison to the brutal pulp style of Himes, whose oeuvre came to an explosive end with his last Harlem novel, *Plan B* (1983). This unfinished novel reached a limit point of explosive violence on the level of content that the novel's style was barely able to contain. If this relationship between the application of critical efforts and the perceived institutional merit of texts is as described here, then judgment itself becomes a rather impotent mode of response (because that which requires response is not perceived as being worthy of response to begin with). Crucially, the fact that criticism's main modus operandi is not—or just barely—in action with regard to these writers paradoxically precludes it from attending to some of the more interesting operations someone like Highsmith engages in, as I will argue in the next chapter.

So, Grossberg's analysis of the logic of mediation with its attendant cultural "logic of lack" (11) helps us explain the larger operation of cultural criticism. In the context of his concern—cultural studies—Grossberg therefore urges us to question its reliance on identifying "mediation with communication" (12) that sees all cultural practices as involving "the production of meanings and representations, of subjectivities and identities" (12). Specifically, Grossberg's analysis suggests that this reliance does not provide a political or ethical tactic that would be capable of living up to the promises it makes in cultural studies work, for it might be the case that "the emerging formations of power may no longer find this logic [of mediation] useful" (14). Thus, the concept of culture as currently deployed by cultural studies not only reduces everything to meaning but also does so as a means to combat a mode of power that might be outmoded by now. And if this is indeed the case, as I am inclined to agree, not the least because of Foucault's rather powerful arguments to this extent, then representation as a locus for politics and criticism no longer offers a promising mode of engagement.[11]

Grossberg's own work has long attempted to account for this shift in power formations. So, for instance, he theorizes rock music as a mode of affect rather than conceiving it in ideological, representational terms. Considering affect a main force deployed by texts to generate intensities, Grossberg attends, for instance, to the sonority of rock music, an affective regime that creates "spaces of non-Kantianism [time, mediation, judgment] and such spaces operate on the surface for all to enter; it operates with a kind of economy of place-making where the logic of mediation does not and cannot operate" (15). What is of interest in Grossberg's work, then, is his effort to take affect more seriously by diagnosing how nonrepresentational forces are always at work—forces that may produce representations but that cannot be explained by that logic.

While Brian Massumi astutely criticizes Grossberg for having muddled the important distinction between emotion and affect, I think Grossberg's argument must nevertheless be taken seriously as an intervention into the field that oftentimes pretends that it has successfully eliminated the pitfalls of literary studies.[12] Just as de Man was able to show that literary studies is far from having escaped Arnold's shadow, so Grossberg conceptually shows that de Man's solution to the problem of judgment merely turned that concept into a new, yet related, problem: that of representation. From a Grossbergian cultural studies perspective, we cannot accept endless deferral as a satisfying solution to the functioning of judgment as the operative force of criticism; further, from this perspective we begin to see now that the logic of representation itself is the problem.

Grossberg, of course, does not deny that representation/mediation exists. Rather, he urges cultural studies to appreciate the possibility that representation might not be "about" representation—that the production of "meaning" is merely one effect "representations" produce, and not the most important one at that. What we consider "representations" are themselves produced by asignifying forces. Or, as he puts it, "Signification and representation are merely two modes—and not necessarily the most important ones—in the regime of mediation, or even of discursive mediation" (7–8). Constantin Boundas's critique of what he calls dominant deconstruction strikes a similar note: "Positioning itself, as [deconstruction] did, ambiguously in front of the process of (the) production (of signs) and (the) anti-production (of the body-without organs), it left the metaphysical primacy of reproduction [viz. representation, mediation] unchallenged. And it is this unchallenged metaphysical primacy of reproductive forces [. . .] that accounts for 'turning everything into a drama' in the deployment of (major) deconstructive strategies" (165). Both Grossberg and Boundas are making the same point with regard to their disciplines (cultural studies and philosophy, respectively), which leads them to ask, in Boundas's words, "with what else [other than representations] does a text generate intensities" (167)? To address this question, both Boundas and Grossberg turn for their answers to the strictly arepresentational thought of Gilles Deleuze, a thinker whose work inhabits cultural studies, as well as literary and film studies, mostly on the margins.[13]

That Grossberg points to Deleuze's thought as a way to problematize some of the more dominant critical paradigms—be it the still lingering deconstructive vein or the cultural studies response to it—is even more remarkable in that he thus marks an interesting and telling dynamic inherent to any discipline invested in interpretation. That is, de Man's critique of literary criticism's continuing judgmental mode of operation might have been able to produce some initial shock waves; yet the very nature of de Man's own practice ultimately allowed the discipline to welcome his critique and make it its own precisely because de Manean criticism (American deconstruction) remains solidly within the realm of representation and interpretation. The critical question remains "what does this *mean*?" even though the oft-repeated response is that we cannot decide or that the textual meaning assumes a plurality of forms. Likewise, the attractiveness of cultural studies, despite its attack on the privileging of texts, is of little surprise considering that it too has much investment in the concept of representation (albeit in a much more political sense), as Grossberg has nicely parceled out. In its attempt to politicize the act of criticism, cultural studies has (partially) turned away from the literary (or cinematic) text but has never really questioned representation as such. In fact, it might not be overstating the case that much of cultural studies has no interest at all in questioning representationalism, since much of its politics are tied to notions of recognition, identity, and thus representation and judgment.[14]

This helps explain why, generally speaking, Deleuze's thought has had considerably less influence on literary and film criticism than deconstruction, New Historicism, or cultural studies. Any quick MLA database search using the term "Deleuze" will produce considerably fewer entries than "cultural studies," "Foucault"/"New Historicism," or "Derrida"/"Deconstruction." Similarly, a perusal of the main cinema journals will not bring forth a vast array of scholarly work that deals with or deploys Deleuzean thought—despite the fact that he wrote two books on cinema, just as he wrote extensively on literature.[15] What then is going on? Why is one not entirely mistaken in suggesting that the academic critical apparatus has largely kept Deleuze at bay? While there may be all kinds of explanations (such as his difficult and constantly changing terminology, the seeming—but only seeming—lack of systematicity of his writing, the sheer breadth of his interest that makes his arguments often rather difficult to follow for readers), I suggest, following Grossberg, that Deleuze's insistence on the asignifying force of language lies at the root of criticism's reluctance to engage his thought. Or, perhaps more to the point, disciplines such as literary or film criticism might be reluctant to take Deleuze's arepresentationalism more seriously because following Deleuze on this point pulls the rug from underneath the disciplines' cherished trinity—representation, interpretation, and judgment—as I have begun to argue in chapter 2.[16] To further this argument, let us turn to one of Deleuze's earlier essays, "The Simulacrum and Ancient Philosophy"—an essay that in its very clarity and concision shatters many well-cherished and naturalized presuppositions of contemporary critical practice, not least because it runs a hard line on the key insight that "modernity is defined by the power of the simulacrum" (265).

Gilles Deleuze: Overcoming Platonism

Taking up Nietzsche's claim that the task of modern philosophy is "to reverse Platonism," Deleuze wants to diagnose what this overturning means and how it could be accomplished ("Simulacrum" 253). It is of course hardly a coincidence that Deleuze becomes interested in the question of Platonism. After all, it was Plato who powerfully introduced representationalism into Western thought. As Jacques Derrida has frequently suggested, the laser beam of Western metaphysics went from Plato all the way to contemporary philosophers such as Martin Heidegger, and I want to add that Plato's arrow of thought has also been caught by the modern practice of literary and film criticism as practiced in academia and popular culture. As such, then, an overturning of

Platonism is not a small task. More specifically, a successful over-turning would seriously question the validity of the entire criti-cal enterprise—or at least criticism in its representational mode. But for our purposes even more crucial is that an overturning of Platonism would also show why judgment, no matter how subtle, cannot be considered a helpful response to a literary (or filmic) text, especially, though not exclusively, in its extreme case: that of violence. So, if de Man has shown that literary criticism con-tinues to rely on judgment and argues for a deconstructive criti-cism suspended in representational ignorance and if Grossberg has shown that representation itself might be the problem, then Deleuze gives us the tool to see how judgment is the operation of representation. That is, symptomatologically reading Deleuze's essay on Plato and the simulacrum allows us to understand why the discipline of criticism cannot escape the realm of judgment as long as it continues to base itself on the economy of representa-tionalism.

What, then, happens in and with Plato's thought according to Deleuze? It is well known that Plato's arguments worked by his division of genus into species. Deleuze, however, contends that the real purpose of Platonic division "is not at all to divide a genus into species, but, more profoundly, to select lineages: to distinguish pretenders; to distinguish the impure from the pure, the authentic from the inauthentic" ("Simulacrum" 254). Perhaps the best-known example of this procedure is Plato's attempt to track down the Sophist.[17] And it is in this context, so Deleuze sug-gests, that we have to understand the function of myth in Plato's thought. If the method of Platonic division is a "dialectic of ri-valry" (254), the ability to distinguish between the authentic and inauthentic, the true and the false, ultimately depends on some a priori ground that allows a subject to make these divisions. And myth, in Plato, becomes this ground. That is, his theory of Ideas—as expressed in the myth of the pure souls—"permits the construction of a model according to which the different pretend-ers can be judged" (255). If the realm of Ideas is the highest good to be aspired to, then it follows that there are a number of different levels of participation, namely, that there are participants who faithfully copy these ideas and participants who do not. That is, Plato's theory of Ideas "constructs the immanent model or the foundation-test according to which the pretenders should be judged and their pretensions measured" (256). What Deleuze relentlessly points out here is the centrality of *judgment* to Platonic—that is, representational—thought. This becomes crucial as soon as Deleuze moves on to discussing those Platonic concepts most relevant to the practice of criticism: the copy and the simulacrum.

In Platonism, says Deleuze, copies "are secondary possessors [or] well-founded pretenders, guaranteed by resemblance; *simulacra* are like false pretenders, built upon a dissimilarity, implying an essential perversion or a deviation" ("Simulacrum" 256). The moral importance of this distinction cannot be overestimated, for the Platonic motivation to differentiate between good and bad copies or, rather, between copies and simulacra, is immanently linked to the desire to promote the inherent goodness of the true pretender (copy) precisely because this pretender is modeled on the purity of the Idea: "The copy truly resembles something only to the degree that it resembles the Idea of that thing. The pretender conforms to the object only insofar as he is modeled (internally and spiritually) on the Idea. He merits the quality (the quality of being just, for example) only insofar as he has founded himself on the essence (justice). In short, it is the superior identity of the Idea, which founds the good pretension of the copies, as it bases it on an internal or derived resemblance" (257). In contrast, the simulacrum's pretension is unfounded, as it conceals its inherent *dissimilarity* from the Idea: it merely pretends to be like the Idea when in reality it is of an entirely different—inauthentic, impure—lineage.

One of the upshots of Deleuze's argument here is that the popular postmodern language of simulation does not make much sense, if we understand by simulacra "copies of copies" as Jean Baudrillard and Fredric Jameson do.[18] The point Deleuze makes is precisely that simulacra are different *in kind* from copies; simulacra are not copies of copies because the former are derived from a different lineage than the latter. Copies are secondary to a prior identity, whereas simulacra give rise to identity as an *effect*: "one [reading of the world] invites us to think difference from the standpoint of a previous similitude or identity; whereas the other [reading] invites us to think similitude and even identity as the product of a deep disparity. The first reading precisely defines the world of copies or representations; it posits the world as icon. The second, contrary to the first, defines the world of simulacra; it posits the world itself as phantasm" (261–62). For Plato, and those thought systems derived from or simply influenced by him, such as (neo-)Platonism and Christianity, the purpose of validating the moral superiority of copies over simulacra lies precisely in the fact that copies resemble—be it a pure Idea (Platonism) or God (Christianity). For instance, Christianity, as Deleuze writes, claims, "God made man in his image and resemblance. Through sin, however, man lost the resemblance while maintaining the image. We have become simulacra. We have forsaken moral existence in order to enter aesthetic existence" (257). Copies—representations—are intrinsically judged as morally good; in contrast, simulacra, and with them aesthetics, have thoroughly been demonized.

Deleuze's analysis, however, does not posit a choice between these two readings of the world. Deleuze is not a poster boy for TiVo users, who can record an entire evening's worth of television talk shows and choose the next morning which one they are in the mood for watching: Leno or Letterman, or perhaps both. Rather, he makes it unmistakably clear that the power of the simulacrum—its very existence—undoes the proposition that we are living in a world structured by representations as primary forces. On the contrary, the simulacrum, "the Being of all beings" (265), "harbors a positive power which denies *the original and the copy, the model and the reproduction*" (262). The simulacrum's power— "the power of the false" (263)—lies in its *constitutive* capacity to structure existence, for it does away with the very possibility to distinguish between copy and model.[19] The simulacrum looks like the model and thus insinuates that it has copied the model, when really the simulacrum deploys an internal difference, a dissimilarity, to produce the effect of similarity, resemblance, and identity. The Colossus of Rhodes looked like a perfectly proportioned hunk of a man only because its proportions were thoroughly dissimilar to a real human being or, rather, to the Idea of a real human being. The power of the simulacrum, then, induces a "vertigo" (262), a dizziness, delirium, or hallucination—a psychic mode that is different from an illusion precisely in that the latter can be measured against a truth whereas the former cannot: a hallucination is not based on something in existence that could be empirically measured, whereas an illusion is.[20]

But the simulacrum constitutes for Plato a problem not only because of its simple inferiority to true copies. Rather, as Deleuze points out, Plato appears to be disturbed by the fact that "the simulacrum implies huge dimensions, depths and distances that the observer cannot master" (258). Because of the impossibility to master, to know, or simply to understand these dimensions—or, in Kantian terms, the sublime—the perceiving subject falsely experiences the simulacrum as a resemblance to the copy, the original. As a result, the subject loses its distinctness from the object of perception: "the simulacrum includes the differential point of view; and the observer becomes a part of the simulacrum itself, which is transformed and deformed by his point of view" (258). Or, as Claire Colebrook glosses this argument, "any specific point of view is not a point of view overlooking some object world, but a proliferation of points, a pre-personal field of singularities. [. . .] We can't subordinate looking, receptivity or the givenness of the world to the site of the subject, as though the world were located *within* point of view. Before the representing power of the subject there is an infinite series of looks or 'contemplations'" (111–12). At stake, then, is a Platonic desire for maintaining the distinctiveness of subject and object; likewise, in phenomenological terms, the problem with the simulacrum is that it falsifies "true" perception in that it leads the perceiver to become conscious of something that really does not exist as such. The violence occurring here, then, is one against a presumed wholeness of perception.[21] The perceiving subject, in his or her encounter with the "aggression of the simulacra" (Deleuze, "Simulacrum" 261), experiences an "affective charge" (261), a "becoming-mad" (258)—something that, from Plato onward, the history of Western (major) thought has been at pains to denigrate, to repress.[22]

According to Deleuze, Platonism "founds the entire domain that philosophy will later recognize as its own: the domain of representation filled by copies-icons, and defined not by an extrinsic relation to an object, but by an intrinsic relation to the model or foundation" (259). As such, it instantiates a movement against the forces of becoming—of affect—and embeds a moral choice, articulated as "a preference for the calm, ordered life of the soul governed by reason to the disorderly and passionate life of the soul moved by poetry" (Patton 33). Life as such is rendered as a stable process of copying in which clearly delineated subjects can be judged based on their ability to emulate the idealistic original. The realm of representation, in other words, is from this moment on immanently constituted by the desire to judge: representationalism cannot be thought without judgment, cannot be done without judgment. Or, in Nietzsche's genealogical terms, the force of judgment so crucial for Plato still affects representational thought in the present. A reversal of Platonism, therefore, is an untimely act, one that by "acting counter to our time [acts] on our time and, let us hope, for the benefit of a time to come" (Nietzsche, "Uses and Disadvantages" 60). Deleuze's interest in revisiting Plato, and in asserting the primacy of the simulacrum, is thus not one of excavating a "truer" reading of Plato. Deleuze is not a practitioner of what Nietzsche denigrated as "antiquarian history."[23] Rather, the point that I think we would do well to heed very carefully is Deleuze's insistence that we have not yet done with Plato(nism). Plato's thought is not one we can look at "objectively" as a historical document precisely because it still operates in contemporary critical practices. The virtual force of Plato's initial affirmative instantiation of representationalism as a moral judgment continues to be actualized today, just as, it seems to me, Arnoldianism is not a matter of a past era we have done with but instead continues to permeate contemporary thought and practice.[24]

↓

It seems, then, that we have answered the question with which we began. As long as criticism, in its encounter with literature or cinema (or other arts), conceives of its object as representations, it is bound to produce moral judgments, no matter how subtle they might appear to be. In this conception, art remains intricately tied to a more or less Arnoldian view of art as moral pedagogy. Further, this conception of signaletic material (cinematic images, literary words, musical notes, etc.) also necessarily insists on the separation of the perceiving subject from the object perceived, for it is this distinctiveness that is necessary for a valid judgment to be made to begin with. For only if the perceiving subject is not affected by the object can one be sure that the perception of it and the attending judgment will be pure, unfettered by the becoming-mad of the force of the simulacrum. However, what Deleuze's reading of Platonism's denigration of the simulacrum suggests is not only that Plato actually recognized the untenability of his own theory; it also shows that our idea of point of view—so crucial to many literary and film analyses—cannot be maintained in a way that suggests the agency of a freely perceiving subject.[25] Rather, the constitutive force of simulation—that which percolates every image—renders the subject as indiscernible from a multiplicity of point of views. The subject is nothing but a sequence of point of views, of affective encounters with the world; or, as Ellis shows in *American Psycho* (and Highsmith in *The Talented Mr. Ripley*), the subject is merely a sequence of masks: taking off one mask reveals nothing else but the delirious surface quality of yet another mask.

But this is a difficult lesson to learn for a discipline so invested in the critic as the subject in charge of interpretation or the author (or reader, as the case may be) in charge of "making meaning."[26]

Whereas de Manean deconstruction was rather easy to incorporate into the discipline precisely because it remained thoroughly invested in representationalism, and whereas cultural studies too could strongly affect criticism because of its (political) interest in representationalism, Deleuze's thought has had a much harder time affecting the discipline as such precisely because it puts into question the very ground on which the discipline depends. After all, the question one needs to ask now is "What can one do if the assumed purity of a critical point of view cannot be maintained?" or "What is one to do now that images in whatever form do not re-present the world, nature, or some true idea?" Of course, some answers to these questions have already been provided, not only by Deleuze himself, but also by some theorists such as Nealon or Steven Shaviro.

What I am interested in here is to provide one further link, one that, I think, is made explicitly by Highsmith's fiction to which I will turn next. That is, if Deleuze shows us that the realm of representation is the realm of judgment, then I would like to suggest that an encounter with violence in literature or film cannot possibly assume the form of judgment—not only because judging representations is oddly recursive (it judges itself by necessity and thus can never assume a moral place outside said representation, as it is more than often assumed by critics), but because judgment, in its immanence with representation, *is* the movement or force of violence par excellence. More precisely, in at least one sense Deleuze's analysis shows that, ontologically speaking, *violence is all there is* in that the primacy of the differential point of view—of difference—functions as a mode that can only be described as violence in that it is pure force. Yet this constitutive violence is not a violence directed against or done to some prior wholeness, to some phenomenological world or Being that we somehow lack or desire to return to because it is free of violence. In fact, understanding violence in terms of "doing violence to" always denotes a representational conception of violence.[27] It seems to me, however, that the movement of perception—including that of images—is driven by the violence of difference. As such it does not make much sense to try to judge this violence, for it is what makes us up. All our capacities are produced by this violence. Yet not all violence is the same. In fact, Deleuze's analysis of Platonism shows—if we understand it as suggesting the pure immanence of the triad representation-judgment-violence—that it matters what kind of violences violence produces. Or what kind of violence we do to violence. We always do violence to difference, but it matters what direction and weight this violence assumes: What effects are produced? What does a specific form of violence enable one to do? What kind of line of flight can it set into motion? In masocritical terms, then, the task is not to escape violence but to regulate it differently.

Not coincidentally, in Deleuze's thought difference is intricately linked to the category of affect. Affect is the force of difference, the force of difference affect. And in contrast to a Kantian attempt to render affect ultimately inferior to concepts and reason, Deleuze's "simulating" philosophy affirms affect as such, welcomes it for what it is: the movement of violence. Affects produce effects; they are about linkages, about the logic of the "and" rather than that of "either/or." Affect indexes the ethical and ontological necessity to continually go elsewhere in an experimental movement of intensification, innovation, and improvisation, but this movement's trajectory always leads *through* the object itself. The task, therefore, is not to subject the object to judgment but to confront it with the question of what it does. The violence of a literary or cinematic work, then, is not subjected to the demand for a "good" and "moral" meaning (à la the discourse surrounding the supposed morality of, say, Steven Spielberg's violent World War II films *Schindler's List* [1993] and *Saving Private Ryan* [1998]). Rather, it is questioned merely for what it does and how it does it: Is it capable to increase the power of the subjects encountering it (and being configured and transformed by it) to act, to think, to move? Or does it decrease these forces? In short, does it further the powers of living or hinder them to unfold? This is the ethical principle underlying a Deleuzean theory of asignification, a critical and clinical encounter with images that views imaging as productive of effects through affects, rather than containing, however multiple or undecidable, truths or meanings. The latter are always merely effects of the prior forces of simulation, affect, violence: that is, of difference.[28] Taking this seriously might produce a way for criticism to engage its objects in a rigorously ajudgmental mode; it would, perhaps, open up a thorough process of rethinking why we study images to begin with and what the promise of art might be for the questions of politics and pedagogy.[29]

This, then, is the task: to delineate—and thus produce—lines of flight through an affective, masocritical encounter with (violent) images, be they written, cinematic, or otherwise. By necessity, this endeavor must take multiple forms, since the object and context of the encounter with it automatically affects and effectuates *different* responses. Both object and subject alter in this affective encounter; we cannot determine the meaning of these changes, but we can map out the (virtual) effects. The crucial question we have to ask about the use of violence in literature or cinema is not whether or not it is moral (good or evil). Rather, the only questions we are left with are to ask whether it works, whether it allows for the production of new thought, and whether it increases a body's capacity to act, to become healthier, to be able to act in and upon the world—a world that, it should be recalled, is ontologically structured by, not against or in fear of, violence.[30]

4 Serializing Violence

Patricia Highsmith's "Empirical" Pedagogy of Violence

As I argued in chapter 2, considerable interest existed in 1999 and 2000 in the film adaptation of Bret Easton Ellis's widely loathed novel *American Psycho*. Virtually simultaneous with the burgeoning anticipation in how feminist director Mary Harron would render what is generally considered one the most antifeminist American novels in recent memory, another novel and its upcoming film version crept into the limelight of public reviews and middlebrow magazine discussions. When on Christmas Day 1999 Anthony Minghella's adaptation of Patricia Highsmith's *The Talented Mr. Ripley* vied for the attention of an American movie audience stuffed with turkey and pumpkin pie, the usual newspaper reviews had begun evaluating the film as a potential Academy Awards contender.[1] Anticipating—and perhaps more significantly, helping to manufacture—the success of the film, cultural outlets such as the *New Yorker* and the *New York Times* preceded the movie's release by rather extended discussions of both the film and Highsmith's work. For instance, the *New Yorker* printed a four-page analysis by Susannah Clapp of Minghella's encounter with Highsmith, "the chilliest crime writer of them all" (94). Likewise, the *New York Times* devoted four consecutive essays to Highsmith and the cinematic rendering of her most famous novel. First, in late November, Michiko Kakutani, the paper's leading book critic, reviewed the reissue of three of the five Ripley novels in a single volume by the Everyman's Library.[2] Then cultural critic Frank Rich published a full-length think piece in the newspaper's

Sunday Magazine section on the timeliness of *The Talented Mr. Ripley* for late-twentieth-century American culture. Finally, David Thomson and Janet Maslin, both among the foremost American (popular) film critics, substantially reviewed the film in the week immediately preceding its release.

I point to these citations mainly to suggest that Minghella's film not only provoked interest in a new work by the acclaimed director of Academy Award–winning *The English Patient* (1996) but also directed renewed attention to Patricia Highsmith, an American writer whose frequently violent, often seemingly misanthropic fiction has long been celebrated in Europe but whose reputation has suffered in the United States largely because of the suspense/mystery/crime label attached to her fiction.

Like many other reviewers and critics (see, e.g., Shore and Dupont), Clapp points out that "Highsmith's critical reputation has been ambiguous" (94) and that her "books were always more successful in Europe than in the United States" (96). Regarding Highsmith's difficulties as a literary figure in the United States, Michael Bronski tellingly points out that the United States has seen "no less than five attempted Highsmith revivals [between 1975 and 1995], each with the re-release of back titles and a flood of attendant reviews and laudatory articles" (42). Incidentally, in the wake of Minghella's film, Highsmith's work underwent yet another comeback. In conjunction with the hardcover publication of *The Selected Stories of Patricia Highsmith* (2001) and *Nothing That Meets the Eye: The Uncollected Stories of Patricia Highsmith* (2002), Norton also rereleased a number of Highsmith's long out-of-print novels, including the classic *Strangers on a Train* (1950), and Bloomsbury published the first major biography of Highsmith, Andrews Wilson's *Beautiful Shadow* (2003). To boot, that same year Highsmith's former lover Marijane Meaker published *Highsmith: A Romance of the 1950s* (2003), a romance novel based on their relationship. Though it is too early to assess the longevity and impact of this most recent comeback, it seems doubtful that it will radically alter her marginal status in U.S. letters.

More crucially for my argument, the interest in Minghella's

film and Highsmith's fiction as articulated in the pages of the larger national newspapers and cultural magazines has consistently been framed around the questions of *morality* and *judgment*. That is, regardless of the critics' evaluative response to the film adaptation of Highsmith's fourth novel, almost all of them felt compelled to point out that the film ends with the murderous protagonist, Tom Ripley, remaining at large. For example, Rich speculates that the studio's motive in releasing the film on Christmas Day attempted to appeal to an audience interested in the star power of the film "before there [was] time for too much backlash over its creepiness, its violence, its homoerotic sexuality and its defiance of the moral closure usually provided by big-budget Hollywood entertainments." Likewise, in reporting on the production of the film, Thomson informs his readers that "*The Talented Mr. Ripley* had problems with its ending. Some people have felt that justice should be served." Here, Thompson alludes to the fact that an unabashedly amoral killer escaping "just" punishment must be considered rather remarkable—even after thirty years of "new violence" in American cinema—given that one of Hollywood's unspoken rules dictates that crime must be punished.[3] Interestingly, Minghella himself considers his film in more traditionally moral terms, *pace* the public discourse emerging from his adaptation. He believes that Ripley's escape at the end of the film constitutes his punishment par excellence. As he claims in an interview with *Sight and Sound*, "I was charmed by the idea of a central character who could commit murder and get away with it. It's not that I enjoy the amorality of that. I wanted to say that *getting away with it is his punishment*" (James, "My Bloody Valentine" 16, my emphasis). Likewise, Bronski argues that, in the final analysis, the film remains "very safe" (43) and conservative—especially compared to the unabashedly amoral universe of the novel. In short, no matter what other issues the critical reception of Minghella's film addressed, the overall reaction to it clearly foregrounded the issue of judgment—specifically the lack of punishment of Tom Ripley—as a key question of interest and concern in the context of the film's treatment of violence.

In the case of Bret Easton Ellis's work, one might argue that the concern with judgment is almost exclusively one for and of criticism. Ellis does not appear to thematize directly the question of judgment as such, for none of his protagonists—most certainly not Patrick Bateman or Victor Ward, the main character of *Glamorama* (1999)—could care less about the amorality of their violent actions. My discussion of *American Psycho* is thus mainly concerned with working out how criticism crucially intersects with fictional productions of violence and what happens when it deploys judgment as its main tool of analysis of this fictional violence. Lest it appear that judgment is always merely an external concern, one brought to the text by (critical) readers and viewers, however, I want to direct closer attention to Highsmith's work as a means of showing that fiction itself has the capacity to—and indeed does—confront the issue and practice of judgment. Patricia Highsmith, I think, might be best read as a clinically cold scientist whose fiction constitutes her laboratory in which she invents different modes of response to violence and, in so doing, tests their effects.

↓

As my brief recalling of the critical reception of Minghella's film adaptation is meant to insinuate, Highsmith's work also has been the focus for a type of criticism concerned with morality and judgment.[4] However, in this chapter I am less concerned with the criticism of Highsmith's work or of its many cinematic adaptations.[5] Instead, I want to work through Highsmith's fiction to see how it problematizes judgment as a mode of response to violence. Indeed, my interest in turning to Patricia Highsmith emerges from the fact that the question of judgment affected Highsmith to such a degree that she can be said to have welcomed it as the defining problematic of her entire oeuvre. In that sense, Highsmith practices what we might call a Foucaultean ethics, for he, too, conceived of his work as a sequential encounter with differing *problématiques* that, in his words, must be viewed not so much as "bad" than as "dangerous" (*Foucault Reader* 343). Michel Foucault, just like Gilles Deleuze, thought that a "problem does not exist, apart from its solutions" (*Difference and Repetition* 163).[6] In other words, the theoretical conception of problems/solutions offered by these two French philosophers casts the existence of both problem and solution on the same plane of immanence. Hence, the only way out is through. You cannot "find a solution to a problem in the solution of another problem raised at another moment" (*Foucault Reader* 343). And this is essentially Highsmith's mode of response to her problematic of judgment. The solutions she offers, novel by novel, story by story, are consistently formulated *through* her encounter with the question of violence—an encounter that, due to its clinical coldness, one may very well call masochistic. That is, over the course of a forty-five-year-long writing career in which she produced twenty-two novels, seven books of short fiction, and her "how to" manual *Plotting and Writing of Suspense Fiction* (1983), Highsmith obsessively reformulated her problematic, repeatedly put it to the test, and, in the process, serially reconfigured the question of judgment as always and already being shot through with the question of violence.[7]

In fact, for Highsmith, the questions of judgment and violence are immanent to each other, something that will become clearer once we examine the movement of Highsmith's overall work rather than focus on any given text as the locus for interpretation. The movement of Highsmith's fiction indicates that her response to the question of violence is less and less characterized by the desire to superimpose some sort of judgment at the end, no matter how tentative, implausible, or irrelevant to the larger effect of her texts it may appear. Most of her early novels still end by passing judgment on the violent main characters. In these novels, judgment is dished out in the form of suicide, capture by law enforcement, or violent death at the hands of someone else. Her work of the second half of her career, however, increasingly turns to Tom Ripley's character (four out of her last ten novels concern him), who continues to escape judgment—by the characters in the text as well as the novels' author. Interestingly enough, Highsmith's own statements made in her 1983 nonfiction book suggest that by then, relatively late in her career, she was able to grasp her fictional endeavor in these very terms. She claims not only that she is "interested in morality, providing it isn't preached" (*Plotting and Writing* 140) but also that "creative people do not pass moral judgment—at least not at once—on what meets their eye. There is time for that later in what they create, if they are so inclined, but art essentially has nothing to do with morality, conventions or moralizing" (25). Indeed, she finds "the public passion for justice quite boring and artificial, for neither life nor nature care if justice is ever done or not" (56). For Highsmith, then, the task is to suspend the emergence of judgment, insisting that its time is always merely that of a time to come, that is, of a future moment that is yet to be determined.

In what follows, I will investigate the trajectory of Highsmith's fiction with an emphasis on the Ripley novels in order to work out how one specific American postwar writer of violent fiction makes the question of judgment her own as a question of violence only to arrive at an increasingly immanent mode of response to this double problematic. Highsmith's violent fiction increasingly conceives of the possibility for responding to violence only as an affective practice, as an encounter occurring on the very plane of immanence that is shot through with violence. This implies that (for Highsmith) judgment, a practice always in need for a representational position outside that which is to be judged for it to be effective and "morally sound," has become an impossibility and implausibility.

In that, her fiction crucially parallels the larger cultural, economical, social, and political development mapped out by Michael Hardt and Antonio Negri in their influential study of contemporary capitalism's mode of power, *Empire*, which itself is crucially informed by Deleuze and Guattari's work. Just as it becomes essentially meaningless for Highsmith to allow for any judgment to be passed on her violent, amoral characters as her work moves into the late 1960s and onward, so Hardt and Negri argue that it is politically meaningless, indeed dangerous, to practice a type of sociopolitical response to capitalism's flows that is not immanent, that instead lays claim to a transcendent position of judgment, which, perhaps, might have provided a viable political position in previous eras of American society. And just as one of the most crucial political implications of *Empire* is that we must become capable of responding differently to this fundamentally new mode of power permeating contemporary society, so Highsmith's work produces an "Empirical" pedagogy of violence. Her oeuvre attempts to affect—that is, to train or habituate—readers so that they become capable of encountering her fictional violence in a different manner: carefully attuned to the changes occurring on the larger sociopolitical plane of Empire.

The following sections will build a map of Highsmith's work, beginning with a telling biographical anecdote, followed by a careful and extended analysis of her most famous novel, which, in turn, will lead to a more general discussion of her work's trajectory and its ethicopedagogical responses in conjunction with the Empire thesis. If the call of the last chapters was to heed "affect" as a crucial force criticism must respond to, this chapter provides one extended example in that it responds to the *intensities*—the speed and slowness, movement and rhythm—of Highsmith's work, with all its interruptions, sedimentations, mutations, and amplifications. Violence, as imaged in Highsmith's work, ends up being increasingly severed from any "meaning." That is, the fictional violence itself operates without being reterritorialized onto the transcendental plane of meaning—of representation—and thus questions those explanatory apparatuses that pretend to "understand" its (nonexistent) meaning.

Violence, Judgment, and Writing

Readers familiar with Patricia Highsmith's work might have come across an oft-cited story that may very well have had formative consequences for her obsessive return to the issues of morality, judgment, and violence. It appears that she was an unwelcome child. According to Highsmith, her mother tried to abort her by drinking turpentine five months before her birth: "She really tried to get rid of it [the fetus]—she told me—*I didn't mind.* She said, 'It's funny you adore the smell of turpentine, Pat.' Because she drank turpentine before I was born trying to have a miscarriage. *I didn't mind one bit*" (Dupont 62, my emphases). In the end, we can only speculate about how seriously she was affected by this knowledge, especially in light of the fact that she made this statement as an adult, thus raising the possibility that her fiction might have affected her view of her biography. It is therefore not the truth value of her biographical statement that should concern us here but her *style* of response to the narrated event itself, for what sticks out in Highsmith's brief recounting of this childhood incident is her double assertion that she "didn't mind." In other words, she was not bothered by this piece of information, by her mother's intentions, and, presumably, by her mother's action. To Highsmith, her mother's violent intentions and consequent actions were what they were—regardless of whether she liked them or not, regardless of whether she considered her mother terrible or not.

Manifesting an instance of truly immanent response, Highsmith replied to her mother's attempt at doing away with her by doing away with judgment. Instead of judging her mother, she counters the knowledge of her mother's violent intentions with a stubborn insouciance that refuses to regard the event as any more painful than it actually was or is. Continually judging her mother likely would have trapped her in an endless Oedipal drama that constantly returned to itself, thus blocking her from truly experimenting with the question of violence.[8] As Deleuze argues throughout his career, creating something of real value is, in fact, always a question of rigorous experimentation; it is never "a question of judging other existing beings, but of sensing whether they agree or disagree with us, that is, whether they bring forces to us, or whether they return us to the miseries of war, to the poverty of the dream, to the rigors of organization"

("To Have Done" 135). As if to illustrate the philosopher's argument, Highsmith's Bartlebyesque "I would prefer not to" type of response manifests the transformation of the singularity of this particular violent event into a productive experimental engine for her fiction, for imaginatively investigating the relationship between violence and judgment.[9]

To repeat, I am *not* suggesting that we turn to Highsmith's biography in order to locate an alleged originary experience that might explain her apparent obsession with violence; doing so would immediately reduce the question of violence to the plane of representation. Rather, I want to call attention to the *style* of engagement itself that this anecdote displays and that, as we will see, crucially resonates with her fictional work. Hence, rather than reducing her fascination with violence to one biographical event along the line of the always popular "return of the repressed" thesis, I think we must heed the *attitude* Highsmith the writer articulates in response to her encounter with personal violence, all the more so because she repeatedly displays the same attitude when she conceptualizes the act of writing. Just like her response to a form of violence she has been privy to herself is marked by a remarkable absence of (moral) judgment, so her attitude toward the creative act of writing about violence is shot through with the imperative to keep judgment and family history at bay. Highsmith dismissed any correlation between her biography and work and quite obviously rejected the "write what you know" school of creative writing promoted by countless MFA programs in the United States that emerged in the aftermath of the success of the confessional writers such as Sylvia Plath, Ann Sexton, or Robert Lowell. She repeatedly declared that her "ideas are not related to where I was born, or to the family, and, I must say, I mistrust writers who use their family because I think they're not imaginative" (Dupont 61). Highsmith essentially articulates that her obsession with the nexus judgment-violence does not so much represent a working through of some kind of Oedipal conflict as it constitutes a response to a singular event in her life (regardless of the degree of its possible fictionalization), one that functions as a provocation along the lines of a Nietzschean arrow of thought that must be caught and shot forth again in a different direction.[10] In other words, I am not suggesting Highsmith lied about this event. Rather, given the timing of the statement's utterance, it seems entirely possible that to Highsmith the event had become yet another violent story to be told—one that does not bear explanatory power but that possesses a certain force to solicit responses. The event, in short, could be considered to function as a provocation, a *problématique*. Rather than seeking it out, it found her, thus transforming her life. The transforming event, though, ceased to be personal for her and remained effective merely as an accident that becomes an experiment in which the world around her participates.

Remarkable in that Highsmith deploys this concept of abiographical writing around the issue of violence—one that habitually tends to be read by critics through the lens of some sort of transcendental signifier, be it located in family or social ones (Oedipus, economic relations, race conflicts, gender issues)—it provides a crucial concept for my purposes in that it links the issue of how critical language responds to violence in fictional texts and the differential philosophy of Deleuze that underlies much of my diagnosis. Whereas Deleuze teaches us a thoroughly arepresentational engagement with language (as argued in the preceding chapter), Highsmith provides a case in point by pushing the idea to its limit case—violence—that tends to direct any response immediately into a demand for explanation, understanding, and judgment. But both Highsmith and Deleuze reject this approach. Just as Highsmith disdains recourse to her biography as a means for explaining her fictional world, so Deleuze proclaims that "to write is not to recount one's memories and travels, one's loves and griefs, one's dreams and fantasies. [. . .] We do not write with our neuroses" ("Literature and Life" 2–3).[11] In other words, if we put these two philosophies of writing in close proximity to the question of violence, we start mobilizing a thought or mode of response that is less interested in what a particular incidence of fictional violence means than in how it operates.

↓

The first thing to be marked about Highsmith's violent fiction is the obsessive quality of her incessant return to approaching the question of judgment as a question of violence—often marked in terms of characters' guilt perceived either by themselves or their surroundings. Highsmith herself is the first to acknowledge the repetitiveness of her fiction: "Well, since I was sixteen or seventeen, I've been writing the same kind of stories" (Hochkeppel 183, my translation). What, then, are these stories, and how does the trajectory of Highsmith's career look like? Are her stories really the same, and, if so, what is the effect of its repetition? Or, if the stories differ in their seeming sameness—especially around her works' key questions of judgment and violence—then what are the specific effects produced by this repetition?[12]

Her most famous character, Tom Ripley, is the title character of five novels that Highsmith published between 1955 and 1991. Given the singularity of this serialization—Highsmith never wrote about another central character more than once—it perhaps makes sense to begin thinking about the questions of judgment and violence as they are posited and affected by this serialization. Criticism on Highsmith has repeatedly argued that Tom Ripley is Highsmith's most amoral character, a man who is unabashedly unconcerned about his frequently violent actions. Kakutani, for instance, complains that the later Ripley novels lack psychological realism and that the increasing improbability of Ripley's actions in the later novels have turned him into "an out-and-out madman: a sadist [. . .] a thrill-seeking murderer." She suggests that this excess of amorality invites readers "to feel smug and morally superior: a fatal flaw in just about any novel." Kathleen Gregory Klein claims that Ripley is not "immoral but thoroughly amoral, he accepts no standards of judgment" (194). Further, "because Tom Ripley, like few other Highsmith protagonists, is a calculating criminal whose behavior is both conscious and deliberate, he poses a dilemma for the reader" (194). Thus, focusing on this series as it functions within the larger context of Highsmith's overall work might provide a productive entry into the problematic of judgment and violence as Highsmith conceives it.

Indeed, as I will argue, the Ripley series not only marks the *intensification* of Highsmith's problematic but functions as breakdowns—points of singularity at which transformations occur—in her overall career. The repetition that characterizes her oeuvre at large is intensified in and through one dramatic persona, but this very intensification is itself amplified through serialized repetition. Each time Highsmith reaches this breaking point, something in her approach to her problematic is being transformed. In this, she develops an ethics of writing—and, in turn, produces an ethics of reading—that is characterized by a patient, experimental, immanent encounter with the problems she faces that I consider exemplary of the kind of masocritical ethics I have been delineating thus far. Highsmith avoids applying wholesale one solution to her problematic in all of her work, for she knows that her problematic constantly mutates, a mutation contingent on her sociocultural environment as well as her evolution as an artist and person. In avoiding this ethicopolitical faux pas, she also invites, if not demands, her readers to inhabit more carefully the trajectory of her work.

In essence, her work attempts to affect readers so that they will begin to habituate new reading practices that allow for specific responses to specific problems. Crucially, this emerging practice of response operates without any recourse to some overriding universal solutions that somehow declare the inherent "badness" of the problem at hand. As it turns out, Highsmith's problematic remains throughout her career how to encounter forces of judgment as a mode of response to instances of violence. As articulated in her encounter with her mother's confession as well as in her "properly" fictional work, it seems that she indeed practiced something akin to a Foucaultean ethics of problematization characterized by producing specific responses based on specific diagnoses. This practice of *problématiques* becomes the driving force of Highsmith's writing, and it is this force that will transform her solutions, that will force her to redescribe the problem, to reconceive of her answers, indeed to posit one answer only to retract from it for a while before returning to it in changed form as a new solution to a new problem.

↓

A preliminary overview in terms of what happens to the violence in her early novels confirms my description of this Highsmithean practice of writing. The three novels she wrote before *The Talented Mr. Ripley* all end in a clean resolution. *Strangers on a Train* (1950) features the accidental death of one murderer (Bruno) and the capture by a tricky detective of the other (Guy). *The Price of Salt* (1952) itself is not concerned with explicit violence (i.e., murder) but nonetheless resolves the story's main conflict about the relationship of a lesbian couple by giving it a happy end. The negative judgment passed on the lesbian lovers by their surroundings is ultimately described and defied as hypocritical.

Of course, in providing a happy end, Highsmith violated the standard of lesbian fiction at the time. As Highsmith describes this matter in the afterword to the novel's rerelease in 1990, now entitled *Carol* (with Highsmith's own name finally on the cover), the "appeal of *The Price of Salt* was that it had a happy ending for its two main characters, or at least they were going to try to have a future together. Prior to this book, homosexuals male and female in American novels had to pay for their deviation by cutting their wrists, drowning themselves in a swimming pool, or by switching to heterosexuality (so it was stated), or by collapsing—alone and miserable and shunned—into a depression equal to hell" (261). Highsmith claims that she initially published the novel using her pseudonym, Claire Morgan, because she wanted to avoid the label of "a lesbian book writer" (261), just as she did not want to be pigeonholed as a suspense author; yet, one suspects that the particular moral climate described in her statement might have had an effect on her "disowning" of the book as well.

Even though *The Price of Salt* does not feature the type of violence most of Highsmith's work is otherwise known for, it features the same basic problematic, albeit in a specific milieu that must be heeded in reading the novel. About thirty years later, Highsmith would return more explicitly to the question she began to tackle in *The Price of Salt*, and this time around she would deploy violence as a means to affect the question differently (see *Found in the Street* [1986] and *Small g: a Summer Idyll*). Finally, in *The Blunderer* (1954), her second novel about violence, an innocent man (Walter Stockhouse) is judged guilty by the police and shot dead by the actually guilty man (Gregor Kimmel), who, in turn, meets violent death as well.

In other words, all three novels find a relatively neat resolution to their respective plots. In contrast, the first Ripley novel ends with Ripley, then "merely" a double murderer, at large, thus allowing for the possibility of future stories about him. What happens in this transformation is that for readers the arrival of pleasure (afforded by the moment when a text invites us to experience the certainty of "sound" judgment) is deferred by the fact that traditional reader expectations are violated (lack of resolution) and, even more painfully for us, that we have been made to feel sympathetic towards the scheming double murderer Ripley. Highsmith, that is, pushes on the concepts of guilt and truth—in short, morality—hard enough for them to crystallize to the point where neither appears to matter anymore. Or, better, where judgment was closely tied to the question of "truth" (including who is guilty in whose eyes), judgment is now rendered as violence.

Just consider the difference between *Strangers on a Train* and *The Blunderer*. The former essentially features Highsmith's only detective story—that is, a story where detection of the truth has considerable narrative force. Only four years later, Highsmith rejects the concept of truth as meaningless as the primary locus for accurate judgment precisely because she can show how the force of "truth" is effective regardless of its validity or truthfulness. As David Cochran writes, Walter, the protagonist of *The Blunderer*, "realizes his technical innocence is irrelevant in face of the fact that he had plotted [his wife] Clara's death [though he never acted on it], whereas Kimmel's actual guilt [he killed his wife] is similarly irrelevant, since he has succeeded in putting the police off his trail" (122) and redirected attention to Walter's *seeming* but not actual guilt. Kimmel does this because Walter, the blunderer of the novel's title, inadvertently reopens the investigation of the death of Kimmel's wife. Because Walter exactly imagines how Kimmel had killed his wife based on newspaper reports, because this imaging event leads his imagination to plot the murder of his wife just as Kimmel did, and because he leaves traces of this imaginary plot in his notebooks, the police eventually suspect both Walter and Kimmel of having murdered their wives.

But, and this is one of the great achievements of the first (and subsequent) Ripley books, Highsmith carefully reconfigures the question of judgment as being about truth by now constructing judgment qua violence as an affective category, that is, a matter of intensities. The transformation occurring, then, moves from the question of judgment as an issue of truth, logos, and reality to the question of judgment as an issue of and for violence, affect, and simulation.[13]

Since this transformation is key to all of her work in that it will continue to resonate in every book, we need to slow down our mapping process at this stage. Before proceeding any further, we should find out how exactly this transformation happens as well as what it does. To this end, the next section will closely examine *The Talented Mr. Ripley*, a novel that allowed Highsmith for the first time to reach a singular point of transformation. This moment of transformation ends up being the constitutive force of the rest of her oeuvre, a body of work that itinerates this transformation as a proliferation of efforts to find responses to her basic problematic. Interestingly enough, the remaining four Ripley novels will allow her to achieve the purest moments of this breaking point, but, as will hopefully become clear, these moments could not have been reached had it not been for Highsmith's incessant repetition of her basic story with all their retractions, hesitations, or, perhaps, accommodations to specific genre expectations.[14]

In other words, the act of repetition itself ends up operating as a pedagogical mechanism. Instead of catering to an existing audience who is already capable of accepting Highsmith's specific response to the question of judgment and violence as mutually informing each other, Highsmith relentlessly produces her audience as yet to come. The larger movement of her work attests that she was very well in tune with the likelihood that readers would not be able to follow her most radical solutions if she were not to train them in how to read her fiction. In essence, she produces what Deleuze describes as "minor literature"—a literature described by the production of speech acts that create themselves "as a foreign language in a dominant language, precisely in order to express an impossibility of living under domination" (*Cinema 2* 223).[15] As an American born in Texas, partly raised in New York, who lived most of her life in England, France, and Switzerland, who was more popular and critically acclaimed in Germany and France than in her native country, Highsmith continued to write in English about fictional American citizens.[16] But she did so in such a fashion that allowed her to develop a violent language about morality/judgment within the dominant moral discourse of American language as articulated in much of the literature of her time, let alone the politico-cultural atmosphere of the 1950s (and even later). But perhaps precisely because Highsmith's situation resembled that of a writer such as Kafka—being an exile in his own language—Highsmith as a writer was "not in a condition to produce individual utterances which would be like invented stories; but also, because the people are missing, the author is in a situation of producing utterances which are already collective, which are like the seeds of the people to come, and whose political impact is immediate and inescapable" (Deleuze, *Cinema 2* 221). Tom Ripley, the literary persona through which Highsmith was able to produce her minor "moral" language—a language that concerns itself with the question of judgment—is itself the product of her repeated encounter with the conditions surrounding the possibility for her writing: anonymous, collective, political. No wonder, then, that Highsmith claimed she "often had the feeling that Ripley was writing it and I was merely typing" (*Plotting and Writing* 76).

Becoming-Violent

The Talented Mr. Ripley introduces Highsmith's readers to Tom Ripley, who subsequently will appear in four more novels as the title character. In these later novels, Ripley will have already succeeded at establishing himself as a relatively wealthy, married, and generally respected man leading a comfortable, quiet life in the countryside not far from Paris. Having gained much of his wealth through his criminal activities, Ripley continues to be affected by his violent past actions. In contrast, our first glimpse of Ripley in *The Talented Mr. Ripley* is of a young man struggling to make ends meet with part-time jobs and small-time criminal activities such as the occasional forging of tax records. His luck begins to change when one day Mr. Richard Greenleaf, a wealthy owner of a shipbuilding firm, persuades him to travel to Italy in order to talk his son, Dickie, into returning to the United States to join Greenleaf's company. Ripley, who is only marginally acquainted with Dickie, initially succeeds at becoming friendly with the latter. Eventually, however, their relationship turns sour, as Dickie loses interest in Tom's company. Responding to this troubling turn of events, Tom murders Dickie and then assumes the latter's identity. The rest of the novel unfolds the consequences of Tom's violent deed, showing us how he manages to hold off both the bumbling Italian police and those personally acquainted with Dickie such as his female friend, Marge, his father, as well as Freddy Miles, a good friend of Dickie's whom Ripley kills as well once he gets too close to uncovering the truth. By the end of the novel, Tom Ripley, now as himself again, has murdered two people, considered the possibility of killing two more, and still remains at large, having successfully deceived everyone about the level of his involvement in these murderous events.

Critical responses to *The Talented Mr. Ripley*, including that of Minghella's film, tend to highlight what Hilfer has called the "protean" quality of Ripley's amoral character and actions. But while it is undoubtedly true that Ripley's criminal success has much to do with his ability to "act," the particular inflection acting is given in much of Highsmith criticism—that is, as an intentional, planned endeavor—has done little to shed light on what, exactly, Highsmith has accomplished with the writing of her first Ripley novel. Describing Ripley's actions as masterful, willing enactments of roles that erase his real identity, these critics refuse to consider the possibility that identity might be nothing else but a series of performances—an endless putting on and off of masks. Likewise, positing Ripley's actions as the outcome of a talented actor planning his actions in order to advance his own cause deploys an understanding of acting based on intentional imitation. This, however, makes it difficult to account for some of the key *affective* moments in Ripley's rapturous development to becoming a violent character that have nothing at all to do with making rational decisions, or masterminding, as Erlene Hubly (123) suggests.[17] Most important, perhaps, the characterization of Ripley as a rationally intending subject allows us to admire his success while distancing us from the more immoral consequences of his actions; we can admire and congratulate Ripley for his great talent while concurrently remaining distanced from the ends to which he puts his talents. Yet, this sort of stiff-arming of the less moral effects ultimately leads to a reaffirmation of this moral space—one not occupied by Ripley but, so it is claimed, perhaps by Highsmith and certainly by the critics—that has been placed under scrutiny by Highsmith in her larger fictional project. In the following, then, I will show how Highsmith reconfigures morality—judgment—in terms of violence as an affective category by more carefully attending to Ripley's well-known talent—acting.[18]

Being initially "bored, God-damned bloody bored, bored, bored" (8) by Mr. Greenleaf's initial proposition to travel to Italy, Ripley soon seems to reconsider his attitude. His intense outpouring of angered emotions—articulated in his mind as boredom—quickly subsides and gives way to the first instance of his ability to act. Listening to Greenleaf's explanations, Ripley soon gets "into the spirit" (8) of the situation and begins responding to the older man's questions more carefully, alternating between truthful statements, slight exaggerations, and flat-out lies. Ripley himself registers his change of attitude. Feeling that his "boredom had slipped into another gear" (9), his "heart took a sudden leap. He put on an expression of reflection. It was a possibility. *Something in him had smelt it out and leapt at it even before his brain*" (9, my emphasis). The significance of what Highsmith describes in her typically "factual, almost metaphorless prose" (Handke 172, my translation) cannot be underestimated for the course of the novel and her work at large, for at this moment Ripley is shown to register an encounter with what a number of theorists, including Blanchot, Foucault, and Deleuze, have called "the outside": Ripley encounters a force ("it") that something in him had smelt out, like a scent of possibility oozing through the smoky bar in which their meeting takes place.

Contrary to many responses to Tom Ripley claiming that he is a protean man planning his deeds by deploying his talent for acting, Highsmith suggests from the very first moments of the novel on that Ripley's acting is not tied to a plan originating in a premeditated mood. Here as throughout the novel, Highsmith narrates Ripley's actions and thoughts in affective terms: his feeling of extreme boredom, his "getting into the spirit" (8), his capacity to be "manically polite" (9)—all of this suggests a remarkable narrative configuration of thought as an *affective* process. Deleuze is enlightening in this context:

> Thought is primarily trespass and violence. [. . .] Do not count upon thought to ensure the relative necessity of what it thinks. Rather, count upon the contingency of an encounter with that which forces thought to raise up and educate the absolute necessity of an act of thought or a passion to think. [. . .] *Something in the world forces us to think.* This something is an object not of recognition but of a fundamental *encounter*. [Whatever is encountered] may be grasped in a range of *affective* tones: wonder, love, hatred, suffering. In whichever tone, its primary characteristic is that it can only be sensed. (*Difference and Repetition* 139, first and third emphases mine)

Deleuze's description of the "something in the world [that] forces us to think" captures what happens to or with Ripley in almost the same terms used by Highsmith: something in Ripley senses something outside of him. More than anything else, Ripley *responds* to a force outside him. This force, and not a rational decision, triggers his response. His actions here and elsewhere can be described as acting only if we conceive of acting not as a process of imitation (representation), for Ripley does *not* imitate something he has observed, remembered, or recognized from the past that he now sets out to emulate.

Instead of the force of recollection underlying the process of imitation, then, it is Deleuze and Guattari's well-known concept of "becoming" that can be said to structure Tom's behavior.[19] Becoming, as they write in *A Thousand Plateaus*, "is never imitating" (305), nor has it anything to do with "resemblance [or] identification" (237). To become-dog you do not have to bark or wag your tail while crawling on all fours. Tom Ripley does not have to acquire the same aesthetic tastes that Dickie displayed to become-Dickie. Further, becoming does not constitute an evolutionary process, be it as a progress or regress; instead, "becoming is involutionary" (238), a "multiplicity" (239), a fascination with "the outside" (240), an affect (257), a capacity to become affected, to enter a "zone of proximity" (293). It is Tom's capacity to respond to the force of chance, his inclination to experiment, that enables him to enter into this zone with the force of the outside: becoming always constitutes "an encounter between two reigns, a short-circuit, the picking-up of a code where each is deterritorialized" (Deleuze and Parnet, *Dialogues* 44). Tom's becoming-Dickie as manifested in the novel becomes possible in response to his being in the middle of things, without a plan but always pushing on a version of selfhood that neither depends on nor desires a stable sense of self, nor pretends that the self exists in any other version but as a momentary sedimentation of multiplicity: "Starting from the forms one has, the subject one is, the organs one has, or the functions one fulfills, becoming is to extract particles between which one establishes the relations of movement and rest, speed and slowness that are closest to what one is becoming and through which one becomes. [. . .] This principle of proximity or approximation is entirely particular and reintroduces no analogy whatsoever. It indicates as rigorously as possible a *zone of proximity*" (*Thousand Plateaus* 272). As the vocabulary Highsmith uses in this opening passage as well as later ones suggests, Tom's ability to "smell" this force of the outside that inspires him to think, to go along with Greenleaf's proposition, operates on an affective level in the sense that an affect is "the effectuation of a power of the pack [or multiplicity] that throws the self into upheaval and makes it reel" (*Thousand Plateaus* 240). Ripley does indeed reel.

So, from the beginning, Highsmith configures her favorite character not so much as a protean man than as a *man of response*. Instead of judging Greenleaf's proposition as absurd (after all, Tom barely knows Dickie), Ripley senses—smells—something he cannot yet put into words but is nonetheless willing to encounter as an experiment. In other words, Tom Ripley takes a gamble. He rolls the dice, betting more on chance than on his own capacity to pull off a sustained hoax. But thought is a roll of the dice, as Deleuze argues: "What the dice-throw represents is that thinking always comes from the outside (that outside which is already engulfed in the interstice or which constituted the common limit). Thinking is neither innate nor acquired. It is not the innate exercise of a faculty, but neither is it a learning process constituted in the external world" (*Foucault* 117). Thinking is always an in-between, an encounter, a response, an entering and inhabiting of a zone of proximity, rather than an imitation. Thinking is an affect, a becoming, not a process of representing. Thinking is "trespass and violence." Here, then, are the initial components of Highsmith's most famous books and character: contingency and the encounter with the outside, thought as affective response.

If we take this response structure of becoming as the immanent mode of Tom's "acting," we will also see how an intensification of this structure affects the way violence operates in this novel. The pivotal moment in the novel occurs when Tom starts assuming Dickie's persona. But, and this cannot be overemphasized, Tom's becoming-Dickie functions itself as a response to a prior moment of judgment: to wit, the fateful suggestion, made by Marge to Dickie, that Tom is a homosexual.[20] Regardless of the validity of Marge's suspicion, one which Dickie will eventually second (80), the point here is that Tom *imagines* and, due to its intensity, *experiences* the effects of being judged: "The sudden weight of guilt made sweat come on Tom's forehead, an amorphous yet very strong sense of guilt, as if Marge had told Dickie specifically that he had stolen something or had done some other shameful thing" (76). This strong sense of guilt, already prefigured by the novel's opening scene (Ripley "had a feeling of guilt" [20] when accepting Mr. Greenleaf's proposition), provokes an intensification of his emotions. Seeing his relationship with Dickie disintegrating as a direct consequence of Marge's judgment (i.e., Marge deploys the negative force contained by the label "homosexual" to drive a wedge between Dickie and Tom), Tom undergoes a violent transformation, throwing Dickie's possessions out of the window in a fit (78). In all this, he "had a curious feeling that his brain remained calm and logical and that his body was out of control" (78).

At this exact moment of affective crisis, Tom spontaneously becomes-Dickie. He begins dressing up as him, assumes his voice, and imagines Dickie's violent rejection of Marge (78–79). Given the absence of any indication that Tom planned this event, we can hardly think of this moment in traditional acting terms—that is, representation and imitation. In fact, somewhat later in the novel, Tom himself articulates that acting is not about imitation: "The main thing about impersonation [. . .] was to maintain the *mood* and *temperament* of the person one was impersonating, and to assume the facial expressions that went with them. The rest fell into place" (131, my emphases). In other words, Highsmith describes Tom's actions—his enacting—as a matter of *style*, as a process of becoming that has nothing to do with representing, imitating, or resembling. Acting as a truthful or realistic act of copying or imitating is subsumed by the prior force of acting as simulation: inhabiting a mood—deploying an affect, a force—constitutes a practice of simulation in that its goal is not to reproduce but to respond.[21] An essential falsehood, then, allows for the production of the appearance of similitude, indeed verisimilitude: one must apply much makeup to appear as "natural" on TV.

Tom's becoming-Dickie happens in response to his feeling of guilt, of having been judged, and this becoming is from the beginning marked in violently affective terms. In this sense, then, Tom's becoming-violent precedes his first actual act of violence— the killing of Dickie. His becoming-Dickie marks his becoming-violent. The indiscernibility of this event actualizes Dickie's death. Long before he finds his death at Tom's hands on a boat trip, Dickie has been sentenced to death, even though neither Tom nor Dickie knew about it. What has taken place here is what Deleuze and Guattari describe as an incorporeal transformation, the actualizing of an order-word that consists of a line of flight and a death sentence. The line of flight instantiated is Tom's becoming-Dickie/becoming-violent, whereas Dickie's death manifests the inevitability of the order-word's second aspect: only if Dickie can become something else as well can Tom become-Dickie.[22]

When they take the fateful train trip from Cannes to San Remo, Tom's frustrations with Dickie, whose indifference, if not hostility, to Tom's presence further amplifies Tom's emotional instability, are pushed to their limit, in the process transforming Tom from a relatively innocent young man in search of a better life into a cold-blooded murderer: "Tom stared at Dickie's closed eyelids. A crazy emotion of hate, of affection, of impatience and frustration was swelling in him, hampering his breathing. He wanted to kill Dickie. It was not the first time he had thought of it. Before, once or twice or three times, it had been an impulse caused by anger or disappointment, an impulse that vanished immediately and left him with a feeling of shame. Now he thought about it for an entire minute, two minutes, because he was leaving Dickie anyway, and what was there to be ashamed of anymore? He had failed with Dickie" (100). Interestingly, the very physicality of this passage—with the prose's rhythm spilling over in the repeated attempts at precise time descriptions—links up with Tom's sense of failure: his having been judged by his friends, suggesting that the inherent force of judgment moves always too fast, is always ahead of itself, forgets the concrete materiality of the situation being judged. This violence of judgment, which does not allow the other to persist without forcing him or her into being, indeed becoming, something or someone else, produces violence.

And Tom responds to this force. He is capable of doing so precisely because he has already become-Dickie, even though he only now realizes this: "He had just thought of something brilliant: he could become Dickie Greenleaf himself" (100). But Tom has long become-Dickie, as Highsmith's narrative makes perfectly clear in that it does not provide any transitional period bridging Tom's "brilliant thought" with his acting upon it. Instantaneously, Tom "began to think of *how*" (100). Not wasting a second on contemplating the consequences of his becoming, Tom intuitively knows that only his actions matter now, regardless of their "meaning." Tom imagines a series of possible murder scenarios, as if he had planned it for a long time. But he has not. That he can imagine so clearly his future enactment of his violent deed directly results from his prior becoming-Dickie, as it is indiscernible from his becoming-violent.[23] And so Tom imagines: "The Water. But Dickie was such a good swimmer. The cliffs. [Tom rejects this idea.] San Remo. Flowers. A main drag along the beach again, shops and stores and French and English and Italian tourists. Another hotel, with flowers in the balconies. Where?" (100–101). No moral scruples because the violence of morality itself has provoked his response, his violence. And then Dickie dies, having been smacked in the head with an oar that continually "hit him in the side of the neck, three times, chopping strokes with the edge of the oar, as if the oar were an axe and Dickie's neck a tree," "slic[ing] Dickie's forehead," and plunging the oar's handle with a bayonet grip into Dickie's side (104). Notably, Highsmith depicts the entire process of Tom's becoming-violent as a response to the force of judgment levied at him and configures the terms of this response as affect. And despite or, perhaps better, *because* of Tom's experience of guilt, he does not pause to consider the morality of his actions.

He responds to the sense that it was the realm of judgment that produces—indeed *is*—violence itself.

Tom's process of becoming does not end here. Most crucially, he is eventually forced to become-Tom again, something that he initially loathes (at one moment he thinks that to identify himself as Tom Ripley "was going to be one of the saddest things he had ever done in his life" [200]) but that becomes acceptable once he intuits that becoming-Tom does not mean a return to his old self: "Hadn't he learned something from these last months? If you wanted to be cheerful, or melancholic, or wistful, or thoughtful, or courteous, you simply had to *act* those things with every gesture" (193). That this acting does not function by imitation he understands a bit later, for he begins to see that regardless of the ultimate truth value of his acts, his "stories were good because he imagined them *intensely*, so *intensely* that he came to believe them" (253, my emphases). In short, his acting is a practice of imagining, which, in turn, is about affect or intensities, about entering a zone of proximity, of becoming.

His second becoming is an effect of his first one, with the consequence that he does not so much return to his earlier existence but to a new one, affected by his prior becoming: Tom now displays a new sense of sophistication, a new sense of being in the world (which will undergo further intensification in Highsmith's subsequent serializing of him) that would have remained impossible had it not been for his prior becoming-Dickie. This intensification will eventually also do away with any remnants of Tom's guilt, as well as with any pretense to realism on Highsmith's part. Even so, throughout the rest of *The Talented Mr. Ripley*, Highsmith occasionally continues to show Tom struggling with a lingering sense of guilt (he has nightmares in which Dickie is still alive, having swam to the shore [166]) that intensifies as a result of his second murder. In the process, Tom's actions become less credible (the police can be only so stupid). But I take Highsmith's "disavowal" of realism to be part of her project's point, for judgment denotes a practice based on realism—if not necessarily in the literary sense per se then in that it requires a comparison to an (imaginary or real) standard or origin, to something that is perceived as true, as real.[24] In contrast, for Highsmith judgment becomes the problem par excellence precisely because it *is* violence. Thus Highsmith redescribes the question of judgment via posing it as an issue of truth and violence (*The Blunderer*) in such a way that the question of violence appears as the most *intense* version of judgment.

Tom's ability to respond to something outside of himself that forces him to think, to imagine, to invent—this is what his acting qua becoming constitutes. In turn, this configuration of Tom's character suggests that Highsmith herself has arrived at one specific solution to her larger *problématique*: beginning with the question of judgment, she renders it as the question of violence, a rendering that configures these two terms as mutually immanent of each other. You can think of judgment only as and through violence. Further, this immanence itself is marked always as an affective process, a movement of instances of becoming. Tom has to become-violent in order to become-Dickie, but becoming-Dickie requires his becoming-violent. Finally, he has to become-Tom to achieve the ability to see his sense of guilt for what it is: productive of and produced by a practice of judgment that is violent at its core. As he contemplates, "if he hadn't misjudged the relationship between Dickie and Marge so stupidly, or had simply waited for them to separate of their own volition, then none of this would have happened" (274). Judgment, in other words, is always a practice that *proceeds with too much speed*—just like violence. It is this quality of judgment that constitutes its violence, that makes it productive of violence.

Empirical Violence

With this remarkable answer found so early in her career, we might expect Highsmith to have wholeheartedly embraced this "solution" to her *problématique* and continue on this particular trajectory of creating likeable, murderously violent characters

ship with his father and a past girlfriend, Keener feels oddly at-
tracted to MacFarland, who appears to remind him of his father.
My point here is that MacFarland's punishment arrives without
Keener, the character readers are most likely to sympathize with,
ever desiring it. Likewise, David Kelsey's suicide in *This Sweet Sickness* seems to serve more generic purposes than anything else,
for by the end of the novel, Kelsey's schizophrenic state of mind
has all but eradicated his physical existence. The extent to which
the pathetic nature and pathology of his life has been established
by Highsmith does not so much solicit readers' lust for revenge
and punishment as provoke pity, if not empathy. Kelsey's life has
been melodramatic enough so that his suicide, his final form of
his punishment, does not make any difference at all.

But this inconsequentiality of the forms of punishment in
these five novels should be of interest to us: ought we not at least
wonder why Highsmith seems to have felt compelled to abandon
her carefully wrought solution to her problematic? Should we not
feel puzzled that she retreats from her crucial achievement to
have brought into mutual presupposition the concept and practice of judgment and violence at the very moment she has been
able to configure them as questions immanent to each other?

Only in Highsmith's novels of the second half of the 1960s do
we once again encounter violent characters who remain at large
by the end of the books, such as Philip Carter in *The Glass Cell*
(1964) and Sydney Bartleby in *The Story-Teller* (1965). *The Glass
Cell* documents the effects prison can have on a man—especially
when he is unjustly imprisoned. In many ways, the story pursues
a quite Pavlovian thesis: if you push a man so much, you will turn
him into a violent being. Much more interesting than this argument is the one offered in *The Story-Teller*. Here, the imagination
of Bartleby, a second-rate writer of crime stories, leads to his enacting of an actual crime: precisely because he has imagined murder so intensely he is first (falsely) suspected of having killed his
wife and then finds it easy to force her lover to swallow a lethal
dose of sleeping pills. Rather than a behaviorist thesis, *The Story-
Teller* argues for the lethal force of the artistic imagination. In

this context, we should note that Highsmith eventually retracted the "thesis" of her first novel, namely, that any person can become a murderer, a sentiment that still circulates as being central to Highsmith's "philosophy." However, Highsmith, acknowledging that she may have thought it when she wrote *Strangers on a Train*, unequivocally stated, "I don't believe that everybody can be coerced into murder" (Cooper-Clark 317). However, the fact of the reintroduction of violent characters who remain at large into Highsmith's fiction has to be qualified immediately by pointing out that in her last two novels of the 1960s, *Those Who Walk Away* (1967) and *The Tremor of Forgery* (1969), no murders are committed to begin with (with the latter potentially featuring a violent death as a result of something akin to premeditated self-defense). Twenty years into her career, then, Highsmith had crafted thirteen novels, of which only three, perhaps four, feature violent characters that escape their judgment. This is worth mentioning if for no other reason than that critics continually emphasize Highsmith's alleged penchant for creating amoral characters that remain unpunished. At least up until this point in Highsmith's oeuvre, this is patently wrong; but this claim somewhat ironically points to the function of criticism and how it is driven by its desire for judgment to such a degree that, at times, it cannot see when it actually occurs.

If, however, Highsmith's writing between 1955 and 1969 constitutes a "return to judgment," then we must heed the very repetitiveness of this seeming retraction of the "solution" she arrived at with the writing of *The Talented Mr. Ripley*. Reading Highsmith's fiction (and not only that from the first part of her career), I am unlikely to be alone in noticing how difficult it is to differentiate between her characters and, when all is said and done, her basic plots. All of this leads to a remarkable difficulty in recollecting specific incidents attached to specific proper names.[26] Importantly, it appears that Highsmith herself must have been affected by this increasing monotony of her work. A sense of boredom might very well have manifested itself by the time she conceived of *The Tremor of Forgery*, her first book about the morality of violence without the clear-cut occurrence of murder. In this book, Howard Ingham, an American writer, spends time in Tunisia to gather material for a movie script. After he finds out that the producer of the movie has died in New York on the bed of Ingham's girlfriend, he abandons his film project but stays on in Tunisia. One night, he hears an intruder trying to break into his house. Not seeing the man but suspecting a hoodlum who has bothered him before, he throws his typewriter at the unwelcome guest, then shuts the door. The fate of the intruder will remain unclear for the rest of the novel: was he fatally injured and carried away by hotel employees who wanted to cover over the incident?[27] Or was he merely hurt and helped by the employees to leave the premises?

Regardless of how we read the novel's key event—whether as an act of self-defense leading to the death of a small-time Arabic crook or as a more or less premeditated act of violence in the guise of self-defense that may or may not have led to a death—the novel is beyond the shadow of a doubt about Highsmith's key problematic, namely, the questions of judgment (morality) and violence, as even the back-cover description of the novel's paperback edition emphasizes: "Gradually, however, a series of peculiar events—a hushed-up murder, a vanished corpse, and secret broadcasts to the Soviet Union—lures [Ingham] inexorably into the deep, ambivalent shadows of this Arab town, into deceit and away from conventional morality. And when Ingham finds an accomplice to murder, or perhaps something more, what is in question is not justice or truth, but the state of his oddly quiet conscience." Most importantly, it is Adams, the patriotic American radioing secret propaganda messages to subvert the Soviet regime, who becomes curious about the (murderous?) incident and presses Ingham to clear his conscience. Suspecting him of foul play, Adams lectures Ingham that he must not abandon his good American morality only because he is now in a world that is not based on Judeo-Christian moral values. Adams believes that Ingham's (alleged) crime will haunt him forever if he cannot bring himself to confess—and thus to ask for punishment

ruption. In fact, Highsmith herself spoke positively of the force inherent to boredom, of its capacity to provoke thought: "I create things out of boredom with reality and with the sameness of routine and objects around me. Therefore, I don't dislike this boredom which encroaches on me every now and then, and I even try to create it by routine" (*Plotting and Writing* 49). In other words, the affective force constituting boredom functions productively in that it is often produced by real or perceived repetitions that lend themselves to a pause, a space for the production of thought. But, and this must be marked, boredom has to be produced by the writer or the world she lives in. (I have already argued this in chapter 2. Tom Ripley, of course, initially acts out of boredom as well.) The affective state of boredom has to be created through routines, through regulating one's practice of writing—and through regulating the writerly encounter with violence. In this routinized, regulated, masochistic interval, Highsmith experiments with her *problématique*, repeatedly testing her insight that violence and judgment consist of forces that are mutually immanent. Hence, Highsmith *had* to write all of these novels to reach the point of intensification she found herself affected by in the late 1960s.

In this context, Julian Symons, one of Highsmith's best commentators, wrote a perceptive passage just before Highsmith published the second installment of her Ripley series: "The return of Mr. Ripley, about which Highsmith thinks at this moment [1969], could solve the problem of correctly articulating her thoughts about social morality and individual behavior by correctly deploying violence without gratuitous sensationalism. Violence is necessary, since her best writerly talents find expression through violence and actuality, and she must find a way realistically to use this" (150, my translation). In this passage, Symons nicely voices his sense of the mood that must have affected Highsmith at the time. He describes the searching mode of operation she must have participated in: Highsmith appears to have been stuck in her search for a way out, for a resolution to her basic *problématique*, for finding a way to deploy violence in such a manner that it does not have to rely anymore on the counter act of punishment or judgment. And I contend that at this moment Highsmith was ready, once again, to turn back. This time, however, her return to an earlier moment in her career is not one that still relies on explicit punishment; rather, she returns to *The Talented Mr. Ripley*, to the book that has begun, if not entirely successfully (after all, Ripley remains plagued by guilt), to configure violence and judgment as immanent forces. That is, rather than a counter act, judgment is immanent to, or shot through with, violence. If Highsmith indeed searched for a way out of her dilemma, if she indeed looked for an exit, then her particular writing practice led her to the insight that, really, there is no exit, that the only way out, if there is one at all, is a process of intensification, of going through. Violence is affect, and only by masocritically heeding the affective force inherent to acts of violence can she determine what is so interesting about the question of violence to begin with. Put more forcefully, only by intensifying her *problématique* can she examine life under domination and experiment with modes of regulating it. This masocritical intensification eventually brings about a pure line of flight: instead of escaping violence, Highsmith's writerly encounter with violence makes the whole plane of representation/judgment/violence flee.

↙

This iteration of a response Highsmith had given some fifteen years prior to her writing of *Ripley Under Ground* (1970) cannot be underestimated as an important achievement of her career, or, for that matter, post–World War II (American) literature, for it occurs at a crucial shift in the development of Western sociopolitical life in general. Michael Hardt and Antonio Negri's entire *Empire* project narrates the battle between forces of transcendence and forces of immanence that have dominated and irrevocably shaped the course of Western civilization since the Renaissance. By the time we get to the post–World War II era, the forces of immanence have, according to the theorists, won out for good, producing what they term "Empire": "In contrast to imperialism,

Empire establishes no territorial center of power and does not rely on fixed boundaries or barriers. It is a *decentered* and *deterritorializing* apparatus of rule that progressively incorporates the entire global realm within its open, expanding frontiers. Empire manages hybrid identities, flexible hierarchies, and plural exchanges through modulating networks of command. The distinct national colors of the imperialist map of the world have merged and blended in the imperial global rainbow" (xii–xiii).

The most important characteristic of this fundamentally new form of social organization—of power—is that all of its forces operate on the same plane of immanence: Empire is the first truly immanent mode of power that Western civilization has faced. As part of this emergence of a new mode of power, of life, of what they call biopolitical production, capitalism itself has been transformed. Empire, and its capitalist economic leg, produces and reproduces itself, with the result that there is nothing but capital, or, as Deleuze and Guattari once claimed, "There is only desire and the social, and nothing else" (*Anti-Oedipus* 29).

The consequence of this shift in social organization is grave for the possibility of politics and intervention. As Hardt and Negri make perfectly clear, nostalgia for a lost world is a loser as a political strategy (and clearly, they direct this polemical argument at their fellow Marxists). Not denying the enormous evidence of oppression and destruction in the contemporary world, they nonetheless insist, repeatedly, that the "passage to Empire and its processes of globalization offer new possibilities to the forces of liberation. [But our] political task [. . .] is not simply to resist these processes but to *reorganize* them and *redirect* them toward new ends. [. . .] The struggles to contest and subvert Empire, as well as those to construct a real alternative, will thus take place on the imperial terrain itself" (xv, my emphases). Again, the only way out is through.

However, in the context of the pedagogical and political practice of criticism that I have been theorizing thus far, this sociopolitical map dawn by Hardt and Negri provides theoretical and pragmatic reasons that explain why cultural criticism cannot af-

ford to hold on to, let alone mourn for, a (moral) position outside. For as long as criticism insists on the availability of this position for itself, it gives up the possibility of "real" intervention.
Hardt and Negri are especially impatient with the commonality
of mournful, nostalgic critical discourse: "Despite recognizing
[all the suffering in today's world], we insist on asserting that
the construction of Empire is a step forward in order to do away
with any nostalgia for the power structures that preceded it and
refuse any political strategy that involves returning to that old ar-
rangement, such as trying to resurrect the nation-state to protect
against global capital. We claim that Empire is better in the same
way that Marx insists that capitalism is better than the forms of
society and modes of production that came before it" (43).

Hardt and Negri compellingly insist that the ethical and political (and thus critical) task of today is finally to heed "the primary
event of modernity [and its eventual instantiation]: the affirmation of the powers of *this* world, the discovery of the plane of immanence" (71). It must be noted, however, that an affirmation
of this moment does not mean that we need to describe or judge
it as "good." In fact, contrary to the frequent celebration of "difference" as "good" in contemporary academia, Hardt and Negri
hold that the "structures and logics of power in the contemporary
world are entirely immune to the 'libratory' weapons of the post-
modernist politics of difference. In fact, Empire too is bent on doing away with those modern forms of sovereignty and on setting
differences to play across boundaries" (142).[28] However, the great
irony inherent in contemporary criticism's desire to valorize difference and cast it as an outside to the bad forces of capital is that
this very desire marks its own impossibility. That is, the fact that
the "outside" has become such a (marketable) catchword marks
the very disappearance of it; or better, it indexes that the outside
has been folded into the inside on the plane of immanence, thus
revealing that the outside is not available anymore, if it ever was,
in the traditional sense of the concept.[29]

To return now to the question at hand—that of judgment, or
morality, as a form of "ethical" response to violence—for my pur-

poses the most telling part of their analysis occurs when Hardt and Negri also turn to the question of morality. They do so in the context of "intervention." Diagnosing how Empire operates, how it intervenes in the social sphere, they claim that its "powers of intervention might be best understood as beginning not directly with its weapons of lethal force but rather with its moral instruments" (35). That is, their analysis bears out that what we commonly understand as brute violence is in many respects much less interesting than the practice that we tend to think of as standing in opposition to violence: moral judgment. Hardt and Negri specifically examine the role played by nongovernmental organizations (NGOs) such as Amnesty International or Médecins sans Frontières, sociopolitical groups seemingly beyond reproach in people's estimation. And, of course, Hardt and Negri's effort at investigating how, exactly, they function in the age of Empire is not to reveal that they are somehow "bad" and that we are all duped by them. Instead, their much more interesting point of intervention is to show that these organizations, commonly perceived as corrective institutions to the more evil forces of global capitalism, form part of the nexus of Empire's operative system. To quote at length this crucial passage:

> Such humanitarian NGOs are in effect (even if this runs counter to the intentions of the participants) some of the most powerful pacific weapons of the new world order—the charitable campaigns and the mendicant orders of Empire. These NGOs conduct "just wars" without arms, without violence, without borders. Like the Dominicans in the late medieval period and the Jesuits at the dawn of modernity, these groups strive to identify universal needs and defend human rights. *Through their language and their action they first define the enemy as privation (in the hope of preventing serious damage) and then recognize the enemy as sin.* (36, my emphasis)

Slavoj Žižek concurs with this assessment, notwithstanding his otherwise negative view of *Empire*: "charity is, today, part of the game as a humanitarian mask hiding the underlying economic exploitation: in a superego-blackmail of gigantic proportions, the developed countries are constantly 'helping' the undeveloped (with aid, credits, etc.), thereby avoiding the key issue, namely, their *complicity* in and coresponsibility for the miserable situation of the undeveloped" (*Organs without Bodies* 179). The institutions traditionally occupying a *moral* high ground, in other words, possess their superior force by producing that which is not moral (sin) and in turn are deployed as a subtle, only seemingly nonviolent, mechanism against immorality. Likewise, given that these institutions tend to be thought of as maintaining a position outside of capitalist greed, of political games, and of human fallibility and corruption, it is stunning to find an analysis that rather convincingly locates these very institutions at the heart of the system to which they are supposed to be opposed. Again, Hardt and Negri at length:

> In Christian moral theology evil is first posed as privation of the good and then sin is defined as culpable negation of the good. Within this logical framework it is not strange but rather all too natural that in their attempts to respond to privation, these NGOs are led to denounce publicly the sinners (or rather the Enemy in properly inquisitional terms); nor is it strange that they leave to the "secular wing" the task of actually addressing the problems. In this way, *moral intervention has become a frontline force of imperial intervention.* In effect, this intervention prefigures the state of exception from below, and does so without borders, armed with some of the most effective means of communication and oriented toward the symbolic production of the enemy. These NGOs are completely immersed in the biopolitical context of the constitution of Empire; they anticipate the power of its pacifying and productive intervention of justice. [. . .] *Moral intervention often serves as the first act that prepares the stage for military intervention.* (36–37, my emphases)

It is hard to imagine a more forceful line of questioning the sheer possibility and, indeed, viability of a recourse to moral judgment as a "proper" response to violence (in the sense of promising to be effective in eradicating or at least containing it). As described by these two theorists, morality—judgment—set the stage for violence to ensue. Indeed, I think it is fair to assert that for Hardt and Negri morality is violence, that the act of judgment based on whatever presumably moral ground equals any given act of violence in their structural functionality and effectivity. Judgment and violence, in short, mutually presuppose, require, and bring to pass each other. Just like in "the process of capitalization *the outside is internalized*" (226), and just like Empire makes breakdowns or crisis its transformative engine, so judgment internalizes violence and casts it as its most intensified form.

Intensifying Violence through Serialization

Patricia Highsmith arrived at this conclusion already in 1955 with her fourth novel, *The Talented Mr. Ripley*. However, the fact that she recoiled from this remarkable achievement, and the even more interesting fact that she returned to it fifteen years later, precisely at the moment when Hardt and Negri locate some of the most forceful alterations in the global sphere that transformed the reign of transcendence into one of pure immanence, must now be seen as being in line with, indeed produced by, this larger sociopolitical development.[30] Occupying the position of an American writer living in various European countries, creating works of fictions always concerned with American citizens living at times in their home country, at times abroad, Highsmith inevitably was affected by the larger global forces described by Hardt and Negri. Yet, just as *Empire* narrates a story of conflict that only slowly resolved itself more decidedly in the post–World War II period, so Highsmith's seeming embrace of the lesson of immanence— that the only response to violence is affect, not judgment—was bound to be a tentative, stuttering one, one that was impossible to maintain with great consistency, for surely the lesson itself was a strange and difficult one to learn. And so it makes sense that Highsmith had to write herself *through* her problematic, had to test out the waters anew and experiment with her "solution," even after her first Ripley success. Contrary to the critical opinion that somehow her Ripley novels are the popular lightweights among her otherwise more challenging work, that, as Russell Harrison argues, "functioned as a kind of breather for Highsmith, a fictional place to which she could repair from time to time when the otherwise quite gruesome business of social interaction in her more ambitious novels became too much" (29), I suggest that these five novels figure as the peak moments in her career, as singular moments of intensification—not in the sense that they are "better" (aesthetically or otherwise), but in that they constitute the culmination of the most fundamental lesson she has taught herself and offers to her readers as "arrows of thought" that, in Nietzschean fashion, we may pick up and shoot elsewhere.

The iteration of her problematic through her oeuvre, then, turns out to be not so much a repetition of the same, as even Highsmith might have thought at one time or another. Rather, her effort to serialize her problematic, first through creating a series of stories remarkably similar on most levels and then through turning her first encounter with immanence into its own series, must be described as what Deleuze and Guattari theorized as *itineration*, a force of repetition that structures surprises, a Nietzschean Eternal Return that allows only that to return which has the capacity to differ.

It is precisely Highsmith's repeated performance of this itinerating force that does not allow us to consider her, as has occasionally been done, as an existentialist writer.[31] For Highsmith, nothing is to be overcome, least of all violence or, in proper existentialist terms, death. For existentialism, the whole point of living is to face up to death, since this is how we gain and confirm our authenticity and assert to ourselves that we are alive and free. Refusing the power of death and behaving morally in a universe otherwise as absurd as the one depicted in Samuel Beckett's theater of the same name become the markers of "true" human action. Yet, the problem inscribed into existentialism is that one can never succeed at this task. Inevitably, our effort to establish ourselves as authentic must fail: we will die. Highsmith's violent fiction, in contrast, is not at all governed by this logic of failure or lack. That we will die is a fact of life to which she ascribes no special power, no teleological force. She simply does not mind that death looms on the horizon for all of us. Hence, her fictional violence is neither a response to certain death nor a means to prove oneself authentic. Violence, as it works in her fiction, is neither that which has to be overcome nor that which demarcates failure. There is no mourning in Highsmith's work. In contrast, violence is that which has to be masochistically *repeated* in order to push it to the limit of what it can do. And precisely when these limits are achieved, a necessary transformation occurs, as I have argued was the case with the first Ripley novel as well as with *Tremor of Forgery*.[32]

Repetition, then, can be considered the pedagogical—masocritical—imperative structuring Highsmith's fiction. Contrary to Immanuel Kant's famous universalizing moral imperative prescribing that one should act only on a maxim that one simultaneously wishes to be a universal law (*Foundations* sect. 1), Highsmith's writing appears to be more Nietzschean in kind in that the repetition of violence at work is characterized not by that which Highsmith desires to be done to herself, for that would not get her anywhere at all other than reproducing the same one more time. Rather, Highsmith's repetition of violence operates by the logic of itinerating intensification where what is repeated is only that which ultimately can return differently. In other words, the serialized repetitiveness of Highsmith's oeuvre does not constitute an eternal return of the same—the quintessential existentialist reading of Nietzsche's most famous concept.[33] Instead, it seems to me, Deleuze's articulation of how the eternal return operates in Nietzsche describes much more fittingly Highsmith's writing practice. According to Deleuze, Nietzsche's imperative, as opposed to Kant's, is, "whatever you will, will it in such a manner that you also will its eternal return" (*Difference and Repetition* 7). He goes on to explain that this ethical test of one's will goes further than Kant's categorical imperative because it does not relate the force of repetition to "the moralizing source in the generality of concepts" (7); rather, "it seems to make repetition itself the only form of a law *beyond* morality. [. . .] The form of repetition in the eternal return is the brutal form of the immediate, that of the universal and the singular reunited, which dethrones every general law, dissolves the mediations and annihilates the particulars subjected to the law" (7, my emphasis). In other words, repetition is "what is," as it were. It is not based on the generality of law but on the specificity of actions, of a kind of practice that most decidedly brings to mind, once again, the specificities of masochism. For does the masochist not precisely will his punishment in such a way that he also wills its return, over and over again, in a (seemingly) infinite way (according to the masochistic contract, it is only the mistress who can put an end to it)? And he wills this infinite return as a means to extend and intensify the experience of inhabiting an interstice within which he is subjected to a sensation of himself as becoming-other to himself—a process of becoming that assumes a degree of consistency (which is crucial to his survival) only because of the specificity of the contract's terms that function as a regulatory framework, albeit one in which he has relinquished his control to his mistress, that is, to the other.

Both Highsmith's fiction and her nonfictional statements attest that her interest in, indeed obsession with, repeating her violent stories does not manifest the desire to create or affirm a moral law. Rather, Highsmith continually responds to the problematic of violence and judgment as it plays out in the moment of repetition. Having arrived early on at a point of transformation where violence and judgment have been described as mutually immanent forces, Highsmith's fiction continually returns to this point, albeit in different guises. And here is the key: instead of writing for a preexisting audience that she assumes to be capable of accepting her description of violence as immanent to judgment, Highsmith's work sets out to produce its own audience, to affect a readership that has yet to come, that has yet to become capable of responding to Highsmith's most fundamental accomplishment in a manner that does not lead them (immediately) back to a moral discourse. The fact that Highsmith was marketed, especially in the United States, as a mystery and suspense writer only deepens this point, for while one might go along with the label to a certain extent, it is quite clear that the overt rejection of punishment as a moral concept goes by and large against the genre's rules and thus, one would assume, against what readers of the genre are used to. Had Highsmith cared to cater to her American readers' needs, it seems that she would have merely repeated the success of her first novel. But she did not, as the following statement, evoking her great short story "The Man Who Wrote Books in His Head," makes perfectly clear: "each book is, in a sense, an argument with myself, and I would write it, *whether it is ever published or not*" (Dupont 63, emphasis mine).[34]

Not to write for an audience—this is what allows her to develop a practice of writing that becomes capable of responding to violence without judgment. It enables her to repeat her *problématique* because she does not (need to) heed her existing audience (and undoubtedly, her gaining commercial independence due to Hitchcock's successful adaptation of her first novel contributed to this ability). But not heeding an existing audience means to write for an audience yet to come rather than "showing us ourselves" (Klein 196), for both "us" and "ourselves" are merely in the process of emerging. It means to produce a future readership by deploying repetition as the most fundamental pedagogical tool available. Here everything comes together: her fiction's repetitiveness, its immanent character, its refusal to judge, its moment of emergence in a post–World War II environment that ever faster operates on a plane of pure immanence, and her refusal to write for anyone—all of this culminates in the production of a pedagogy that does not desire to speak "for" anyone, that does not insist on a moral position that would help to authenticate one's preexisting identity or being, and that does not want to represent anything or anyone at all.[35] Instead, Highsmith's pedagogy—her training of her own (American) readership that is only gradually in the process of emerging (the number of films based on her work now in production perhaps suggests the quickening speed of this process, but it remains to be seen how, exactly, these films will respond to her writing)—operates by the force of the Eternal Return. Again Deleuze on Nietzsche's concept:

> Eternal return cannot mean the return of the Identical because it presupposes a world (that of the will to power) in which all previous identities have been abolished and dissolved. Returning is being, but only the being of becoming. The eternal return does not bring back "the same," but returning constitutes the only Same of that which becomes. Returning is the becoming-identical of becoming itself. Returning is thus the only identity, but identity as a secondary power; the identity of difference, the identical which belongs to the different, or turns around the different. Such an identity, produced by difference, is determined as "repetition." Repetition in the eternal return, therefore, consists in conceiving the same on the basis of the different. (*Difference and Repetition* 41)

And because "only the extreme forms return—those which [...] extend to the limit of their power, transforming themselves and changing one into another [...] that which passes into something else and becomes identical" (Deleuze, *Difference and Repetition* 41), it eventually had to be the violence of Ripley that was serialized. For it is in the first Ripley novel that violence and judgment transform themselves into each other and become identical, thus forming a new, extreme form of both violence and judgment that thus become capable of returning.

The second half of Highsmith's career, therefore, is dominated by the itineration of her problematic through Ripley's character: *Ripley Under Ground* (1970), *Ripley's Game*, *The Boy Who Followed Ripley* (1980), and *Ripley Under Water* (1991) cumulatively intensify the achievement of *The Talented Mr. Ripley*. So, for instance, in *Ripley Underground*, Tom's actions still bear resemblance to something like realism. To protect the discovery of his involvement in an art forgery scheme, he kills the man whom he fears is about to expose him. This instance of violence, then, seems to have a rather straightforward, "understandable" motive, unlike the violence in the next three novels, which appears to be increasingly random, "meaningless," and plainly expressive of what seems to be Tom's psychosis. Yet, even in *Ripley Under Ground*, the notion of motive is questioned, most compellingly when Tom asks himself about why he killed Mr. Murchison: "He wouldn't have killed someone just to save Derwatt Ltd. or even Bernard, Tom supposed. Tom had killed Murchison because Murchison had realized, in the cellar, that he had impersonated Derwatt. Tom had killed Murchison to save himself. And yet, Tom tried to ask himself, had he intended to kill Murchison anyway when they went down to the cellar together? Had he not intended to kill him? Tom simply could not answer that. And did it matter much?" (89–90).

For Tom, the answer to the last question is "no," as the rest of the novel clarifies. And the repeated, serialized affirmation of this "no"—expressed in this novel through Tom's words and thoughts, and in the course of all five Ripley novels through Highsmith's style—intensifies Highsmith's configuration of morality as violence.

With each subsequent Ripley novel, Highsmith pushes the amorality of her solution to further, "unrealistic" extremes. But this is precisely the point. The very fact that Ripley's violent actions become increasingly less plausible, that is, "realistic," indicates that, at least for Highsmith, the demand for realistic representations of violence is the problem, not the solution, for realism itself traditionally functions as a moral law, a general concept, that is supposed to determine the social acceptability of violence in fictional form. Hence, the violence of Steven Spielberg's *Schindler's List* or *Saving Private Ryan* are received as "good" and socially constructive, whereas the violence of the "Quentin Tarantino school of violence" tends to be condemned because of its hyperrealism or lack of realism, respectively.[36] Highsmith's Ripley series, in conjunction with the interjections of her other novels, shows that morality and realism have little purchase on the force of violence because the latter is a question of affective force. To attempt to "understand" Ripley is therefore as misguided as, to return to an earlier evocation, the effort to explain the Holocaust precisely because the way "understanding" and "explaining" predominantly function violates the singularity of the events. That is to say, to do violence to violence is, inevitably, the only mode of response available to us, which means not so much that we should not try to understand or explain but that these practices and desires will not provide a solution determined as a way out. Just like Ellis's *American Psycho*, *Empire*, or Deleuze (and Guattari's) philosophy, Highsmith's masochistic pedagogy of violence insists that there is no exit, that all we have is immanence, and that this ontological fact requires us to respond to it: responsibility as response-ability.

We might think of this particular trajectory of Highsmith's fiction somewhat akin to a pedagogical manual—an how-to-respond-to-violence serial novel—that produces an untimely audience for Highsmith, which would explain why her work has for the longest time lacked the popular and academic success it has long enjoyed abroad. This yet to come audience has first to be generated *in* immersing themselves in her unusual treatment of the question of violence for them to become capable of learning how to withhold judgment—the type of response dominating critical reading and viewing practices affected by a long tradition of representational encounters with language. In other words, what may be significant about Minghella's adaptation of *The Talented Mr. Ripley* is precisely its (potential) marking of the arrival of a particular type of reader (or viewer) who first had to emerge with the capacity to be affected by Highsmith's peculiar penchant for running the question of violence through that of judgment. It must be pointed out, of course, that this emergence is produced by innumerable forces operating in conjunction with one another and does, in fact, not depend on any given subject to have read any of Highsmith's work. Rather, Highsmith's work symptomizes a larger movement—that of Empire—to which it stands in mutual reciprocation. But regardless of whether the virtual force produced by and through the incessant repetition of Highsmith's endeavor has begun to be actualized—that is, whether or not it has now started to succeed at producing an American audience capable of welcoming her fiction's particular way of responding to violence by showing how it is always the question of judgment par excellence—it seems to me that any encounter with (fictional) violence could profit from heeding Highsmith's attitude. To Highsmith, judgment never provides a satisfying, productive entry into the question of violence—an (intuitive) insight that she embraced with increasing force as her writing career matured.

If performance, or rather performativity, is crucial to the question of violence (i.e., both Highsmith's practice of writing with its attendant production of future readers through habituation via the Eternal Return in the Deleuzean and Nietzschean sense and Ripley's enacting of his violence), as I have suggested in this chapter, then we might now want to turn to a more specific instantiation of violent *acting*.[37] And where better to turn to than Martin Scorsese, the acclaimed American director who also responds to the problematic of judgment as a problematic of violence? But, more precisely, Scorsese responds to his problematic most compellingly, forcefully, and famously through and with the help of the serialization of his cinematic avatar—the actor Robert De-Niro.

Becoming-Violent, Becoming-DeNiro 5

Rendering Violence Visible on Screen

First Prologue: A Poster on a Wall

A dark, run-down hallway with stone walls oozing a sense of filth and danger. A man in a black jacket, pointing at you a .38 Special in his right hand, a .44 Magnum in his left. The latter's long barrel is so imposing that you almost can feel the cold, hard steel getting uncomfortably close to your head. Framed by these two firearms, clearly ready to shoot your brains out, is the assassin's demented face. His eyes, two crazy half moons, anticipate imminent joy. His mouth, merely a crescentlike dark opening, is contorted in a grin. And then there is the Mohawk. . . . Together with his eyes, it renders the assassin's face beyond good and evil. The only hope you have left is that he might have forgotten to load the guns. Think again, sucker!

Second Prologue: Are You Talkin' to *Me*?

As I repeatedly claimed in the previous chapters, violence has remained a remarkably undertheorized concept—and that is despite, or rather because of, its ubiquity in contemporary American culture. A recent critical argument has given voice to this paradox. Film scholar William Rothman articulates the paradox resulting from the simultaneity of the "despite" and "because" of the previous sentence. He argues that "America is a less violent place than it used to be [but] Americans *believe* that violence is escalating out of control, that it is threatening the moral fabric of our society, and that the proliferation of violence in the mass media, especially the graphic violence in today's movies, is a cause, and not only a symptom, of this threat" (37). If Rothman's paradox is valid—and I think there is no shortage of evidence for it—then I want to suggest in this chapter that this paradox exists because of a widely accepted conceptual distinction between "theory" and "practice." In terms of violence, this oppositional division between theory and practice that permeates contemporary culture enables and ultimately validates the seemingly commonsensical declaration that one knows violence when one sees or experiences it. The very notion of self-evidence implied by this claim casts a theory of violence as redundant precisely because of the alleged phenomenological obviousness of violence (i.e., its practices and practical manifestations).

In response to this all too often unquestioned conceptual binary between theory and practice (of violence), I want to affirm Michel Foucault and Gilles Deleuze's insistence that theory *is* practice, or that practice *is* theory, that, as they argue, "practice is a set of relays from one theoretical point to another, and [that] theory is a relay from one practice to another" (206). For it is perhaps only by reconfiguring the "paradoxical" debate surrounding the *problématique* of violence that we might be able to effect a significant change in criticism's commonplace (judgmental) response habits to violence (in cinema or fiction). I suggest, therefore, that we now turn to a practitioner of, in this case, film violence in order to gain *through* this practice of violence one specific theory thereof. Which brings me back to the first prologue.

The poster described above currently faces me, hanging on the wall above my computer, drawing me into a zone of proximity with its prominent face and the affective charge it forcefully exerts on me:

Are you talkin' to me? Are you talkin' to me?
Then who the hell else are you talkin' to?

Well, I'm the only one here . . .
Who the fuck do you think you're talkin' to?!

Of course, the poster is not "talking" to me, or to anyone else for that matter. But it keeps fascinating me; it continues to engage me every time I look at it. More precisely, what affects me is a singular moment of violence this poster renders sensible. This affectively tangible sensation of violence is presented not through depictions of blood or spilled guts, blown-up cars, or a nuclear cloud mushrooming over a destroyed cityscape. Instead, the violence of sensation is triggered by and through the face of Travis Bickle, famed main character of Martin Scorsese's landmark film *Taxi Driver* (1976).[1] Or rather, the affective charge exerted upon me directly emits from the face of Robert DeNiro—an actor whose face has violently branded itself into the collective (un)conscious of movie audiences more than that of any other (American) movie actor in recent memory.[2]

Expressing his admiration for DeNiro's capacities as an actor, film scholar James Naremore argues in his seminal study *Acting in the Cinema* that DeNiro is not only a "thoroughgoing naturalist [but] also a sophisticated theorist" (267). Concurring with this assessment, I feel nonetheless compelled to reformulate Naremore's insightful characterization and claim that DeNiro might very well be our best *theoretician* of violence (at least in cinema) precisely because he is the most consistent and frequent *practitioner* of screen violence (in the sense that he participates in and experiments with it). And in his evolving role as America's great theorist of violence DeNiro has gradually become the undisputed face of violence in American cinema, indeed in American culture.

Analyzing *how* DeNiro has "facialized" violence should therefore advance the task at hand—namely, to rethink (criticism's ability to respond to) violence qua violence, as an affective, asignifying regime of intensities and sensation that solicits audiences' fascination more than their desire, let alone capacity, to "understand" when exposed to it in film or other cultural productions.

Why fascination? Because it expresses a particular attraction to a kind of image that cannot be circumscribed by the standard psychoanalytic concepts of the voyeuristic gaze and its sadomasochistic implications. For, as Maurice Blanchot argues in his response to the question "Why fascination?" that he posits in the context of *The Space of Literature*, "when what you see, although at a distance, seems to touch you with a gripping contact, [. . .] when what is seen imposes itself upon the gaze, as if the gaze were seized [then what] is given us by this contact at a distance is the image, and *fascination is passion for the image*" (32, my emphasis). Blanchot encourages us here to heed fascination as a passion, a degree of intensity, a becoming-affected by something or someone else. This becoming-affected has not necessarily anything at all to do with a desire to dominate or be dominated (which, for psychoanalytic film theory, are desires that tend to come as an inseparable pair). Attending to this fascination—most often registered on and expressed through a *face* (think of a child's astonished, dumbfounded gaze triggered by something unfamiliar, or her gaping mouth in response to, e.g., a magician's trick)—I suggest with literary critic Jeffrey Karnicky that fascination's value lies in preventing "interpretation of a certain kind" (*Contemporary Fiction* 58), one that always turns too quickly to the desire to "understand" and "judge" the image rather than encounter its operative force on its own terms.

Diagnosing the process of DeNiro's becoming-violent through his facialization of violence, thus, is meant to attend to the force we call fascination and that we most often witness on and through the face of someone else. However, faces, as Deleuze and Guattari argue, cannot be assumed "to come ready-made. They are engendered by an *abstract machine of faciality*" (*Thousand Plateaus* 168).[3] Faces are maps, or surfaces. Thus, our diagnosis of DeNiro's becoming-violent must delineate the development of his faciality—his giving face to images of violence—over the course of his career. But because "you don't so much have a face as slide into one" (177), we must do more than just map DeNiro's changing "face." If a face is not to be had, then a specific process—Deleuze and Guattari call it "faciality"—must produce it. "Faciality" diagrams processes of territorialization of multiple forces that include those of the entire body that "comes to be facialized as part of an inevitable process" (170). Our masocritical diagnosis must therefore also heed the discourse most closely associated with DeNiro as an actor: that of so-called Method acting with its attendant psychological concepts of acting out and working through.

The prominence of what is commonly called "the Method" in American cinema of the post–World War II era has led to an (popularized) association of acting with mimesis (imitation, representation). However, I will show that DeNiro's method is of a different kind, one that has emerged out of the history of Method acting but that has made some crucial alterations. Attending to this difference, I think, will result in a conceptualizing of enacted violence that questions and ultimately bypasses any psychoanalytic understanding of it. The latter reads violence and its multiple occurrences (practices) as immoral acting out of repressed desires or memories that are triggered through the process of mimesis (which is how critics tend to read Tom Ripley). Psychoanalytic discourses respond to the "disease" of acting out by advocating the rational, therapeutic process of working through (theory) as the necessary (and only) "cure." Based thoroughly on a representational understanding of acting that has emerged from the popularization of the Method, psychoanalytic film criticism tends to hold as superior theory to practice, working through to acting out, mourning to melancholia. In contrast, DeNiro's practice theorizes a different conceptualization of violence—one that deploys acting out and working through as fundamentally affective, and thus immanent, processes. If working through and acting out stand in an immanent relation to each other, however, then the standard judgment levied against violence as a "bad" acting out becomes impossibly useless, indeed self-defeating, precisely because working through always and necessarily turns out to be an acting out.

The Violence of Mourning and Melancholia

The blockbuster comedy *Meet the Parents* (dir. Jay Roach, 2000) opens with Randy Newman's familiar soundtrack voice cheerily intoning, "When you're a fool in love," while documentary-like shots of the happy face of a young woman appear on screen. Subsequently, we are introduced to male nurse Greg Focker (Ben Stiller) who is getting ready to propose to his girlfriend, Pam Byrnes (Teri Polo), an elementary school teacher whose face was just "documented" in the film's opening shots. Typical for a commercially marketed romantic comedy, the good intentions of the groom to be are interrupted—in this case by a well-placed phone call. Overhearing the ensuing phone conversation, Greg gradually realizes the imprudence of his plan to propose to Pam as long as he has not yet obtained the consent of Pam's father.

After a few additional comedic scenes involving the trials and tribulations familiar to any air traveler, we witness the couple approaching Pam's parents' considerable suburban property. As they pull their rented Ford Taurus up to the house, Pam instructs Greg that he should "take it easy with [his] sarcasm," since his humor would be "entirely wasted with [her] parents." At this moment, an ominous melody intones, and the camera cuts from a medium-close tracking shot of the moving car to a low-angle close-up of a second-story window. From the curtain peers the calm, clean-shaven face of Pam's father, Jack. His dark eyes, contorted into intense slits, are separated by two vertical creases on his forehead. The imposing Romanesque nose accentuates the line of the eyes' downcast gaze. And the frowning thinness of the tight-lipped mouth, framed by two deep furrows pointing downward, finishes the visual composition of a face that in its expressiveness suggests the potential for ensuing violence. The camera then directs our attention back to the arriving young couple, this time from Jack's perspective up high. We faintly hear the couple chattering, indicating that our "ears" are with Jack behind the window, his presence still undetected by Greg and Pam. The camera cuts one more time back to Jack, his face unchanged. This very repetition, however, intensifies the facial expression, pushing its gloominess to the point where we might expect it to explode.

When we next see Pam reprimanding Greg for attempting to smoke (Daddy does not like smoking!), we *already* know that Ben Stiller's character is in trouble. In fact, like so much else during the course of the movie—including the information that Jack is a former CIA agent specializing in testing suspects on their statements' truthfulness—we do not need this piece of information to sense that Greg will have a difficult time with Jack. Thus far, we have been introduced only to Jack's *face*, but we really do not need any further proof for Jack's potential for becoming-violent. For, after all, Jack's face, so effectively introduced in the previous shots, belongs to Robert DeNiro.

One year prior to his most commercially successful movie to date, DeNiro starred in another popular Hollywood comedy, *Analyze This* (dir. Harold Ramis).[4] Whereas in *Meet the Parents*, DeNiro did *not* actually play a violent character (at least, Jack is never shown to exert physical force, and we have no evidence that he used it offscreen), the earlier comedy's main device plays on its audience's knowledge of some of Robert DeNiro's most famous roles. Just as in *Mean Streets* (dir. Martin Scorsese, 1973), *The Godfather II* (dir. Francis Ford Coppola, 1974), *Once Upon a Time in America* (dir. Sergio Leone, 1984), *The Untouchables* (dir. Brian De-Palma, 1987), *GoodFellas* (dir. Martin Scorsese, 1990), and *Casino* (dir. Martin Scorsese, 1995), he plays a character involved with the mob; and just as in some of his other famous roles in classics such as *Taxi Driver*, *Raging Bull* (dir. Martin Scorsese, 1980), *Cape Fear* (dir. Martin Scorsese, 1991), or *Heat* (dir. Michael Mann, 1995), his character is explicitly associated with his willingness to "off" people who stand in his way. Yet, unlike all these films, *Analyze This* plays DeNiro's violent character—powerful crime family racketeer Paul Vitty—for laughs. That is, in contrast to any of DeNiro's canonical performances, the expression of violence (and its actual occasion) does *not* depend on it being acted out in a sensational manner for it to be effective. Instead, as the film's psychoanalytically inflected title indicates, in this movie violence discharges its affective force on the level of sensation through its occurrence in the form of a working through.

Or does it?

↓

In *History and Memory after Auschwitz*, cultural historian and theorist Dominick LaCapra sets in motion Freud's well-known differentiation between mourning (working through) and melancholia (acting out) as a means of delineating two different kinds of responses with which Holocaust survivors deal with the memory of Auschwitz—an intensely traumatic event that "continues to be the 'leading image of evil' in our times" (Knox).[5] LaCapra's (psycho)analytic language strongly bears on the present discussion, not because I mean to imply that the violence of Auschwitz is of the same kind as that of Hollywood films, but because his analysis *symptomatically* expresses a certain tendency of the general discourse on violence in contemporary U.S. culture. As we have seen in earlier chapters, the language of acting (out) is often used in conjunction with violent events of "lesser" nature than Auschwitz. Tom Ripley's violent character, for instance, is frequently read in conjunction with his ability to "act," that is, to impersonate or imitate others. And in Bret Easton Ellis's violent fiction, (the action of) characters such as Patrick Bateman or Victor Ward from *Glamorama* are often narrated through a language resonating with (cinematic) acting. (In fact, Victor Ward actually believes that he is an actor in an elaborate snuff film.)[6] In the idiom of (pop) psychology, for example, we frequently find claims stating that, say, the teenage killers of Columbine "acted out" repressed fantasies. For instance, in what I take to be a typical moment in the discourse surrounding this tragedy, Caroline Schomp posits to her *Denver Post* readers the following question: "What went wrong in the families of the gun-toting, bomb-wielding children that those children needed to *act out* their alienation and hostility so cataclysmically" (B11, emphasis mine). What often is assumed, indeed implied, yet not explicitly articulated in such questions or statements is that in these discourses on violence "acting (out)" denotes a "bad" thing. LaCapra's academic writing symptomatically exemplifies how crucial this linkage between acting and morality has become—a linkage so naturalized that it seems to be beyond contestability and as such has significant consequences for the question of film violence.

LaCapra argues that one's (critical) response to traumatic events inevitably entails an *affective* component. In fact, to achieve a "healthy" response to trauma, LaCapra posits as imperative the subject's need to "undergo at least muted trauma and allow that trauma (or unsettlement) to affect one's approach to problems" (40). Yet, he continues to embellish on his insight into the affective quality of response by essentially wanting to downplay, if not flat-out denigrate, its feasibility. So he writes that "one should not remain at the level of acting-out or absolutize the latter in the form of an attempt actually to relive or appropriate others' traumas [. . .] Even if trauma cannot be fully overcome, as it may not be for victims of limit-cases or even for attentive secondary witnesses, it may be counteracted by the attempt to work through problems, mourn the victims of the past, and reengage life in the interest of bringing about a qualitatively better state of affairs" (40).

In this typical passage, LaCapra ascribes meaning—or, more tellingly, moral value—to two different types of *practice*. Indeed, Freud himself is quite explicit about the moral valuation inherent to these two terms. In "Mourning and Melancholia," he links melancholia to abnormal sadomasochistic behavior patterns emerging from unresolved Oedipal conflicts and thus characterizes the melancholic as "pathological" (153) and "obsessional" (161). And yet, Freud declares at the beginning of his essay—*before* he reductively maps the melancholic onto Oedipus—that melancholia is judged negatively and mourning positively *only* because of the lack of existing information about the former and the abundance of knowledge about the latter. As he writes, "It is really only because we *know* so well how to *explain* [mourning] that this attitude does not seem to us pathological" (153, my emphases), as melancholia does. That which is familiar and thus possible to rationalize—that which we believe we *know*—is deemed normal. According to Freud, however, this happens only because of the frequency with which a phenomenon occurs and thus becomes available to us as an experience and, eventually, knowledge. In other words, even for Freud there is nothing "naturally" better about either mourning or melancholia. Rather, the determination of value clearly derives from a specific process of socialization in which the repeated enactment of power relations habituate—normalize—certain flows of desire as morally acceptable and others as unacceptable to the social order. Given that Freud himself calls attention to the social processes productive of epistemological beliefs that are eventually reterritorialized as "natural" moral values, it is all the more remarkable that Freud nonetheless ends up "forgetting" his own insight and instead explains melancholia as a lack, as a morally problematic deviation from a "normal" response to trauma.

LaCapra's frequent repeating of the claim that "with reference to trauma, acting-out may be a necessary condition of working-through" (45) merely gives voice to the inherent moral(ized) quality of Freud's original distinction. Unsurprisingly, then, *all* positive valuations in LaCapra's argument are reserved for the process of "working through." If acting out turns out to be necessary at all, then only begrudgingly so, and merely as a means to a higher (read: healthier and morally superior) end. In the passage quoted earlier, working through emerges as a mode of response counteracting the effects of an acting out. Or, in explicitly ethical terms, LaCapra overtly describes working through as enabling "ethically responsible action and critical judgment" (186). Ethics here, however, is conceived of as morality, as has become obvious from an earlier passage in which he argues that mourning allows "for critical judgment and a reinvestment in life, notably social life with its demands, responsibilities, and norms requiring respectful recognition and consideration for others" (45). This Kantian-Habermasian terminology belies his later insistences that his distinction does not connote a moral discourse underlying it.

Once we recognize his sophisticated academic discourse as symptomatic of a more general discourse that regards violence as an immoral acting out of repressed desires, LaCapra's diagnosis becomes even more interesting for our present purposes in that he regards melancholic acting out as intrinsically "mimetic" (45) and defined by "repetition-compulsion" (45) that "blocks [the superior work done by] mourning and working-through in general" (54). Or, as indicated in the longer quotation earlier, acting out is equated with appropriation and reliving, that is, imitation and re-presentation. LaCapra expresses here what we can observe in most discourses dealing with occurrences of violence: namely, that violence is considered a mimetic acting out (an imitation of "represented" actions that is perfected through an obsessive repetition of, say, listening to Marilyn Manson songs or watching *Natural Born Killers*), which is inevitably to be judged as morally bad.[7] So, acting equals mimesis equals repetition. And, in turn, this tripartite equation inevitably ends up selling a "moral" stance by appealing to the necessity of the work of mourning. This appeal, however, comes packaged with an entire apparatus of social control that is offered "for free"—so free, in fact, that one cannot choose *not* to accept this freebie, just like the extra 10 percent of "free" toothpaste cannot be cut off from the rest of the tube for which one has to pay. Only the work of mourning, facilitated by the psychoanalyst (or the priest or the critic), so the chorus of contemporary cultural criticism intones, will bring to light—and subsequently cure—the underlying causes for a subject's "unfortunate" acting out.

↯

Deleuze and Guattari have long provided a compelling critique of the psychoanalytic conception of the unconscious as a theater—a stage that expresses hidden desires through representations.[8] However, LaCapra's reliance on a negative concept of desire (i.e., desire as lack) does not merely suggest the continuing grip that psychoanalysis holds over contemporary discourses (which at least partially explains the dominance of confessional memoirs on contemporary American bestseller lists). Rather, it indexes the importance for anyone interested in film to heed the power of the argument's ability to moralize acting—one of the *constitutive* practices of (nondocumentary) cinema. Specifically, the type of argument put forth by LaCapra easily leads to a view of acting as a mimetic procedure, which, in turn, will give rise to further repetition compulsions. And if criticism is not directly levied at the mimetic behavior of mimicking or copying, then it directs itself at the "abnormal" compulsion to repeat, as "real world" consequences are feared to occur on the plane constituted by repetition.

Deleuze and Guattari are, of course, not alone in their critique of psychoanalysis. In fact, one could show how *Analyze This*—a postmodern comedy that knowingly spoofs many of DeNiro's famous violent mobster roles—cinematically deconstructs LaCapra's (and psychoanalysis's) binary articulation of acting out and working through. A close analysis of the film would indeed reveal that the film repeatedly plays with these two concepts. To point only to the most prominent examples from the film, the relationship between psychotherapist Ben Sobel (Billy Crystal) and mobster boss Paul Vitty is from the beginning structured around a conflict between two desires: that of psychoanalysis's categorical imperative to talk or work through, and the Mafia's demand that its members shut up and be able to act out the violence its business requires. The film maps out the specific effects of these two practices, revealing that working through, far from being a morally superior category, is always constituted by an acting out. And the latter is a fundamentally nonmimetic practice, since it always articulates a singular response to a given situation. We learn this most clearly in one of the film's key scenes in which Sobel has finally gotten Vitty to initiate his process of mourning. Far from producing "positive" effects, however, all this does at the moment is endanger their lives. Vitty ends up so immobilized as he sobs on his therapist's shoulders that he cannot "get shooting" when he and Sobel are being fired at by assassins supportive of his enemy, rival Mafia boss Primo. Working through without the ability to act out, according to *Analyze This*, is nearly worthless. In fact, Sobel himself is smart enough to realize this, as he fires Vitty's gun in self-defense. However, even though Sobel shoots, he does not hit anybody: acting out requires that you practice, that you work through the specific task at hand.

Without advocating violence by any means, *Analyze This* depicts through DeNiro's Methodically enacted character's relationship to a psychoanalyst that the two response mechanisms to the experience of violent trauma—melancholia and mourning—are constitutive of, rather than distinct from, each other. That is, this film cinematically foregrounds that working through always entails an acting out and acting out always performs the process of working through. Importantly, as I will argue later in this chapter, in the section "Analyze the Face," *Analyze This* accomplished this, just as *Meet the Parents* a year later or films such as *GoodFellas*, *Casino*, or *Heat* a few years earlier, by emphasizing the "faciality" of DeNiro's becoming-violent. For the moment, however, I merely want to mark that *Analyze This* complicates the processes of acting out and working through by insisting that acting—indeed, the very ability to act—is a necessary and arepresentational structural component of both mourning and melancholia. It thus pulls the smug rug of morality from underneath the very concepts that are supposed to provide a double articulation thereof. But if even an event as seemingly innocuous as a mainstream Hollywood product can provide a relatively astute critique of contemporary culture's psychoanalytically inflected understanding of "acting," then why has the equation acting equals mimesis taken such a tight hold of (popular) American culture?

A Brief Genealogy of the Method, Part 1

That LaCapra configures acting as a mimetic operation—an acting out akin to the process of what psychoanalysis calls the "return of the repressed"—should not be considered coincidental or a choice peculiar only to LaCapra's potentially unschooled critical eye when it comes to the question of what acting is or how it works. Quite the opposite is the case. In postwar American culture, the general concept of acting has undoubtedly been inflected by a more specific notion of acting: to wit, Method acting, which itself is shot through with the language of imitation. It does thus not come as a surprise that LaCapra's psychoanalytical concepts deploy the language of acting qua representation. And yet, a closer look at the Method will show that its current configuration as mimesis is rather peculiar.

My goal here is not to work through the long history of acting, with its attendant theories and practices regarding both stage and cinema acting.[9] A few comments on the history of Method acting are in order here, though, because this specific instantiation of acting has dominated American post–World War II acting to such a degree that it has become the most influential form of acting of the last fifty years.

It should be pointed out, however, that this claim holds true mainly for what is known as realist film. While many forms of realism exist in the history of cinema, one can crudely differentiate between at least two. First, the type of "seamless" realism produced ever since Hollywood cinema perfected the shot/countershot shooting style that ends up "naturalizing" film images as representing an unmediated "real" world (see Bordwell, Staiger, and Thompson, *Classical Hollywood Cinema*, for the canonical work on classical Hollywood cinema style) is clearly the dominant mode of American filmmaking up until this day. The second type of realism could be called "aesthetic realism," which historically can be traced to the French poetic realist directors and was eventually theorized by French film critic André Bazin. Whereas Hollywood realism reduces reality to the one it shows us on screen (all the while leading us to believe that what we see on screen is reality in its totality), aesthetic realism foregrounds that, in the words of Susan Hayward, "realism produces realisms" (299).[10]

In any case, Method acting has so permeated American culture that, to use the words of rhetorical theorist Gregory Ulmer, "even those who are not familiar with the theory [of Method acting] are familiar with the product, Hollywood acting" (114). Ulmer implicitly suggests here that audience's familiarity with Method acting does not depend on theoretical knowledge (i.e., their conscious awareness of it). Instead, the Method is familiar to us because of an ongoing process of habituation to which cinema audiences are subjected. Audiences are repeatedly exposed to (affected by) the Hollywood machinery and its star system. And according to Naremore, Method acting would be fundamentally unthinkable without this star system (212) because the Method's success depends on the camera's ability and willingness to provide the audience with close-ups of the minutest facial gestures of the actors who try to express real, genuine emotions. That the effectivity of Method acting depends on the audience's ability to see the actor's facial gestures up close explains why, as Hirsh puts it, "the Method is primarily and ideally a film technique" (*Method* 292) and as such depends on as well as produces star images. Or, in Deleuze and Guattari's language, "the power of film [operates] through the face of the star and the close-up" (*Thousand Plateaus* 175). This is particularly remarkable given that the Method originated as a tool for stage actors, as I will explain.

Our very un- or undertheorized familiarity with Method acting requires, therefore, all the more that we pay closer attention to how the Method—that which has become synonymous with American (film) acting in general—operates. To simplify only slightly, the Method has evolved through three basic stages. First, it was essentially "invented" in and by the early teachings of Russian fin-de-siècle theater director Konstantin Stanislavski. Second, Stanislavski's system was introduced to the American stage in the 1920s through his emissary to America, Richard Boleslavski, whose teachings influenced two famed acting teachers, Lee Strasberg and Stella Adler—though with vastly differing results. Third, infights among the members of the Group Theater (1930s) around the issue of "affective memory" among others, led to the lifelong split between Strasberg and Adler. As Foster Hirsch argues, "Along with Boleslavski, most of his listeners at the Lab [American Laboratory Theater, originally called Theatre Arts Institute] grew disenchanted with the technique [of the Method]—but not Strasberg, who was drawn to it because it confirmed his readings in Freud and because he felt it led to the kind of truthful acting style he was interested in" (*Method* 75–76). Subsequently, in 1949, Strasberg took over the Actors Studio, "that most famous of all American acting places" (Hirsch, *Method* 109), which was founded in 1947 by, among others, Elia Kazan, who subsequently directed Marlon Brando in *On the Waterfront* (1954).[11] In charge of the studio, Strasberg relentlessly promoted "affective memory" as the Holy Grail of realist acting. In contrast, Stella Adler founded her own conservatory, where she waged an enduring battle against Strasberg's limited yet increasingly influential interpretation of the Stanislavskian system. I ultimately want to call attention to Adler's influence on DeNiro; but it is the role of Strasberg, and the original context within which Stanislavski codified "what actors before him had [merely] thought" (Hirsch, *Method* 37), that explains LaCapra's (and most everyone else's) conception of acting as a mimetic acting out of un–worked through (repressed) desires.

The main question Stanislavski asked himself was how he, as a director, could coax theater actors into recreating real life on stage as truthfully (read: realistically) as possible. Having read French psychologist Theodule Ribot's description of what he called "affective memory," Stanislavski began to experiment with this concept as a tool (rather than a dogmatic program) for his actors to activate emotions, feelings, and memories that otherwise would merely lie dormant beyond their conscious awareness. As Hirsch reminds us, Stanislavski's directing practices closely resemble that of Freud's psychotherapy: "Like Freud, who was conducting his own experiments at about the same time and whose ideas mature just as Stanislavski began to codify his system, the Russian director's concern was in reaching the subconscious. Like Freud, Stanislavski asked: What truths lie beneath our conscious minds?" (*Method* 40). The actor's goal, then, becomes to engage in a process of "what if." The actor is supposed to ask him- or herself, "*What if* the situation in the play were really happening—how would I react?" (38–39). The application of "affective memory" merely constitutes the most intensified version of the "what if" scenario, an intensification, however, that leads actors down memory lane of their own lives where they might find long-repressed instances that somehow are supposed to help them understand the character's motivations, beliefs, and emotions. Needless to say, giving oneself over to the process of affective memory can be an arduous and painful task, often requiring long periods of time before the actor is able to connect personal experience or memory to the requirements of the play.

Scholars such as Naremore and Hirsch have made much of the fact that Stanislavski himself had later moved away from deploying the "affective memory" technique as a tool for soliciting performances from his actors. Specifically, Stanislavski grew eventually fond of "the method of physical actions" (Hirsch, *Method* 39) that emphasizes the behavior and motivations of the character rather than the actual experiences of the actor. In other words, Stanislavski moved from emphasizing an actor's interiority to stressing the importance of the theatrical encounter—the ability of his actors to respond to the characters' needs as defined by the play itself.[12] The point I want to mark here, however, is simply that the Method emerged in tentatively codified and multiple form at the very moment when psychoanalysis took hold of the Western imagination—itself only intensifying the gradual process of subjectification around the emerging notion of the self that Foucault has described so well in *The Order of Things*.

Lee Strasberg is generally held responsible for popularizing Stanislavski's Method for the American stage and, eventually—via the detour of some of his more famous students at the Actors Studio such as James Dean, Paul Newman, Jack Nicholson, Al Pacino, Faye Dunaway, Diane Keaton, and Jane Fonda—for American cinema. But we must immediately qualify this claim by specifying that Strasberg's Method—the acting style American culture is most familiar with through the omnipresence of Hollywood's star system— relies almost exclusively on the "affective memory" method.

In fact, the irreconcilable clash that eventually occurred among Stanislavski's American disciples was triggered by Strasberg's unwillingness to heed Stanislavski's own insights that made him move beyond this psychoanalytic technique. Because "Strasberg took from [Boleslavski] what he wanted to, hearing what he wanted to hear" (Hirsch, *Method* 76), Strasberg's Method ended up consisting of what Naremore rather unsympathetically describes as "a series of quasi-theatrical exercises, often resembling psychological therapy, designed to 'unblock' the actor and put him or her in touch with sensations and emotions" (197). Naremore, a proponent of a more avant-garde, Brechtian type of acting that Strasberg himself disliked, criticizes Strasberg's psychoanalyticlike Method because it ends up reproducing an ideology of "romantic individualism" (200). Just about any cinematic biopic of recent memory depicting (troubled) "geniuses"—*Shine* (dir. Scott Hicks, 1996), *Pollock* (dir. Ed Harris, 2000), *Before Night Falls* (dir. Julian Schnabel, 2000), and *A Beautiful Mind* (dir. Ron Howard, 2001) immediately come to mind—testifies to the ongoing popularity of Strasberg's method's belief in the necessity of working through the experience of pain for the production of great art.

And this is precisely my point. American postwar cinema has been filled with performances informed by Strasberg's method to such a degree that it has become almost impossible to think of acting in other terms than those codified by psychoanalysis. This does not even depend on whether or not a given actor actually attended the Actors Studio workshop. The very notion of what constitutes great film acting has been thoroughly shaped by countless Hollywood films that featured celebrated performances by actors who were trained in or applied Method acting techniques. The performances are recurrently described as being the most truthful to the human spirit, to what it means to be truly human. Or, with Naremore, through "the rather parochial teachings of the Actors Studio, Stanislavski's approach had been narrowed down to a quasi-Freudian 'inner work' fueled by an obsession with the 'self'" (199). This approach to acting has so permeated American cinema and the discourse surrounding it that the Method has not only become synonymous with American film acting but also with mimesis. Method actors (are now believed to) imitate their own real-life experiences in order to render the characters to be played life-like and believable, that is, "realistic." Hence, a director like Hal Hartley frequently puzzles audiences and critics alike with films such as *The Unbelievable Truth* (1990), *Amateur* (1994), *Flirt* (1995), or *The Girl from Monday* (2004) because he consistently solicits performances from his actors that are anything but "realistic" or "naturalistic," thus not really allowing the world to know who the actors "are."

A Brief Genealogy of the Method, Part 2

So, this brief genealogy of the Method indicates why LaCapra can claim that acting out is about the obsessive compulsion to repeat mimetically. After all, the discursive formation that gave rise to the Method is shot through with psychoanalytic concepts, themselves articulating and thus perpetuating the increasing cultural and social interest in the self that intensified throughout the nineteenth century. Yet, what has been forgotten in all of this is precisely that the Method—with the emphasis on its connotation of "methodical"—has from early on had a second history, a second theory, a second practice. This second theory and practice was relentlessly advocated by famed acting teacher Stella Adler. Robert DeNiro, who studied with Adler at her Conservatory for Acting in Greenwich Village *before* he became associated with Stanislavski's Actors Studio, credits her with "having [had] a big influence on [him]" (Interview). Whereas Strasberg almost exclusively read Stanislavski's Method in terms of "affective memory," Adler never ceased to stress Stanislavski's later preference for the method of "physical actions." Hence, Adler was known to admonish her students to avoid bringing the character down "to your own small selves" (Hirsch, *Method* 214). Instead, as DeNiro explains in an interview with James Lipton, host of Bravo TV's *Inside the Actors Studio*, Adler relentlessly encouraged her students to break down a script, to analyze it with great care, and to think about what the character is about.

Like Strasberg, Adler accepted that acting is about work and that the rehearsal environment ought to resemble that of a "laboratory setup" (Hirsch, *Method* 206), a descriptive term suggestive of the machinical, processlike character immanent to the art of acting. Yet, unlike Strasberg, Adler continuously encouraged her students to "explore the given circumstances of the play rather than those of their own lives" (Hirsch, *Method* 215). Along these lines, Hirsch nicely sums up the two teacher's differences:

> On how an actor confronts language in a contemporary realist drama, Adler [. . .] hews the Studio line. But where Strasberg encouraged actors to enrich the author's words by writing a subtext triggered by emotional and sensory memory, Adler tells students to remain within the place and situation of the play. "Create the place; work with props—a prop will make you act; reach out to your partner; prepare a past for your character—if you don't build a past, you insult the stage and me." "Stanislavski said not to start with language, start with movement. Acting is action, action is doing: find ways to *do* it, not to say it." Adler's idea is that the actor claims personal possession of the playwright's words not through self-analysis, as at the Studio, but by *stepping out of himself*, allowing his imagination to take flight from clues the author has planted. (*Method* 217, final emphasis mine)

Leaving aside the fact that Adler distinguishes between doing and saying (*pace* J. L. Austin and, subsequently, post-structuralists who show that saying is doing), I think we begin to see the emergence of a completely different conception of acting.

↓

Consider, for instance, DeNiro's performance in *Mean Streets*, Martin Scorsese's first great, influential film.[13] Our first view of DeNiro's character, Johnny Boy, comes about five minutes into the film. We watch as he suddenly emerges from behind a house-front and drops something into a mailbox. As he nervously zig-zags away, he keeps turning back while moving forward. A few seconds later, the mailbox explodes. While one could argue that his act of random vandalism marks Johnny Boy as a violent character from the outset, I suggest that it is not the explosion itself that stands out in this scene as an expression of violence but the *style* Johnny Boy displays. In this scene, as well as throughout the movie, Johnny Boy moves with a "devil-may-care flamboyance" (Dickstein 81). His movements are concurrently expressive of a joie de vivre and explosive recklessness, and it is this irresistible combination of a certain lightness of being and impending violence that brands itself into our minds. And on top of that, there is that hat: reminiscent of the type of stylish hats that characters in the gangster movies of the 1930s would wear, Johnny Boy's hat features prominently in each frame. In fact, we note his hat because the film refuses to shoot DeNiro in lingering close-ups, and the grainy quality of the film stock does not allow for close scrutiny of his facial expressions, let alone his eye movements. But we do see that hat. The way DeNiro makes Johnny Boy carry himself as more important than he really is in the context of the local Mafia hierarchy (the film's opening scenes have established that it takes place in a Mafialike milieu) crucially depends on his engagement with the hat. We sense from this very first scene that Johnny Boy is an impatient upstart who is bound to become-violent sooner rather than later. In other words, we have yet to see Johnny Boy commit an act of violence (that is not "merely" a rather boyish act of vandalism), but we have already the image of violence firmly implanted in our brain. Violence here is a becoming-hat, which tends to be recalled by viewers in that memory territorializes this becoming onto DeNiro's face—or, rather, it effects a becoming-face of DeNiro in the sense that he "slides into it."

From this first appearance on, Johnny Boy, more than any other character in the film, embodies a kind of visceral force that is so exuberant it captures the viewers' fascination. This fascination, however, cannot be reduced to sadomasochistic desires. After all, we have yet to see him interact with anyone other than some inanimate objects. We are simply fascinated by the way DeNiro manages to act out Johnny Boy's potential for violence— which will eventually be realized—without having recourse to tried and true cinematic (or other) images of violence. We thus tend to remember Johnny Boy as a violent character not because he eventually threatens a made guy with a gun who ultimately returns the favor and has him shot. We think of Johnny Boy in violent images because of his hat, the way he wears it, what he does with it, and its eventual absence (he loses it in a bar fight that, not coincidentally, is triggered by someone asking him about where he got his hat), which actually speeds up his impatience, thus precipitating his eventual downfall. Violence as rendered by DeNiro in this film, then, is about an encounter with a prop—a hat. It is a becoming-hat that sets in motion an image of violence as linked to speed, to physical action, to the agile body of DeNiro-cum–Johnny Boy. And this becoming-hat continues to manifest itself even in the eventual absence of the prop itself. Thus, the film not only dramatizes how the nonmimetic version of the Method works but also reminds us that a process of imitation does not trigger the eventual acting out of violence. Finally, the production of an image of violence as a becoming-hat is anything but self-evident; it calls attention to the fact that we do not necessarily know violence when we see it precisely because this claim to common sense presupposes that we know what violence "is" and how it manifests itself.

↓

Adler's method, as exemplified by DeNiro's performance in *Mean Streets*, has very little to do with the ideology of the self, with imitation, or with an acting out of repressed memories. Unlike Strasberg's version of the Method, Adler's is not about the privileging of the (habit to say) "I"—of prioritizing the ego's (illusory) ability to be identical to itself. Instead, Adler's conception of the Method is primarily about intensities of movement, action, doing; most importantly it is about an actor's ability to enter a zone of proximity with the outside: "I is another," as Deleuze, quoting Rimbaud, aphoristically writes (*Kant's Critical Philosophy* viii).

Ironically, Adler's method might have been best articulated by one of Strasberg's studio members. Best known for her role as Edie Doyle, the love interest of Brando's Terry Malloy in Kazan's *On the Waterfront*, Eve Marie Saint argues that the "Method is not playing yourself—that's one of the misunderstandings people have about the studio. [. . .] The Method helps you to observe, to see life, to look outside yourself" (Hirsch, *Method* 221). The Method puts the self under erasure, or at the very least casts it as a serious *problématique* in the Foucaultean sense. I think that this feature of the Method cannot be emphasized enough, for it produces a concept of thought (as practice) that dismantles a Cartesian notion of the I as formulated in his famous dictum, "I think therefore I am." Whereas the latter insists on the self-identity of the I, and thus the primacy of the process of representation and identification, the Method's insistence on movement, and thus time as it passes in the interval of this movement, configures a subject's self as constantly changing. As Deleuze writes about this kind of self:

> It is a passive, or rather receptive, "self" that experiences change in time. The *I* is an act (I think) that actively determines my existence (I am), but can only determine it in time, as the existence of a passive, receptive and changing *self*, which only represents to itself the activity of *its own* thought. The I and the Self are thus separated by the line of time, which relates them to each other only under the condition of a fundamental difference. My existence can never be determined as that of an active and spontaneous being, but as passive "self" that represents to itself the "I"—that is, the spontaneity of the determination—as an Other that affects it. ("Poetic Formulas" 29–30)

So, practicing his or her ability to respond to external clues seems to me the most crucial lesson to be learned from the Method— and it is this lesson that we must heed if we want to be able to say anything at all about violence in cinema and the effects it may or may not produce.

Violence, perhaps the most ontologically "natural" thing (and as such, something we cannot but respond to), is simultaneously the least naturalistic phenomenon precisely because actors can reasonably access violence—and render it visible—only by going outside of themselves, or rather, by affirming that their "I" is always "another." The actor's "I" never provides the locus of experience from which to draw the affective force that is to be imitated in order to become-violent on screen. That is, an actor cannot really hold a knife to the throat of a random person on the street only to "know" what it feels like to be violent so that she can then draw on this experience—via the process of imitation rooted in (remembered) knowledge—in front of the camera. He cannot take a .45 and hold up a convenience store and, after he gets what he pretends to want, shoot the clerk. Nor can actors really give themselves over to the position of a victim: in general, you cannot volunteer to be threatened with a gun in a real-life situation, and you most certainly will not volunteer to be shot at in the head a few times only to be able to experience "real" pain that then can be represented for an audience. Hence, actors who are supposed to render violence realistically on screen are forced to make a connection with something other than their own experience, memory, or psyche. They have to step outside of themselves, thus allowing themselves to experiment with the outside—in form of a hat, for example—as a means for rendering violence visible.[14] And if taken seriously, this experimental imperative leads violence to emerge as a continual variation of its own concept—a variation that always varies itself, whose self-differentiation is immanently generated, always differing in its affective charge that is produced through the deployment of Method-ical repetition.

Only a year later, for example, DeNiro would not act- out violence through a becoming-hat; instead, as the young Don Corleone in *The Godfather II*, he inhabits an odd space of silence. Of course, his silence was prescribed by the script (which also asked him to deliver his lines in Italian). But this silence is mostly ef-

a reliving or an appropriation of a previously lived experience. A certain type of criticism of DeNiro's acting is thus rather misplaced. That is, at times critics have accused DeNiro of playing it safe since his last great "acted out" Method role in Scorsese's *King of Comedy* (1983) as the remarkably unfunny wannabe comedian Rupert Pupkin. In pursuing a great number of cameo roles (*Angel Heart* [1986] or *The Untouchables*, e.g.), so the claim goes, DeNiro has lost some of his edge as a performer. In an odd ironic reversal, it is *critics* who mourn that DeNiro's is not "acting out" anymore. They mourn that DeNiro has allegedly given up his trademark intensity with which he imbued his visceral acting out for a more intellectualized "working through" of his violent performances. They seem to yearn for DeNiro's physical bravado with which he filled his performance of boxer Jake LaMotta in *Raging Bull*, or even the remarkable physical changes that Travis Bickle is made to undergo on his way from dissatisfied yet unsure cab driver to becoming a killing machine, a killer cyborg, if you will, whose weapons are mechanically linked to his every movement. Expressing the sense that DeNiro has lost some of his famous intensity, his willingness to act out, biographer Andy Dougan wonders whether DeNiro has "now learned to fake acting" (247). But to accuse DeNiro of "faking it" presupposes in a Strasbergian sense that acting is a process of imitation, of mimetically representing a real, authentic self that provides the locus for a performance. Yet, intensity is a matter of simulacral production—all the way down—rather than phenomenological authenticity. In this sense, it is impossible to "fake" acting, for Adler's conception of acting does not rely on a logic of the copy (representation) but instead mobilizes what I discussed in chapter 3 as the logic of simulation that functions as the constitutive engine of all production, including (or especially) of representations.

Put differently, what DeNiro learned from Adler is that intensity is not about acting out or excess; rather, intensity is a state that quite often inheres and subsists *within* a style of encounter. Method acting as practiced by DeNiro, therefore, is about a careful experimental, indeed masochistic, encounter with the outside, with a methodical repetition of specific practices—a repetition that, like in a lab, allows the actor to work through a specific acting problematic. This type of acting can be considered as constituting what Deleuze and Guattari call a becoming. We must be very clear at this point, however. DeNiro's eventual becoming-face, which is merely the most recent instantiation of his continually varying becoming-violent, has nothing to do with a Hegelian understanding of becoming. For that matter, it has nothing in common with the story of becoming as it has functioned throughout the history of Western metaphysical thought.

Becoming is a process not so much about dialectical change or acquisition of a state of affairs as about something akin to implosion, an intensifying of affectivity, a movement with its speed and slowness that is not describable by the notion of "quickness" as such. Becoming, as Deleuze and Guattari have argued, is the hardest thing to do (and explain) precisely because Western thought has conceptualized, and pedagogically employed, becoming as a dialectical process. Traditionally, becoming is conceived of as a constant war between two struggling opponents that is resolved only by a third term that has "become" the synthesis of the previous two, sublating both and thus producing a new, higher level of development. Understood this way, one would think that DeNiro's becoming constitutes a story of progress, a teleological consolidation and as such an improvement of his acting skills that eventually culminates in DeNiro's becoming someone else.

But a story about the way DeNiro prepares himself for an acting job illustrates that for DeNiro (Method) acting has little to do with this type of becoming, a becoming ultimately rooted in the concept of mimetic representation. In 1973 DeNiro was still an up and coming actor, having just landed his first important success with his portrayal of Johnny Boy in *Mean Streets*. That summer, he prepared for a stage role in the short-lived one-act play *Schubert's Last Serenade*. Julie Bovasso, the play's author, describes DeNiro's method in a *Newsweek* magazine interview: "Bobby arrives at his characterizations by what sometimes seems like a very circuitous route. He wanted to do one scene, for example, while chewing breadsticks. I was dubious but I agreed and for three days I didn't hear a word of my play—it was all garbled up in breadsticks. But I could see something happening; he was making a connection with something, a kind of clown element. Then at dress rehearsal he showed up without the breadsticks. I said, 'Bobby, where are the breadsticks?' And he said simply, 'I don't need them anymore'" (qtd. in Dougan 60). Bovasso's observation expresses perhaps even better than DeNiro's own comments regarding his acting technique what, exactly, transpires in the process of acting. Deleuze and Guattari note in *A Thousand Plateaus* that DeNiro himself has described his walking style in *Taxi Driver* as crablike (274). Elsewhere, DeNiro apparently remarked that he had "seen some of his roles as a crab, a cat, a wolf, a rabbit, a snake, and an owl" (Dougan 234). Deleuze and Guattari crucially explain that DeNiro's likening his style of walking to that of a crab has *nothing* to do with imitation; DeNiro did not end up being "like" a crab, nor "like" a cat meowing, a wolf howling, or a snake swallowing its prey whole.[15]

Instead, Bovasso and DeNiro's descriptions of his acting process must be understood in terms of what Deleuze and Guattari call a becoming-animal, or, perhaps more appropriate for Bovasso's observation, a becoming-breadstick. This becoming names DeNiro's necessary encounter with something that allows him to enter a zone of proximity with the character he has to imagine and then render visible on screen or stage. Much has been made of DeNiro's elaborate research activities—so much so, in fact, that Rob Fraser has a point in suggesting that "For a time, it seemed as if [. . .] history would remember Robert DeNiro [mostly] for the obsessive detail with which he researched each role" ("Performing Miracles" 5). But not enough has been made of the fact that DeNiro's preparation far exceeds this hands-on empirical research. It is all too easy to view DeNiro's research as a process expressing his desire for, and thus leading to, imitation; both his own characterization of his becoming-animal as well as Bovasso's breadstick story testify that this is not so. This is not to deny the importance of researching a character. For one, DeNiro himself obviously places much value on it. In fact, he believes that the ability to research a character as much as possible is an ideal situation, "but it doesn't always work out" (Interview). I suggest that in the case of violence, (DeNiro figured out that) it can *never* work out.

Instead, DeNiro's methodological obsession—especially evident throughout the first fifteen years of his film acting career—instantiates a process of learning, of inhabitation, of making connections not through mimesis but by response. This describes a pedagogical process not unlike that of the swimmer who learns how to swim not by imitating the swim teacher but by responding to the ever-changing signs emitted by the ocean's waves (Deleuze, *Difference and Repetition* 22–23). That is, learning "takes place not in the relation between a representation and an action (reproduction of the Same) but in the relation between a sign and a response (encounter with the other)" (Deleuze, *Difference and Repetition* 22). Or, in DeNiro's own words, an "actor's body is like an instrument and you have to learn how to play an instrument. It's like knowing how to play the piano. There ought to be acting schools that take you in as small children, the way they do with music. A person doesn't need experience to learn technique. Technique comes first, then as you grow older and get experience you will apply it to what you know" (qtd. in Dougan 106).

How much more powerfully could DeNiro have refuted our common wisdom about (Method) acting? To enact pain, you do not have to have experienced some childhood trauma or an excruciatingly tiring divorce. Acting is about technique—mechanics, if you will; it is about something that has to be learned through continual practice, rather than institutionalized self-reflection. As DeNiro's own assessment of the acting process indicates, in order to act you have to do it; you have to affirm action, knowing that you might "fail" and thus be forced to do it over, again and again, until you discover that which is genuinely new, or that which seems to work best for the demands of the script and the character to be played. DeNiro himself puts it this way: "If I just jumped in and did it and took the leap [I'd] arrive at that place where you thought you had to go through all kinds of, you know, you just arrived there, believe it or not. [. . .] You gotta get out at the end of the day and do it. And if you make a mistake you do it again" (Interview). In other words, whatever experience the actor will gain is secondary to the *process*—the Method—of acting itself.

Conceived this way, acting has little to do with psychologized interiority; instead, the "activity of the actor is less to imitate a character in a script than to mimic in the flesh the incorporeality of the event" (Massumi 64). It is about entering a disciplined encounter with—a becoming-fascinated by—the outside that constitutes the necessary condition of possibility for rendering an (violent) image visible.[16] In DeNiro's own words, "Actors must expose themselves to the surroundings and keep their minds obsessed with that. Sooner or later *an idea will creep into your head.* A feeling perhaps, a clue, or maybe an incident will occur that the actor can later connect to the scene when he's doing it. I always look at everything [. . .] even if it's boring" (qtd. in Dougan 106, my emphasis). According to DeNiro, then, acting is an encounter with the outside: the actor is responsible to welcome this outside, this idea that will creep into the actor's head (or, in Tom Ripley's case, a scent that attracts his olfactory interest). Such a process is, of course, precisely akin to the masochistic processes described by Deleuze. The practice of masochism forces, and through repetition habituates, the "suspended subject" to look at everything, to wait, to endure time until an idea creeps up; it thus requires the masochistic subject to affirm boredom, for most of the time nothing at all happens. But it is *in* the repetition of time passing without action that one is made capable of experimenting with a specific *problématique* and thus is enabled to invent a novel mode of thought, a new image, a new mode of response. Being suspended by boredom, the masochist begins to abstract clichés from his surroundings, gradually intensifying the situation he is suspended in, until the moment of transformation occurs (which is never guaranteed). Boredom (cinematically embodied in the time-image, or duration) functions thus as an intensifier, an affective state that may be necessary to inhabit in order to produce a line of flight, or transformation.

And it is hard to imagine a case for which this analysis rings more true than the case of violence. For how else, I wonder, can an actor render violence visible than by giving himself over to the process described by DeNiro? Of course, most actors do not follow DeNiro's advice, but this is why DeNiro, and not another actor, has come to embody the face of violence in American cinema. For the point made by DeNiro is that expressing violence on screen or stage is not about digging deep inside yourself so that you can narcissistically act out your repressed anxieties or anger; nor is it merely about imitating real life violence by researching violent people or events. Presenting violence on screen, in other words, has not necessarily anything at all to do with experiencing or having experienced it. Violent images are expressed through a specific, and always varying, process that requires clinically cold diagnosis (problematization) rather than the application of solutions developed in the context of a different problem—that is, the slowness inhering in boredom, rather than the quickness of action. In other words, it is the violence inhering boredom that functions as an immanent enabling force to render new images of violence—violent images that differ from the clichéd images of violence in all too many action films. And such problematization never proceeds from a critical position external to the object of encounter. The inevitable process of becoming-affected or fascinated by the object ensures—for better and worse—the critic's own participation in the *problématique*. Action—critical or not—does thus not result from imitation but from affectation.

Analyze the Face

It is hardly a coincidence that DeNiro is described as "a great listener and a great observer" (Dougan 45). DeNiro himself explained once that, researching for his violent role as the young Don Corleone for *The Godfather II*, he repeatedly watched Marlon

Brando play the old godfather in the trilogy's first part. Rather than wanting to imitate Brando's performance—which he knew would be futile—he studied the movie over and over to "see some little movements that [Brando] would do and try to link them to my performance. It was like a mathematical problem where you have the result and you try to make the beginning fit" (qtd. in Dougan 64). DeNiro explained his strategy for rendering the young Don thusly: "I wasn't intimidated by [the role and the fact that Brando had indelibly drawn the picture of the older Don Corleone only two years prior]. I just thought it's a *problem* [. . .]. I kind of liked the fact that I had *boundaries* and I had to *connect* it to something. It wasn't like I had to look for something; it was there. I just had to *continue* it" (Interview, my emphases).[17] Elsewhere, DeNiro expresses that Method acting depends on creating linkages between different parts of him and the character, with the linkages often being provided by neither but instead by an animal or an inanimate object. DeNiro's much-discussed time consuming research methods, then, are much less expressive of a dangerous psychological anomaly indicating a troublesome mimetic process of repetition, of, as LaCapra has it, "melancholic acting out," than a necessary component of his acting process. This process has to be learned anew every time, requiring singular Method-ical *responses* rather than wholesale "solutions."

↓

DeNiro's violent and celebrated becoming-obese in *Raging Bull* is but one way of acting out the Method, and it is most certainly a way of acting out that depends on a careful regimen, a controlled, disciplined diet plan that simultaneously ensures the actor's health and his ability to radically change his physical appearance in one and the same film. And while Scorsese's film features many violent images (after all, it is a film about a boxer), it might very well be the shock produced by the radically different *bodies* of DeNiro that fascinates us. The film certainly seems to bank on this effect, for it opens with a juxtaposition of two violent images:

that of a well-trained, lean, muscular body (we cannot yet see to whom the body belongs, though we suspect it is DeNiro as the young LaMotta) "dancing" in the boxing ring and that of the fifty pounds heavier, fat, older Jake LaMotta (also played by DeNiro) whom we see rehearsing a joke in the dressing room of his night club. The radical disparity of bodies "within" the same actor's body, I think, captures an image of violence that fascinates and thus sticks with us more than all the brilliant mise-en-scène realism of Scorsese's camera work and Thelma Schoonmaker's editing employed to capture the violent action in the ring. Becoming-violent here is imaged through DeNiro's becoming-obese (where his obesity manifests itself not just in his being fat but also in his gestures moving with a degree of slowness inherently responsive to his increased weight).

In his perceptive essay "Methods and Madness," cultural critic Louis Menand argues that *Raging Bull* is, in many ways, about our inability to understand (Jake LaMotta's) violence, for neither of the two common explanatory paradigms—biology and culture— quite suffice to describe in a satisfactory manner why a person acts so violently. Film critic David Denby pushes the same line of argument a step further. Denby asserts in his review essay "Brute Force" that "DeNiro appears to be the first great actor in American movies to have consciously rejected audience rapport" because "De-Niro doesn't want us to identify" (44). Instead, so Denby claims, DeNiro's "brilliant performances are a way of saying, 'don't try to understand me, because you can't. I'm not the same as you—I may be better or worse, but I'm not you'" (44). Both Menand and Denby articulate the sheer impossibility of "understanding" violence—an impossibility that is rendered tangibly visible through DeNiro's acting style.[18] Indeed, we need to heed Denby's assertion that DeNiro refuses to be understood precisely because violence—that which DeNiro most consistently has to render cinematically—is more about soliciting fascination rather than understanding. DeNiro's acting out of violence is (always) marked as particular becomings that continually vary the image of violence as a result of a serialized working through of the *problématique*.

↓

DeNiro's acting, in other words, marks the noncommonsensicality of violence. Consequently, acting, as exemplified by DeNiro, has really nothing to do with tapping into one's psyche or one's past, as Dougan suggests when he claims that DeNiro's "Method training would have encouraged [him] to bring his own pain to the part" (74). Not surprisingly, Dougan then asserts, "Any therapist would confirm that to understand the pain and play it so convincingly DeNiro would have had to have endured at least some part of it" (75). Dougan's psychobiographical analysis sharply contrasts with DeNiro's own description of the Method acting process, however: "Building a character," DeNiro argues in his description of what he learned from Stella Adler, "is not about neuroses or playing on your neuroses. It's about the character [. . .], the tasks of the character, without going about it as if it's all about you" (Interview). Experimenting with the problem of how to render his many violent characters, therefore, requires time and effort; he had to work through the problematic over and over, but the only way he possibly could work through these varying problems was by acting out serialized responses. But whereas psychoanalysis tends to view working through as preferable to and distinguished from acting out, DeNiro's case shows that every working- through always already consists of an acting out, and that acting out is constituted by the need to work through a problem.

Consequently, one might best describe DeNiro's method as a case in point for Deleuze's observation that postwar cinema is that of the seer, not the doer (*Cinema 2* xi). Acting, as exemplified by DeNiro, is not so much about pure action as it is about seeing, about waiting, observing, entering a specific mood through experimentation and, perhaps, an intuitive recognition that mimesis as a tool is overly dependent on action.[19] If we have learned to think of Method acting as being obsessed with activity—research, interviewing, acting out of inner fears or other emotions—then I think DeNiro productively counters this problematic characterization in that he consistently shows in his own practice that acting out is, if anything, a process that cannot be thought and done without a concurrent working through, and vice versa.

What differs, then, is not the moral quality of acting out or working through but their intensities and the way the process of both is accomplished and what is effectuated. How, exactly, is the (violent) character rendered, and through what is the violence made visible? Or, with Deleuze and Guattari, "*what circumstances trigger the machine* that produces the face and facialization" (*Thousand Plateaus* 170)? And it is DeNiro's career-long engagement with this problematic that, I think, confirms and simultaneously expands Naremore's assessment of DeNiro being a "thoroughgoing naturalist [but] also a sophisticated theorist" (267). For the "also" in Naremore's assessment suggests a distinction between practice and theory, between his practicing naturalism and his ability to theorize a given problematic. Or, to return to LaCapra's terminology, Naremore's "also" inadvertently confirms the easy opposition between acting out (practice) and working through (theory). As DeNiro's multiple encounters with violence make clear, however, the theory *is* the practice, the practice the theory. As if taking place in a lab setting, acting is a process of working through specific experimental problems. To work through, to think through (theorize about) the problem, however, the actor ultimately has to find ways of acting out the problematic. For only the doing will ultimately show whether the problem has been "solved," whether it has been transformed into something else, perhaps a new *problématique* that enforces the questions "If violence has been this, then what else can it be?" or "How else can it be rendered?" or "What else can it *do*?"

So, and this brings us back to *Analyze This*, LaCapra's diagnosis of acting out as mimetic and opposed to working through is always too fast, since it does not pay attention to how, specifically, acting works and what it does. As I have been suggesting throughout this chapter, the face plays a crucial role in the process of acting precisely because it has the capacity to territorialize our fascination with what we see, even if it is at times not the face itself that initially makes a violent image visible, as is the case in *Mean Streets*, *The Godfather II*, *Taxi Driver*, or *Raging Bull*.

↙

Analyze This undoubtedly dramatizes this point in its best-known moment: Vitty and Sobel's first meeting. Vitty, having just entered Sobel's office, wants to ensure that his visit remains a secret, lest his underworld friends and foes get wind of it and think him weak. He playfully yet determinedly makes Sobel understand that the psychoanalyst does not know who he is ("You know me?" "Yes I do." "No you don't." "OK" "Seen my picture in the paper?" "Yes I have." "No you didn't." "I didn't even get the paper."). He then pretends that he visits Sobel on behalf of a friend who has problems and "he's gonna have to probably see a shrink."

But Vitty is a poor liar, and after a few sentences, Sobel responds to Vitty's story by declaring: "I'm going out on a limb here. I think your friend is you." At this moment, the camera cuts back to a medium close-up of DeNiro's face in which we detect the slightest opening of his eyes, immediately casting a darker, threatening shadow over his face. A reverse shot of Crystal's face confirms that Sobel too has registered the subtle, yet important, shift of mood, for his face now expresses less confidence and more fear (for his life) than a few seconds before. Has he possibly exceeded his boundaries? The camera cuts back to DeNiro's face, as he begins to perform a moment of acting that by now has become justly famous. His face gradually assumes a happy, relaxed expression, with DeNiro's eyes narrowing to two small slits framed by joyful horizontal furrows of laughter, as his only slightly opened, narrow-lipped mouth intones: "You, yooou, [wagging his index finger at Sobel], yooooou got a gift my friend. You got a gift." As Sobel is reluctant to accept Vitty's praise, their dialogue continues:

> **Vitty:** Oh yeah!
> **Sobel:** No I don't.
> **Vitty:** Yes you do. [in a teasing, sing-song voice]
> **Sobel:** No I really don't.

With the camera on DeNiro's face, we now see it change its expression once more, now back to its original state of lingering violence, with DeNiro's eyes wide open again, the wrinkles of joy gone and the deep furrows on his forehead back in all their glory. "Yes you *do!*" Vitty extols, the insistence in DeNiro's voice simply adding to what his face has already established, namely, that he has made Sobel an offer of praise that must not be refused.

↙

On one level, this scene contrasts Vitty's desire for a quick solution with Sobel's refusal to accept responsibility for anything that does not conform to his institutionalized belief in the force of mourning. (And to some degree he is proven correct, in the sense that Vitty's anxiety, which, according to the mobster, had just disappeared, returns shortly thereafter.) But on another level, this scene, through the power of acting as singularized by DeNiro's face, is *about* the constitutive force of acting (out) itself. What else is this scene but a showcasing of DeNiro's acting powers? And what else is shown but the repetitive compulsion that governs acting? Indeed, what else is illustrated but an (violent) intensification caused by the process of repetition, of repeating the acting out (enacting) of the same line that, through its repetitiveness, introduces difference, a difference that in its constitutive force affects any attempt at working through?

As the rest of the movie comically dramatizes, working through, far from being morally superior to, or indeed distinct from, acting out depends on a process of repeated acting out, on a compulsively serialized return to a practice that is not about memory but, in fact, about what Nietzsche has conceptualized as active forgetting. John Rajchman, glossing Deleuze, explains it thusly: "There is a 'unmourning' that requires more work, but promises more joy. [Melancholy] might then be said to be the sensation of an unhappy idealization, and the real antidote to it is to be found not in rememorization and identification [working through, or mourning], but in active forgetting and affirmative experimentation with what is yet to come" (132–33).

For Vitty to be able to function in a manner appropriate to the logic of his world and current situation (regardless of whether it agrees with our understanding of social codes and norms), he must forget the guilt he feels about the role he played as a young kid in his father's death. Similarly, DeNiro as an actor must actively "forget" some of his past "tricks" that he has used to become-violent in order to reinvent—or to invent again new, differing—images of violence. DeNiro must, in a sense, forget that many of his previous instances of becoming-violent registered as a bodily violence: Johnny Boy's exuberant yet threatening movement accentuated by a hat, Travis Bickle's physical disciplining of himself accentuated by his becoming-crab, or Jake LaMotta's becoming-obese, DeNiro's most famous physical becoming.

The affective impasse Vitty experiences results from an interruption of his body's capacity to act. The question raised by the problem is what his body has to be capable of doing, and the potentially multiple solutions are provided by the *problématique* itself rather than by some prescribed, normativized answer. This does not mean that violence is "good" or that working through is "bad." But *Analyze This* dramatizes that the violence immanent to the compulsion to repeat—to act out—is not merely a perhaps necessary, though really deplorable, step to a healthier response mechanism to violent trauma called mourning. Instead, the film—especially the aforementioned scene that most effectively deploys the violent power of DeNiro's face—insists that this violence is *constitutive* of the process of working through. In other words, *Analyze This*'s facialization of violence through DeNiro's performance deconstructs the institutionalized moral distinction between acting out and working through and thus seems to suggest violence's immanence to life, to action. Through its repetitions on both the level of narrative structure and DeNiro's enactments of a wise guy, it affirms that working through is a process of violent acting out, or of affirming a repetition of that which returns as difference.

A New Pop Iconography of Violence

The "facial" scene in *Analyze This* suggests that DeNiro has acquired the capacity to express his character's menace through a type of acting that in its extreme minimalism and calmness might be considered the culmination of a long process of working through the Method mode of acting out. While viewers may not be privy to a more foregrounded acting process (acting out), they are made to witness the pure immanence of what all too often is conceived of as pragmatically and morally distinct processes: working through and acting out. And our capacity to witness this clearly results from DeNiro's career-long, repetitive giving over of himself to the problem of how to render violence through acting. Without any master plan behind it, without any preconceived solution, or even without any pure recognition of what he was doing, DeNiro performatively "solved" his problem by repeatedly confronting it, trying to find different ways of encountering the question of violence as posited by his characters. In other words, DeNiro's performance has little to do with "consciousness," which is not to deny that he is an intelligent, thinking actor.

Repeatedly working through the problem, however, meant for DeNiro that he frequently had to act violently, that he had to act out. This active repetition with a difference of DeNiro's attempt to find ways to render violence—to show on screen how violence works and what it does—manifests this continual variation, a variation that ends up being varied itself as a result of an enacted experimentation. It has become visible in his early Method acting days in which his body provided his central frame of reference (*Mean Streets*, *Taxi Driver*, *Raging Bull*), to his later, perhaps more mainstream days of cameo roles (*The Untouchables*, e.g.), to his more recent roles in which the focus for DeNiro's violence has almost completely shifted from his body to his face.

↓

Consider, for example, DeNiro's performance of Jimmy Conway in *GoodFellas*, his sixth collaboration with Scorsese. As opposed to his earlier roles in his friend's films, this one is "merely" an important supporting role. Yet, it is precisely the support he lends—especially in juxtaposition to Joe Pesci's volatile character, Tommy—that once again something interesting emerges regarding the imaging of violence. For the first time in his career, one would be justified to characterize DeNiro's face as handsome. Undoubtedly due to the skills of make-up artists working for the film, this "mature" handsomeness nonetheless appears as if it had arisen out of the accumulated acting experience of the last twenty years. His facial beauty is one of extreme calmness and serenity, as opposed to the shiftiness expressed on Johnny Boy's or Travis's face, for instance. From the film's first scene (we soon discover that it is a flashback), of course, *GoodFellas* does not leave any doubt about Conway's violence. Together with Tommy, Conway is shown to kill a body that they believed to have killed already hours earlier (a scene that the film shows an hour into the film). Whereas Tommy stabs the corpse four or five times with his mother's impressive kitchen knife, Conway fires a few bullets in it for good measure. Likewise, the film features a number of other sequences in which Conway is depicted as violent: killing, we learn, is "just business" for him.

Yet, DeNiro's performance is particularly effective in its ability to present us with yet another becoming-violent because his character's calmness differentiates him so well from Tommy's more obvious nihilistic madness. This time it is Pesci who, in a career-making performance, gets to "act out" violence in its most volatile form. Had DeNiro tried to match Pesci's frantic acting out, the film would have been less compelling in its affectivity. Of course, DeNiro was most certainly directed, not only by Scorsese, but also by Nicholas Pileggi's script; but for all intents and purposes, it is his performance of Jimmy that marks the first time of DeNiro's becoming-face as we know it today. For after this performance, his violent roles have by and large ceased to work through his body (with the major exception of *Cape Fear*). In *Casino, Ronin* (dir. John Frankenheimer, 1998) or, most recently, *The Score* (dir. Frank Oz, 2001), as well as in the comedies, DeNiro's characters exude varying degrees of (aging) facial handsomeness that have caught our eyes and thus have territorialized all of his previous becoming-violents onto his face: becoming-attractive, becoming-violent.

↓

In a sense, we can describe DeNiro's acting career as a becoming-facial and his process of acting as a continual becoming. The emerging face of DeNiro as showcased in the two comedies *Meet the Parents* and *Analyze This* is constituted by this process of repetition, of producing variety within this serialization, of intensifying the process of acting in order to ensure that variation itself continually varies. DeNiro's faciality has thus emerged because of his consistent (if unintentional) acting out *while* working through, or working through *while* acting out. It has emerged out of a Method that practically theorizes acting as nonmimetic, as having as little to do with imitation or representation as it has to do with judgment—which are concepts and practices that, as I have argued in chapter 3, always presuppose each other and thus cannot be thought or practiced separately.

Hence, we are led to conclude that DeNiro's style of becoming-violent, in all its different shapes and forms throughout his career, has nothing at all to do with a mimetic process triggering an acting out thereof, as is so often alleged by critics of onscreen violence. Instead, violence is an affect produced through engaging a process, a practice of seeing, of becoming-affected, of intensifying moods to the point of breaking. To get there, DeNiro had to figure out—not once or twice, but every time anew—how to enter this acting space. ("Failure," as DeNiro himself asserts, is part of that process.) Only by working out this problem could he arrive at specific solutions; and only by acting through it could he "ensure" that his variations on the same theme (occasionally) varied themselves.[20]

All of this is to say that the continual variation that DeNiro infuses into the image of violence results from a process of *subtraction* rather than addition. In a sense, acting out is always about a certain way of exceeding, of adding to a given. If my map of DeNiro's different forms of becoming-violent is persuasive, however, it seems that we can claim that, at least as a significant tendency, his early emphasis on addition, on a physical acting out—all the while shot through, constitutively, by a working through—gives way to a stress on working through, on a certain calmness (and attractiveness, one might add) that emerges through the power of an aging, well-trained, immensely controllable, and thus effectively affective face. As a formula, then, DeNiro's continually varying forms of his becoming-violent can be said to have been effectuated by subtracting the one element that we most often associate (and fear) with the concept of violence: blood. DeNiro's algorithm for becoming-violent can thus be named as "violence less blood"—a formula that indexes film criticism's need to become fascinated by imagings of violence in places or occasions *other* than those marked by severed heads, blood-drenched bodies, or buildings blown to smithereens.

Of course, this shift in DeNiro's Method-ical performance style is not complete by any means. For instance, in *Cape Fear*, DeNiro once again returns to imaging violence through an emphasis on his body. Famously, DeNiro flaunts innumerable prison tattoos on his muscular body. Just as we remember his obese body in *Raging Bull*, or his cyborglike appearance in *Taxi Driver*, so it is his becoming-tattoo that has lingered with us as the main image of violence from Scorsese and DeNiro's most commercially successful collaboration.[21] Likewise, as my first prologue meant to suggest, DeNiro's face has already been enormously effective in rendering a new image of violence in *Taxi Driver*. The point here is that becoming-violent does not have to be limited to one instantiation per performance. Rather, multiple forms of becoming-violent occur, but as a matter of emphasis it seems clear that

DeNiro has imaged violence predominantly through his body in the first two decades of his career, whereas he has rendered it visible predominantly on his face in the last ten or fifteen years. Yet, that DeNiro has become the face of violence in post–World War II American popular culture significantly results from the process of facialization that overcodes his physical becoming-violents. As Deleuze and Guattari write, "the face is produced only when the head ceases to be a part of the body, when it ceases to be coded by the body [. . .]—when the body, head included, has been decoded and *overcoded* by something we shall call the Face" (*Thousand Plateaus* 170).

Interestingly enough, popular culture was quick to register this shift in DeNiro's imaging of violence—one that instantiates the process and effects of faciality precisely because his face emerges out of what happens to, and is being done with, the actor's body at large. For a long time, the famous mirror scene from *Taxi Driver*—"arguably the most quoted scene in movie history" (Taubin 56)—has governed pop culture's image of DeNiro, and thus of violence, just as much as his becoming-obese in *Raging Bull*. Countless films have overtly acknowledged the power inhering the mirror scene, and actors in the post–*Raging Bull* years have been unable to escape the enormous obsessive power displayed by DeNiro's Jake LaMotta performance.[22] Yet, comedy skits evince that DeNiro's most recent becoming-violent—his becoming-face of American (film) violence—has taken hold of popular culture. It is hardly a coincidence that the "face" scene from *Analyze This* has almost instantly become a favorite moment in many contemporary comedians' repertoire when they impersonate DeNiro. For instance, Jimmy Fallon of *Saturday Night Live* put this DeNiroean acting moment to good comedic purpose during the "Weekend Update" segment of the longstanding NBC show. In his playfully negative review of *Meet the Parents*, he parodied just about all of the facial (and vocal) tics that are now easily recognizable as trademark DeNiro (October 14, 2000). In fact, DeNiro "spontaneously" responded by participating in Fallon's shtick one show later (October 21, 2000): while Fallon imitated DeNiro's face, De-

Niro mocked Fallon's own mannerisms and slowly "threatened" him into recanting his review.

So, in and out of context, this scene articulates pure, raw violence through its enacting. Without ever saying so much, everyone—Sobel, the viewers of *Analyze This*, and Jimmy Fallon's audience, *whether or not* they have seen this particular movie—is affected by (and senses) the violently threatening sensation inhering in and rendered by this moment of acting. And while the vocal intonation of the scene is effective and contributes much to its success, I suggest that it is not really needed, as opposed to, say, Marlon Brando's husky voice in *The Godfather* when he, as Don Corleone, declares that his offer cannot be refused. The close-up of DeNiro's facial acting quite literally does all the work necessary to imbricate this moment with all the violence of sensation that can be mustered without actually having to show—act out—(sensational) versions thereof.

Becoming-Violent, Becoming-Minor

Michael Mann's *Heat* presents us quite possibly with DeNiro's best violent performance outside of a Martin Scorsese film since his celebrated role of the young Don Corleone. At the time of the film's release, much clamor was provoked by the fact that it featured for the first time the two preeminent Method actors of their generation in the same scene: DeNiro and Al Pacino.[23] While one could say much about their different acting styles, I simply want to highlight that Mann's script provides us with one final image of how DeNiro's facialization of violence has emerged as a constitutive function of contemporary screen violence.[24]

In the celebrated face-to-face sit-down scene between the two legendary actors, Pacino's character, Vincent Hanna, a righteous and accomplished yet dissatisfied LA detective, expresses a certain admiration for his criminal opponent, DeNiro's Neil McCauley, as they are sitting across from each other at a table in a crowded coffee shop: "You know we are sitting here face to face like a couple of regular fellows and if I have to go out there and put you down, I'll tell you I won't like it. But if it's between you and some poor bastard whose wife you're gonna turn into a widow, brother, you are going down." Pacino's character assumes a certain fraternity with DeNiro's precisely because of their face-to-face encounter. While Hanna acknowledges that he will not hesitate to kill McCauley, he clearly thinks that the value of their face-to-face establishes a relationship with each other—that they share something—*outside* of their "professional" relationship, which is structured by violence. McCauley, however, will have none of that. Rather than conceiving of the face-to-face as (perhaps more ethical, most certainly less violent) outside of their cop-criminal relationship, he insists that the face-to-face does not change anything: "There is a flip side to that coin. What if you do get me boxed in and I will have to put you down? Cause no matter what, you will not get in my way. We've been *face-to-face*, yeah. But I will not hesitate, not for a second" (emphasis mine). Yes, they have been face-to-face, but so what when the face itself has become the most powerful image of violence?

(It is almost as if the film wanted to refute a liberal-minded reading of Levinas's concept of the "face-to-face" that uses it to establish a version of ethics dominated by recognition and intersubjectivity, or the need to *recognize* and thus respect the otherness of others. This reading strikes me as questionable, however, for two reasons: one, Levinas's "face-to-face" is not about an encounter with another human but with God; and, two, Levinas is quite explicitly arguing against "recognition" as the basis for ethics. For Levinas, ethics, performatively provoked in the face-to-face encounter, is a one-way street in which the subject is *subjected by* the other: "Subjectivity is being hostage" [*Otherwise Than Being* 127]. Not only does the other not care whether I recognize it but in fact I am always and already in debt [that I can never pay off] to the other. The subject is always already subjected to and by the other, and it is this brute fact of the subject's *passivity* in her relation to the other to which Levinas ascribes ethical force. Ethics, so Levinas argues, is "a calling into question of my spontaneity" by the presence of the other [*Totality and Infinity* 43]. Hence, for Levinas ethics can never be about seeing through another's eyes, for this perspectival understanding of responsibility is akin to a kind of subjective imperialism in which seeing through the other's eyes ends up in controlling the other's vision. In short, the intersubjective interpretation of Levinas's face-to-face amounts to a particularly insidious instantiation of violence, not a method for escaping violence.)[25]

In this sense, then, *Heat* dramatizes a rather dangerous habit of film criticism of violence: namely, the film shows that critics look for violence and its potentially dangerous effects in all the wrong places precisely because they pretend to know what violence "is," just as Hanna thinks he knows what a good old fraternal face-to-face talk is. It is up to McCauley—whose violence is made manifest *through* DeNiro's faciality—to suggest otherwise; it is left to the one who has become the face of violence in American culture to speak critically of these assumptions.

And in the end, suggesting otherwise seems to me the key to DeNiro's accomplishment with regard to his ability to become the face of violence in American post–World War II culture. For this "otherwise" is effected not by attempting to step outside as a means to oppose a given set of circumstances; nor is it brought about through a process of imitation. Instead, DeNiro's Methodical acting clearly operates by repeatedly going *through* that which is best known: Method acting. Inhabiting the Method allows an affectation from inside, very much akin to what Deleuze describes as a "minor treatment" of "History," of "doctrine," of "dogma" ("One Less Manifesto" 243). If the Method has normalized a particular style of acting with the result that acting is now hard to be conceptualized without having recourse to representational concepts, then the immanent reworking—its minorizing—of it seems to bear the potential of not only revealing the "error" inherent in that equation but of actually affecting the major mode to the degree that another mode of thought becomes available. We might even liken this minorizing of Method acting to Francis Bacon's painterly practice of immanently reworking figuration in order to produce the Figure: neither Bacon nor DeNiro outright reject representation (i.e., figuration, narrative); rather, they intensify its logic, making it continuously vary from itself in order to image and make affectively available the sensation of violence as well as the violence of sensation.

We can thus begin to think of acting—clearly an enormously crucial concept operative in the discourse surrounding screen violence, as well as literary violence as indicated in chapters 2 and 4—as a fundamentally asignifying and amoral operation. As such, it inheres in both processes of working through and acting out, thus rendering these two practices as immanent and, consequently, morally neutral. Yet, despite this moral neutrality, working through and acting out are expressive of different values (in the Nietzschean sense): they are *ethically* different precisely because of their different vectors of force on the same sliding scale of intensities. Attending to the process of what Deleuze and Guattari call "faciality," then, allows us to diagram how a multiplicity of forces constitutive of the acting process territorialize in specific registers, therefore giving rise to different and differing images of violence. Crucially, the process of (affective) becoming I have mapped out in this chapter works by and through repetition. DeNiro's face functions thus merely as a visual marker of a much more complex process, one, however, that has very little if anything at all to do with mimesis. Critical responses to the quality of faciality of DeNiro's face cannot have recourse to moral judgments: for how does one judge a face? A face is what it is, which means it is nothing but continual variation.[26] So, whereas LaCapra's mimetic version of acting allows us merely to reproduce moralizing clichés about screen violence, mapping out the specific effects and affects of DeNiro's becoming-face of American violence enables us to say something about what violence does in American cinema, or at the very least in DeNiro's films.

Not coincidentally, therefore, this chapter has focused mostly on DeNiro's Scorsese films as well as three films following their last collaboration to date. As others have pointed out, it is almost impossible to think of DeNiro without also thinking of Scorsese, perhaps the greatest American director of violence. Theirs is—

more than a "cinema of loneliness," as Robert Kolker's landmark book of the same title claims—a cinema of violence or, better, a cinema of violent becomings. But diagnosing the surface forces and movements of DeNiro's acting—its faciality—allows us to respond more precisely to violence qua violence, without having to regress to psychoanalytic categories of interiority, subjectivity, or identification as Dougan does; or to the category of historical context as Kolker, as well as Leighton Grist in *The Films of Martin Scorsese, 1963–77: Authorship and Context*, do. Of course, the violence of DeNiro's characters, especially in his first three or four Scorsese films, is some sort of response to what happened in the United States in the 1960s. But, and this is an important qualification, the historical context does not tell us anything about how the violence functions, how it works, what it does. And I contend that unless cinema studies—as well as literary or cultural studies, not to mention more "empiricist" enterprises—has a better grasp of the answers to these questions it will remain difficult for criticism to say anything at all about other operations such as "context" and "cause and effect."

Until criticism will have invented tools to take on violence on its own terms, it really cannot extrapolate anything at all about questions that clearly depend on—and all too often presume that we already know—answers to the questions of the affective effectivity of (screen) violence. And given that one of the main concerns with screen violence is audiences' fascination with it, it seems to me absolutely necessary to attend carefully to the process of facialization precisely because it provides a way into the very location (and the processes by which it comes into being) that sets in motion and captures—deterritorializes and (re)territorializes—viewers' becoming-fascinated. Highlighting violence as a process of faciality, thus, suggests that our contemporary attraction to cinematic violence might not just be one based on blood and other more overtly acted out, sensational forms thereof. This is not to discount the attraction blood has for us as well. But it is to insist, with Deleuze and Guattari, that DeNiro's becomings (including his becoming-face) suggest that, quite possibly, "the face has a great future, but only if

it is destroyed, dismantled. On the road to the asignifying and asubjective" (*Thousand Plateaus* 171). Criticism, it appears, must begin
to attend to the facialization of violence in order to overcome it.
This would potentially entail *an overcoming of Hollywood cinema itself*—as Jean-Luc Godard has recently insisted with increasing can-
tankerousness—since its success relies, though not exclusively, on
its ability to institutionalize star images through fetishized close-
ups of their faces.[27] If movie violence is in any form related to real
life violence, it has more to do with the facialized system of Hollywood itself than with viewers' uncontrollable desires to imitate
and to act out their repressed desires.

In any case, what the example of Robert DeNiro as both a theorist and practitioner of violence suggests is that such violence is
itself closely connected to the *problématique* of pedagogy. Pedagogy, however, should be understood less as a matter of "learning
from" than "doing with." I am not attempting to defend cinematic
or fictional violence because we have something to learn from it;
violence does not teach us anything about anything other than
itself, meaning, violent images do not teach us something about
something else precisely because imaged violence is not primarily a representational operation. Rather, the pedagogical quality
of imaged violence resides in the latter's force: in its solicitation
of our response-ability—a mode of response that demands repetition, habituation, that is, masochism as the pedagogical and
ethical imperative of criticism. I attempted to exemplify this in
this chapter by structuring the argument around a series of more
or less repetitive movements—movements of repetition that, I
hope, created through their very repetitiveness a certain diagnostic intensity, so much so that these repetitions' recurrences
were those of difference itself: a sense of different and differing
articulations of violence, all of which immanently worked out and
through the equally varying acts of imaging violence performed
by DeNiro. To elaborate on this masocritical intervention further,
I will turn in the final chapter to the *problématique* of response-
ability as a pedagogical ethics of violence rather than a representational (moral) response to violence.

6 Don DeLillo's "In the Ruins of the Future"

Violence, Pedagogy, and the Rhetoric of Seeing 9/11

On the morning of September 12, 2001, I was scheduled to teach an American studies mass lecture course on "Violence in Twentieth-Century American Culture." Like most people, I had spent the previous day glued to the television, trying to catch as great a variety of coverage of the events of 9/11 as possible. The next day, at 9 a.m., I approached my classroom with a considerable amount of trepidation. I knew from some colleagues that I would have the option to cancel class, allowing students to seek grief counseling or other means of finding emotional comfort and support. Yet, though I did not know what exactly I should or would do in class that morning, somehow I felt that canceling class was never an option for me—due in large part to the subject matter of my course. After all, *I* was supposed to be the one who had something intelligent to say about violence in the context of American culture.

After explaining to my students that they would be excused if they preferred to leave, I tentatively directed our attention to the attacks of the previous day. While I expected that my students might not be willing to engage in a discussion of the events so soon, I discovered that they were only all too eager to address this violent event, having themselves already engaged in hours-long conversations with their friends and families for the past twenty-four hours. More precisely, I found out that they wanted *me* to address the events. As one student plainly put it, they were hoping that *I*, the teacher, would tell *them* what the events of 9/11 "mean." A bit stunned by their demand that I provide them with the meaning of the event, I had no choice but to refuse to comply with their touching request, not least because I did not know myself what to make of the attacks. Rather than pretending that I would have a coherent explanation, I instead suggested that as a class we might do well to take seriously our collective *inability* to articulate—for ourselves as well as to one other—in coherent fashion the "meaning" of 9/11.

That is, I prodded students to heed our discussions of some of the material we had covered in class up until this moment—materials that in their collective force offered us various tools for thinking about violence (about what it is, what it does, why it happens, etc.); specifically, I suggested that we might want to take seriously our shared *sense* of uncertainty in response to depictions of violence in texts as varied as, for instance, Dashiell Hammett's *Red Harvest* (1929), William Wellman's *Public Enemy* (1931), *The Autobiography of Malcolm X* (1965), Sylvia Plath's poem "Daddy" (1965), or hip-hop songs by Public Enemy and N.W.A. In response to the question of what we are supposed to make of these various versions of violence, more often than not our responses tended to be that it is anything but easy to come to terms with them precisely because of the way the violent images function and are deployed in these texts. Thinking, for example, about the function of violence in Plath's poetic language, Malcolm X's prose account of his brutal life experiences, or Public Enemy's revolutionary lyrics set to violently grating soundscapes complicated any attempt to simply condemn violence wholesale.

Over the course of the next few class sessions, I kept returning to our sensation of uncertainty or doubt. I argued that we might very well be on our way to develop a productive response to 9/11 by affirming the very fact that we simply do not know what to make of the event. I further proposed that our situation was not so much defined by a lack of response but by the fact that we had already responded: our response, it turned out, was simply expressed in and by our collective sense of uncertainty. And interestingly, the very existence, let alone acknowledgment, of this lack of certainty had in itself, as one student confessed, the effect of something akin to an instance of violence. Affirming one's sense of uncertainty, hesitating in the face of what appears to call forth an unproblematic judgment, and deferring a quick emotional fix in light of tragedy, so we discovered, is invested with real affective force. That is, we sensed the violence of sensation, as well as the sensation of violence, notwithstanding the fact that at that moment we were collectively unable to represent the event in form of a coherent narrative. What this particular student expressed to us, I later came to understand, is precisely what Patricia Highsmith's fiction teaches us: that it is not at all easy *not* to respond to violence without seeking immediate recourse to judgment (or, in more general terms, categories that are familiar to us). Differently put, *not* immediately judging an instance of "obvious" violence that appears to be calling for nothing but quick and determined judgment shifts one's own intensive investments from one register to another—the violent rush experienced by asserting a stance of moral righteousness to the violent vertigo experienced by an encounter with one's self as not always already being in control (however illusory such a sense of control may actually be). It was the difference between these two levels of intensity and, perhaps, the very unfamiliarity with the latter that instilled in us a very real sense of (one's sense of self) being violated precisely because the event itself enforced upon us the violence of sensation.

Instead of telling students "what's what," then, I worked with them to see whether we may actually have something to gain from deferring such responses. (I should hasten to say, however, that we did discuss more sociohistorically oriented explanations of the event—explanations that, to my mind, have considerable force. Nevertheless, despite the compelling quality of such explanations, students were not "satisfied" with them, since they did not get rid of their sense of affective uncertainty.) For a brief while, at least, I felt that my students and I managed to encounter 9/11 by practicing such a state of suspense. For a brief moment, that is, I think we managed to create a collective space in which we encountered a very real moment of violence without reducing it to its representational quality or to a self-help discourse dominated by expressions of subjective experience.

Masochistically suspending, however momentarily, the demand for understanding performatively confronted us with a very real moment of violence: namely, the affective violence of uncertainty. My point here is of course that these are two incommensurable moments of violence: the frustration and pain involved in not knowing how to respond is not at all the same as the pain experienced by the real victims of 9/11 and their friends and families. But the affective state induced by suspending the moment of certainty constituted an angle of entry, or line of flight, into the event that almost by necessity forced us to heed its specificity, its primacy—something we accomplished precisely by deferring our most immediate demands and desires (which, in the end, are mostly about us rather than about the other).

By masochistically intensifying the moment of uncertainty (rather than relieving it by providing an answer, however convincing), we were collectively forced to give ourselves over to a moment of violence, namely, the violence of sensation. Far from being representative of, let alone identical to, the violence of 9/11, our affective encounter with the violence of sensation—embodied in our sense of uncertainty—was productive, I think, because it performatively emphasized the very *difference* of these two forms of violence, while nevertheless exemplifying how they relate to each other. The latter form of violence was nothing "like" the former, but in its very dissimilarity—because of its arepresentational quality—our masochistically habituated encounter with the affective violence of uncertainty allowed us to aim at this other form of violence. Neither positing the violence of 9/11 as "incomprehensible" nor reducing it to a representational resemblance, our pedagogical, masocritical encounter with the event was characterized by maintaining the interval between two different degrees of violence, which, though infinitely different, are crucially related *in* this very sensation of difference. In short, however intuitively and with however much ad hoc coaching on my part, we tried to affirm our response-ability—the fact that we always already respond and are response-able to the event—by means of *suspending* and thus reconfiguring the most clichéd habits of response, namely, the tendency to territorialize the primacy of the object or event onto the plane of subjective familiarity and knowledge.

Of course, much of what I just described is now filtered through twenty-twenty hindsight and reflection on my part. Undoubtedly, the reality of my classroom practice in those first ten days or so after 9/11 did not operate on such high theoretical grounds. Yet, getting my students to experiment with this notion of suspense and thus frustrating their expectations of themselves and me did, I believe, expose all of us to an encounter with violence on its own terms—without having to "experience" its most terrible manifestations, just like Robert DeNiro does not have to "experience" how it feels to shoot someone or getting shot at himself in order to enact cinematic violence. If this is indeed what transpired, then I consider this brief period a pedagogical success.

Yet, the fragility of my pedagogical success became clear to me soon after George W. Bush's address to the nation—a rhetorically powerful speech in which he offered with remarkable clarity and force his response to my students' initial desire to be told what to make of 9/11. According to the president, the matter was, and still is, quite simple: 9/11 is nothing more, and nothing less, than a matter of good and evil. And while it may be easy to belittle such a seemingly simplifying response to the (either merely assumed or real) complexity of 9/11, it is impossible to deny the rhetorical effect of this declaration, as I quickly witnessed in the context of my classroom space. Whereas a great number of students initially had gone along with my attempt to defer judgments such as those eventually offered by the forty-third president of the United States, this willingness began quickly to disappear once the force of Bush's rhetoric took hold of the larger public discourse on 9/11. Increasingly, the very students who had initially given themselves over to experimenting with suspending judgment embraced with considerable conviction just such judgments; in my view, this change of attitude occurred to the great detriment of our collective ability to continue our discussion of the issue on a level of complexity that I believe is necessary for any discussion about violence if it is to serve any purpose other than moralistic proselytizing.

Lest I ever thought of myself as an überteacher, the effect of the presidential pronouncement made it painfully clear to me of just how difficult it actually is to habituate and sustain a mode of response to violence that not only defers familiar clichés but, *in* deferring, actually arrives at a moment of lasting, indeed perpetual, transformation of our very ability to respond to violence. Just as Highsmith must have struggled not only with developing but also sustaining a mode of response to violence that does not immediately operate on the plane of judgment, so I experienced firsthand on a pedagogical level how difficult it is to affect others with a style of response to violence that violates habitual or "common sense" modes of response that we have internalized as a result of institutional processes. Of course, I am not suggesting that my students failed where I succeeded; doing so would presuppose that there is a right way of responding, which, in turn, presupposes the primacy of the very representational regime that I have attempted to slow down throughout this project. Quite obviously, a multiplicity of forces affects the ways we respond, which is why response is always a question of singularity. My point here is simply to acknowledge the difficulty of *not* surrendering to the rhetorical seduction of the language of judgment that we are all exposed to all the time. Hence, to me the pedagogical task is to find ways of suspending the desire to give in to that seduction, however briefly, as a means to experiment with what happens when the clichés of responsibility are reconfigured from within the demand that one must judge an event such as 9/11 as *response-ability* (ethics).

↓

The purpose of this personal narrative was not to solicit sympathy from my readers for the predicament I faced; nor did I mean to present myself as someone who was properly humbled and thus divested of any notion that I may own all the solutions to the *problématique* of violence. For even if I had once felt that I possessed sufficient answers, the experience of teaching this course made it perfectly clear—if I had ever been in doubt—that having the answers does by no means guarantee that anyone else will be affected by them, just like Caspar's proprietary version of ethics in the Coen Brothers' *Miller's Crossing* was anything but a guarantee for keeping violence at bay.

No, the purpose of this brief narrative was to raise a question that surely should concern those of us who (still) teach literature and film—a question that is equally pressing today as it was in the immediate aftermath of 9/11. In its most basic form, this question is simply about the value of teaching literature and film. At a time when our collective (un)consciousness understandably preoccupies itself with what at least *appear* to be events of era-defining proportions, it seems to me that one could be excused for wondering how (the teaching of) literature and film could still be relevant to events that seem to have little if anything to do with the writing, reading, viewing, and producing of images. September 11, 2001, one might be inclined to argue, exposed film and literature classes as highly questionable deployments of sociocultural energies. Discussions of authorial or directorial intentions, characters' psychology, texts' representational veracity, and the always popular debates about the "meaning" of it all—these and many other typical academic discussion foci may appear now as, at best, soothing diversions from the realities of life; at worst, teaching literature or film in a time of crisis may seem like the self-indulgent privilege of an intellectual elite whose practices bear little relevance for the "real" world. Likewise, institutionally reinforced claims for the subversive force of this novel, that film, or the critical readings themselves increasingly assume the shape of deluded solipsisms made by those wishing their practices had a more tangible impact on the world. And there appears to be no obvious reason for excluding this present study—one that has focused only on literary and cinematic texts—from this suspicion of irrelevance. Put differently, after 9/11 one might argue that students and teachers—indeed, all citizens—would be better off studying history and political economy rather than reading fiction or watching movies.[1] Or, to paraphrase one of my students during the immediate aftermath of 9/11, why bother with the fictional when reality itself provides more than enough challenges? Rather than engaging imaginary violence, should a study such as this one not concern itself with the causes and effects of real-world violence such as, for instance, spousal abuse, rape, murder, terrorism, or war?

Perhaps.

My hesitation here is meant to acknowledge the obvious importance of analyzing, for instance, the historical transformations Islamic and Western cultures have undergone in response to capitalist processes that have by now all but mapped themselves onto the entire earth. Nevertheless, I want to argue *for* the space of film and literature because I think they bear the *pedagogical* potential for activating an *ethical* mode of encounter with violence. In order to show that the space of literature and film indeed provides a productive linkage to the question of real-world violence, I would like to conclude this study with an extended discussion of one specific writerly response to the violence of 9/11: Don DeLillo's essay "In the Ruins of the Future," which appeared in *Harper's Magazine* in December 2001. What I am going to suggest in these remaining pages, then, pertains to the question of how a pedagogical engagement with (contemporary) image events of violence might performatively provoke an encounter with the unfolding of the consequences of 9/11 that heeds the event's "irreducible singularity" (Baudrillard, "Spirit of Terrorism"), something that can be argued to be conspicuously absent from most engagements with this event. The role of engaging the questions of how images work and what they do, I shall argue, requires now, more than ever, an *"aesthetic stance,"* to use Nietzsche's phrase ("Truth and Lying" 252, my emphasis).

In the Ruins of the Event: Suspension No. 1

In the first few months after 9/11, *Harper's Magazine* asked Don DeLillo to write an essay on the terrorist attack. That *Harper's* asked the author of novels such as *Players* (1977), *White Noise* (1985), *Libra* (1988), or *Mao II* (1991) is hardly accidental, for "terrorism has played an important part in nearly every novel [he] has written to date" (Allen). Indeed, "terror, like an airborne toxic event, floats across the deceptively shiny surfaces of DeLillo's fiction" (Scanlan 229) and often manifests itself in his examination of the writer-terrorist relationship.[2] The appearance of DeLillo's essay in the December issue made it one of the earliest nonjournalistic, yet analytical responses given to the events of September 11, 2001. However, what makes the essay truly remarkable is not merely what it says about 9/11 but how, *in responding to* the event, it simultaneously puts the notion of response at stake. Resisting the demand to speak with moral clarity and declare what the event "means," his essay instead shows that response is always a question of response-ability, or the ethical *how*. DeLillo stylistically configures response-ability as always and necessarily a question of how rather than what, (e)valuation rather than representation, the power of the false rather than the regime of truth. What DeLillo's response thus teaches us— its most significant intervention in the post-9/11 discourse—is that present-day attempts to image an (traumatic) event's sense cannot possibly operate exclusively on the level of its content (the representational "what") without attending to the *rhetorical* mode of presentation, the ethical "how." Or rather, what DeLillo shows, and what I will elaborate on, is that what an event means is always already shot through with how it appears. If anything, it is this very insight that I hope to have performed and illustrated throughout this masocritical study when examining how specific texts themselves confront the *problématique* of violence and how to respond to its various degrees of intensity.

DeLillo's style of response does not occur in a vacuum, however. Rather, his narrative encounter with 9/11 actualizes a mode of *seeing* the world that the French cineaste André Bazin once conceptualized in terms of an ontophenomenological theory of cinema. Bazin advocates a film aesthetic mainly relying on the long shot, deep focus cinematography characteristic of the neorealist mise-en-scène. Countering earlier realisms, especially Sergei Eisenstein's influential theory of dialectical montage, as "making reality the servant of some a priori point of view," Bazin favors a cinematic aesthetic stance toward reality that artfully responds to the world image in its "wholeness" (2:64, 97).[3] The event's wholeness, however, is not posited as a transcendent category; instead, the cinematic stance mobilized by, for instance, Luchino Visconti, Roberto Rossellini, or Vittorio De Sica "divide[s] the event up into still smaller events and these into events smaller still, to the extreme *limits* of our capacity to *perceive* them in time" (Bazin 2:81, my emphases). For Bazin, perception itself is up for grabs, since his theory of cinema—as a theory of vision—ultimately concerns the very limits of perception as a concept. Whereas phenomenology begins and ends with conceiving the subject as the locus for and horizon of perception, Bazin theorizes the very limit at which the perceptive act transmutes into an act of *seeing*—a mode of response to the world that, in Bazin's hands, puts the perceiving subject at stake.[4] *Seeing*, in other words, is less a matter of (in)correct perception than a question of how subjects can respond to events.

Bazin suggests that modes of seeing inhere in events rather than originate in a perceiving subject. However, inhering does not connote a previously existing authenticity of the event so much as posit point of view as a relation of force, as an effect of the event's actualization. As Claire Colebrook argues, "any specific point of view is not a point of view overlooking some object world, but a proliferation of points, a pre-personal field of singularities" (111). She writes that, consequently, "perspective and point of view are enabled by style. Style is not the expression of the human point of view; the human is an effect of a certain style" (113). For Bazin, the event does not contain a truth to be uncovered or recovered. Hence, abstracting clichés from the event to push it to its

extreme limits necessarily precedes the need for structuring images through dialectical montage processes. Whereas Eisenstein
assumes an a priori emptiness of the screen that must be filled
with dialectically ordered images arranged from a preexisting
human vantage point, Bazin's cinema thought implies that the
screen *virtually* is filled with images even before the film projector
plays what the camera's eye has artfully "captured." The neorealist
mise-en-scène's task is, therefore, to abstract images stylistically
from the fullness of the screen.[5] This mise-en-scène thus renders
visible the event as nothing but a conjunction of singular view-
points preceding the objects to be viewed.

Dialectical montage cannot help but begin with subordinating
the event to a subject's point of view—first to the director's and
then to the subjected viewer's. In contrast, the neorealist visual
process of abstracting images actualizes from the event modes of
seeing that take the latter elsewhere: *seeing* as a rhetorical actualization of futurity rather than a perceptive capturing of an event's
inherent authenticity, which is then offered for judgment, *seeing*
as an experimental mode—not as creative discovery of what is
but as an ethical production of the yet to come.

Instead of the thesis-driven mode of inducing conscious perception through dialectical montage, DeLillo, as we will see, mobilizes a neorealist aesthetic that Bazin calls "a phenomenology"
(2:65), which holds "more an ontological position than an aesthetic one" (2:66). The differentiated modes of seeing constitute
a subject's point of view or mode of experience. Thus, an aesthetic
stance that responds to the event a subject encounters must be
considered first and foremost ontological in nature. Yet, at the
heart of Bazin's answer to the question "What is cinema?" lies the
way this ontology is *engaged*—the way it is (made to be) viewed
through artifice. For Bazin, the ontology of seeing consists of
myriad different modes of seeing. These modes, or force relations, continually become image events that eventually manifest
themselves through how specific subjected viewers actualize—
(are made to) see—them. Hence, if cinema desires to encounter
reality, it has no choice but to begin from within the acts of see-

ing. Bazin can therefore claim that the neorealist aesthetic stance "knows only immanence" (64). This aesthetic stance begins and ends in the middle, positions the act of viewing amidst the event's force relations, and, leaving the act there, tries to habituate the subject to encountering the middle so that the subject becomes able to *see* the world—itself always a becoming-middle—as it "is" before judging it.

In the Ruins of Epistemology: Suspension No. 2

To suspend judgment of the world and to restore our "belief in this world," as Deleuze (*Cinema 2* 172), evoking Bazin, once demanded—this ethical recipe ultimately generates the paradox of a cinematic realism that is profoundly aesthetic.[6] Producing realism in order to render visible the world's ontological wholeness without immediately capturing the world on the plane of judgment "can only be achieved in one way—through artifice" (Bazin 2:26). Cinema must *aesthetically* extract from the world its most constitutive material processes—acts of seeing. The notion of "masochistic freezing" might best describe this process of extracting and is perhaps most famously rendered at the end of Francois Truffaut's *The Four Hundred Blows* (1959), when the sudden zoom-in-on-freeze-frame image of the film's youthful protagonist, Antoine (Jean Pierre Leaud), lucidly, indeed clinically, puts into questioning, masocritical suspense that which he, as well as the viewer, sees or has seen.[7]

The absence of such an aesthetic stance—configured in and as an effect of such a process of masochistic freezing—perhaps explains why *9/11*, the documentary by the French brothers Jules and Gédéon Naudet, while haunting in its own right, comes across as "being there" almost too much, in the sense that the film's images capture the moment of terror so well as to foreclose response-ability that does not begin and end with what the viewing subject already knows. The film offers images for our perception that do not further our capacity to see the event in a manner different from the ways we have perceived it before. At best—and this is no small accomplishment—the documentary intensifies existing feelings of horror as we hear falling bodies impact the ground with a fatal thump. Ultimately, however, the film seems to reinforce rather than transform, perhaps because it does not risk the question of *seeing* itself. It does not see that, as Deleuze puts it, the "difference *in* the origin does not appear *at* the origin—except perhaps to a particularly practiced eye, the eye which sees from afar, the eye of the far-sighted, the eye of the genealogist" (*Nietzsche and Philosophy* 5).

In contrast, DeLillo's writerly eye concerns itself with these rhetorical acts of imaging and seeing. Indeed, DeLillo's literary eye, in its attentiveness to the question of imaging, actualizes the neorealist conception of seeing as articulated by Bazin, thus crucially transforming (the image of) the event 9/11.[8] Always the astute observer of contemporary narrative possibilities and necessities, DeLillo shows that literary language does not remain unaffected by the language of visuality that has encroached upon the public throughout the twentieth century.[9] Crucially, however, DeLillo—unlike countless commentators who argued that 9/11 was "like" a Hollywood disaster flick—does not have recourse to the language of images as a simile or metaphor. Instead, imaging processes propel his narrative to "analyze [reality] in a cinematic way" (Virilio, *War and Cinema* 65), although his medium of expression remains language.[10] While his "reflections on terror and loss in the shadow of September," as the essay's subtitle states, alternate in eight sections between more abstract, perhaps more "properly" essayistic musings and detailed, almost impressionistic (imaginary?) lists of stories emerging from the attack on the World Trade Center, DeLillo's language performs the meandering look of the neorealist camera eye, following no narrative in particular, yet many at once, thus intensifying the very experience and concept of narrative as a mode of *seeing*.

Unlike the dialectical desire to perceive—or capture—reality representationally to alter it, DeLillo's narrative strategy intervenes in the world by *seeing*, or rhetorically (re)inventing, it, which is why his encounter with 9/11 has nothing to do with a lack of the Real, either in the Kantian or Lacanian sense.[11] The essay invents a view of reality that invites readers to shape and reshape reality into different impressions of equal value, which combine to a speculative series: this happened and this and this *and* . . . .[12] Thus, the essay attempts rhetorically to position the readers so that they become capable of *seeing* that which cannot be perceived in the event's endless televised images—images that through their proliferations first intensified the public's affective responses to a point of utter confusion ("What happened?" "Why?" "What am I supposed to think?") before this affect found itself territorialized onto the plane of judgment, of "correct" perception (George W. Bush's "the evil ones"). Operating alongside and within television's powerful perceptual apparatus of capture in order to mutate its most mind-numbing and moralizing effects, DeLillo's essay instead allows the event to emerge with a "crystalline ambiguity," to use a phrase Lawrence Weschler (qtd. in Taylor 3) once ascribed to Art Spiegelman's graphic novel *Maus* (1986)—also an attempt to render the singularity of an irreducible event.[13] DeLillo's essay lucidly responds to the mood of 9/11 and to its aftermath—without reducing it to a simple explanation or meaning—by mobilizing *seeing* as a narrative mode that works from within the image event instead of imposing itself on it. Yet, the essay does not avoid montage; rather, its splicing together of various images, stories, and styles of narrating the event provides an artificial means to serialize the ontological eventness of 9/11. In so doing, the essay shifts from the epistemological register of the post-9/11 public discourse to an ethico-ontological register that primarily addresses how an event demands its own mode of response.

A compelling pedagogical consequence for teachers of literary and cinematic images, DeLillo's essay posits alongside all other ruins the ruins of a version of literary and film studies that continues to pretend that it can protect itself from the world. I am thinking here, for instance, of Valentine Cunningham's *Reading after Theory* in which the author goes to bat for the primacy of

texts over all theorizing about them because "theory does violence to the meanings of texts" (88). While Cunningham's argument against the "anything goes" (82) practice of theory is well
taken, his solution—*tact*fully to protect the *meanings* present in a
text by heeding the "presence, the rights, the needs of the human
subjects, in texts, in the originations of texts, in the reception
of texts" (142)—strikes me as symptomatic of the very problem
from which literary and film studies suffers to begin with: namely,
the ongoing configuration of signaletic material as well as reading
and viewing practices in terms of signification, representation,
and meaning. It is surely no coincidence that his discussion of the
history of theory all but ignores Deleuze, the one post-structuralist thinker who cannot at all be said to conceive of language and
images representationally.[14]

Concurrent to positing the ruins of this type of critical approach, DeLillo's essay also insists that social constructivism does
not suffice as an ethical mode of encountering images, since to
assert that everything is socially constructed comprises merely
one more instance of declaring the "whatness" of an event. (One
might also point out that social constructivism is itself socially
constructed, something that is frequently overlooked by propo-
nents of social constructivism.) Deploying images as response-
able to (rather than for) the world, DeLillo's essay leans hard on
Kathy Acker's argument that "*to write* should be *to write the world*
and, simultaneously, *to engage the world*": instead of protecting
itself from its responsibility to the world or merely showing how
something is socially constructed, "In the Ruins of the Future"
renders the event *otherwise*, subjunctively—masocritically—
submitting microversions of the event without insisting on their
ultimate veracity. This rendering otherwise with its attending diagnostic rhythms and movements echoes those of Highsmith's
career-long attempt at getting at the relation between judgment
and violence through repeatedly testing that relation in a series
of microcases; DeLillo's rendering otherwise also resonates with
DeNiro's actorly practice that is characterized by a continual
variation of his own enactments of screen violence as a means

to release the multiple forces permeating both the sensation of violence and the violence of sensation. All these examples perform what I have been calling masocriticism—something that I too have been trying to practice, throughout this book as well as in this chapter, with its digressions and tentative efforts to approximate, to approach the event of 9/11 through DeLillo's essayistic response to it.

In the Ruins of Point of View: Suspending Plots

Perhaps the most important aspect of DeLillo's engagement with 9/11 is his alternating between various narrative points of view. Indeed, the essay is overtly preoccupied with the question of how to narrate and thus *see* the event itself. Note, for instance, his countless uses of "narrative," "story," and "counter-narrative" when naming the event and the possibility of responding to it. DeLillo's essay even invokes the need for us to respond to the event by actively rewriting it. The cold war narrative favored by the Bush administration "ends in the rubble, and it is left to us to create the counter-narrative" (34), DeLillo writes, prefacing the random, fleeting impressions he then proceeds to list: "There are a hundred thousand stories crisscrossing New York, Washington, and the world. Where we were, whom we know, what we've seen or heard. There are the doctors' appointments that saved lives, the cell phones that were used to report the hijackings. Stories generating others and people running north out of the rumbling smoke and ash. Men running in suits and ties, women who'd lost their shoes, cops running from the skydive of all that towering steel" (34). But it is not enough simply to give voice to the "stories of heroism and encounters with dread" (34), though they do form part of the process of creating a counter-narrative: "These are among the smaller objects and more marginal stories in the sifted ruins of the day. We need them, even the common tools of the terrorists, to set against the massive spectacle that continues to seem unmanageable, too powerful a thing to set into our frame of practiced response" (35), or what he later calls "slant of our perceptions" (39). The ultimate task is precisely to alter "our frame of practiced response." For only by doing so, the essay suggests, do we stand a chance of encountering 9/11 as a singular event without having recourse to what Foucault and Deleuze dub the "indignity of speaking for others" ("Intellectuals and Power" 209). Speaking "for" others too often serves as a disguise for speaking one's own point of view, thus eradicating that which is other. That is, DeLillo's stance here suggests the necessity of altering our capacity to respond.

The essay tries masocritically to induce in the reader a certain kind of response-ability through rhetorically intensifying its narrative rhythm. It alternates between what appears to be a dialectical movement of impressionistic close-ups of the event and distanced, intellectual analyses of what happened—but without ever arriving at a resolution of this movement. If the rhythm of DeLillo's essay can be described as dialectical, then only in the sense of Theodor Adorno's *Negative Dialectics*, which proceeds "immanently" (5) or chiasmically, casting event and response as immanent to each other.[15] In short, DeLillo's essay deploys a style of response—an ethic of movement—that appears to emerge from within the rubble of images circulating around the events of 9/11: this, then this, then this, *then* . . . , serializing itself ever further into the event's materiality.

Thus, the essay functions as a transformative relay that provokes responses to the event by mobilizing a specific aesthetic stance that does not pretend to do justice to it—even if the event is (necessarily) available for a discourse of justice. The essay presents merely an asignifying series of images rather than a series of just, or moral, images, to paraphrase Jean-Luc Godard, a cinematic "seer" influenced by Bazin. That is, as Deleuze glosses Godard's slogan "Pas une image juste, juste une image," "a 'just image' is an image that exactly corresponds to what it is taken to represent; but if we take images as 'just [a series of] images,' we see them precisely as images, rather than correct or incorrect representations of anything" (*Negotiations* 190n1). In this sense,

DeLillo's image events resonate aesthetically and ethically with those of neorealist cinema: faced with the impossibility yet necessity of responding to events that exceed immediate explanation, both kinds enact their response-ability to show how intensively inhabiting—suspending—an event can bring ethical responsibility to it.

Unlike most 9/11 documentaries, which establish their trustworthiness by giving voice to personal experience—something that tends to lie outside evaluation—DeLillo's essay rhetorically affects his readers by not allowing them to trust any of his narrative voices as qualified to do justice to the event. Ostensibly nonfiction that generically requires the writer to tell it as it is (or, in any case, not to make up false stories), it commences innocuously enough by situating 9/11 seemingly objectively in the last decades' globalization processes. But even in this first section, the third person account is already complicated by its explicit juxtaposing of different narratives—the West's and the terrorists': "In the past decade the surge of capital markets has dominated discourse and shaped global consciousness. Multinational corporations have come to seem more vital and influential than governments. [. . .] Terror's response is a narrative that has been developing over years, only now becoming inescapable. It is *our* lives and minds that are occupied now" (33). Whereas in 1976 Wim Wenders's film *Kings of the Road* could postulate that the "Yankees have even colonized [Germany's] unconsciousness" through relentlessly proliferating popular culture images, thus giving voice to a perceived movement of colonialism even within the so-called First World, the situation, at least from a U.S. standpoint, has now crucially changed. Although the United States continues to circulate images—at a greater pace than ever—DeLillo writes that it is now "our world, parts of our world, that have crumbled into theirs, which means we are living in a place of danger and rage" (33): "they" are now colonizing "us."

But this juxtaposition does not hold. Section 2 of the essay immediately narrates a different kind of story. Instead of affirming the dialectical us versus them rhetoric that was encroaching on the essay—First World versus Third World, United States of America versus the Taliban, West versus East, globalism versus tribalism—DeLillo narrates that the terrorist "planted in a Florida town, pushing a supermarket cart" (34) is not affected by the "sight of a woman pushing a stroller" (34) because "he does not *see* her" (34, my emphasis). Incomprehensible to most of "us," the terrorist does not see the woman and is thus not touched by the image's affective impact—because he exists in a different narrative "format" (34) and mood that differ from ours. Whereas "our" narrative format has a logical plot (think classical Hollywood cinema), the terrorist pursues the "apocalypse" (34)—a narrative where logic and understanding, or knowledge, have no purchase on the event. Thus, DeLillo's narrative intimates, the dialectic of recognition that permeates public debates of 9/11 does not hold as an explanatory apparatus because the other does not even acknowledge—is not capable of acknowledging—our self. The other bypasses us. The terrorist's self is already other to our concept of the self; the terrorist's self is non-self-identical to itself: the I of the self is always already an other.[16]

DeLillo's competing narratives suggest that attacking the other's self is bound to fail from the beginning because that self does not exist as we configure it. "We" can bomb "them" out of their caves, but their selves have already mutated into something else, fleeing to a different location, even if these selves have yet to be produced: "For many people, the event has changed the grain of the most routine moment. We may find that the ruin of the towers is implicit in other things. The new PalmPilot at fingertip's reach, the stretch limousine parked outside the hotel, the midtown skyscraper under construction, carrying the name of a major investment bank—all haunted in a way by what has happened, less assured in their authority, in their prerogatives they offer" (39). The other has already become other to itself: it now percolates within "us" and our technology, effecting transformations within "us" that cannot help altering the very possibility for eradicating "them."

DeLillo has always been an untimely writer. His fiction re-

sponds to specific social events by articulating their future transformations and effects, actualizing the as of yet virtual future,
which is, in the Bergsonian sense articulated by Deleuze in *Bergsonism* (chapter 4) and *Cinema 2* (chapter 4), always copresent
with the present itself. The developments of the so-called war on
terror since 9/11 tragically proved once again DeLillo's qualities
as a prescient seer: as confirmed by the attacks on London in the
summer of 2005, for instance, the terrorists are not "them" but
"us"—in our midst, homegrown, nationals of the very country
they attack, just like DeLillo suggested merely a few months after 9/11. The great failure of the "war on terror" has been its inability up until recently to conceive of terrorism as a viral war
machine. Terrorism was *always* a decentralized operative force;
what has changed since 9/11 is only that this constitutive decen-
tralization has intensified *in response to* the war on it. Any hit on
any one of its cells generates others elsewhere because the very
cell structure of terrorism is constituted *differentially*, similar to
Eisenstein's theory of montage, which insists that a "shot is [not]
an *element* of montage [but] is a montage *cell*" (37), propelling the
entire montage system forward by internal conflict and collision,
just like a combustion engine moves the car from *within* rather
than without.

To put this in a slightly different register that is nevertheless
central to DeLillo's essay, 9/11 has also destroyed the neoliberal
dream of globalization as citizen-consumer utopia. The event has,
in a certain sense, brought back tribal forces, but this reintroduction of tribal power is, as Michael Hardt and Antonio Negri's *Empire* illustrates, not so much a return than an intensification of
globalization itself. Globalization is not opposed to what media
pundits demean as "medievalism," nor is it a progressive movement away from medievalism, as we are continually assured. On
the contrary, globalization is infused with and affected by medievalism, constituting its most intensified moment yet: the global
self is always already the tribal other going global.[17]

However, the reader is ultimately not asked to take this analysis at face value, as if it represented the meaning or truth oozing

from the event. Quite simply, the event cannot be reduced to an atmosphere of mass paranoia à la *X-Files* narratives in which the protagonists must always fear that their bodies have already been injected with alien corpuscles. For paranoia is simply the most comforting narrative available in response to trauma, positing the self as persecuted by the outside, the other.[18] The other serves as the explanatory force par excellence to reinforce the self as a self-contained entity that controls itself by suspecting everything else. But paranoia is just another plot, and, as DeLillo asserts in what might be taken to be his thesis (if having a thesis were not to go against his essay's performative, pedagogical force), "Plots reduce the world" (34). Plots reduce the world because the act of plotting constitutes the virtual seed of destruction: to wit, al-Quaeda's plotting ended in the planes' perfectly staged and executed double impact on the twin towers. Thus, DeLillo's essay does not plot an explanation that would offer readers a safe reconstitution of the world; instead, the essay indicates that plot constitutively partakes in the problem, as a "vision of judgment" (34) preceding the event. And what else is judgment if not a world-reducing plot?

But plots also reduce the world because they can be easily explained and used as explanations for "evil." For instance, in Oliver Stone's *JFK* (1991), the "plotting" reduction of the president's assassination to a tightly knit conspiracy scheme serves as a seemingly compelling yet ultimately simplistic explanation of the "evil" done; conversely, the conspiracy plot itself promises to be explainable simply by locating those involved in the plot. In stark contrast, James Ellroy's novel *American Tabloid* (1997) engages JFK's assassination not by reducing the event to *one* plot but by amplifying the very idea of plot itself: "You want plot? I'll give you plot!" so the book seems to declare in bold tabloid letters as it provides the reader with hundreds of them. Consequently, reading Ellroy's novel does not leave one with the impression that figuring out "what" happened will lead to an understanding of "why" it happened; instead, by intensifying the very idea of plot(ting), the novel subjects the reader to the provocation that the *belief* in plots is itself a problem rather than a solution. Or rather, both DeLillo's essay and Ellroy's "response" to Stone's *JFK* show that plots inevitably reduce the world; indeed, as DeLillo has reiterated throughout his work, they "tend to move deathward" (*White Noise* 26) or, again, "move toward death" (*Libra* 221).

That plots reduce the world also on a phenomenological level is dramatized by Richard Grossman's brilliant experimental novel *The Alphabet Man*.[19] The plot of the 420-page narrative about a schizophrenic poet/killer can be summarized in one paragraph, which the novel itself eventually provides us on page 426, that (seemingly) clearly maps out what happened to whom and why. Yet the very fact that the plot summary *succeeds* 420 pages of narration does not so much indicate the sadism of the author or narrator who relishes the thought of having frustrated readers with this weird, violent, and confusing narrative only to mock them with a straightforward account of it. Rather, concisely stating the plot calls attention to the very fact that readers' *experience* of reading the novel cannot be summarily accounted for through having recourse to plot as an explanatory mechanism—just as the deployment of the moral category of "evil" does not sum up the experience of the public's initial *affective* response to the event of 9/11. The intensifying vertigo induced through the novel's structure and all its aesthetic narrative devices, in addition to the obscure content, which is ostensibly a mystery story, has continually affected the reader so that she does not know where she is at any given time in the narrative. The reader is other to herself at any moment, just as the novel's main character, the psychotic Clyde, is continually other to himself in psychosis. To name the plot is thus not merely the least interesting thing to say about the novel but it fundamentally misses the affective intensity generated for readers by the encounter with, that is, *in* the reading of, the text.

That plots reduce the world, however, is not a problem in itself. Rather, what counts is the *style* of reduction. *JFK* reduces the event of November 22, 1963 to an "explanation" thereof, whereas *American Tabloid* and "In the Ruins of the Future" "reduce" their respective events to their most intensified moments, abstract them. Thus we read in DeLillo's essay, "The cell phones, the lost shoes, the handkerchiefs mashed in the faces of running men and women. The box cutters and credit cards. The paper that came streaming out of the towers and drifted across the river to Brooklyn back yards: status reports, résumés, insurance forms. Sheets of paper driven into concrete, according to witnesses. Paper slicing into truck tires, fixed there" (35). DeLillo's essay takes these reduced events to their limits: "*a* pregnant woman, *a* newborn, *a* dog" (37, my emphases). Deleuze and Guattari call these limits "haecceities"—verbs in the infinitive, proper names, dates, indefinite articles—which "consist entirely of relations of movement and rest between molecules or particles, capacities to affect and be affected" (*Thousand Plateaus* 261). A haecceity names the event because it "has neither beginning nor end, origin nor destination; it is always in the middle. It is not made of points, only of lines. It is a rhizome" (263). In DeLillo's asubjective, amorphous space of narrative serialization, *seeing* is itself rhetorically actualized from within the event and away from the territorializing force of subjective and subjectifying acts of explanation based on "truthful" perceptions. Thus, DeLillo's haecceitic narrating begins to render seeable the public's initial affective response to 9/11 and its hallucinatory eliding of expository claims. Differently put, recourse to plot as predominantly an explanatory mechanism of the event's whatness fundamentally misses the point that plot—or systematicity—is itself constituted by affect or intensities, that is, continual variation.[20]

In the Ruins of Analogy: Suspending Likeness

DeLillo's essayistic encounter with 9/11 rigorously teaches us this last point. For while we as readers are inclined to believe that the essay's initial third person account is reasonably objective, the essay quickly undermines this impression. Section 4 narrates the story of Karen and Marc, the first and only proper first names used in the essay.[21] In the essay's rhythm, this new narrative seems a mere close-up, calling our attention to a specific instance among the many stories—for instance, that of the "two women on two planes, best of friends, who die together and apart, Tower 1 and Tower 2" (34), or that of "the saxophonist playing softly" (35)—that were only alluded to earlier. Yet, two-thirds of the way into this section, the narrator undermines our confidence in him. Having just described Marc's actions during the attack (he self-lessly helped other tenants in his building), the narrator states:

> Marc came out to the corridor. I think we *might* die, he told himself, hedging his sense of what would happen next.
> The detective told Karen to stay where they were.
> When the second tower fell, my heart fell with it. I called Marc, who is my nephew, on his cordless. (37)

We are surprised to discover that the narrator has told a much more personal and presumably subjective story than we have been led to believe thus far. Curiously, within a few lines, the narrative voice shifts from third person omniscient to an odd mixture of narrative point of views. Why, for example, does the narrator not say, "He thought he might die" (indirect discourse)? Or, why does the narrator not provide direct discourse (i.e., "'We might die,' he told himself"), as he did in the passage just preceding this one, which describes the moment Marc experiences the unthinkable: "When [Marc] heard the first low drumming rumble, he stood in a strange dead calm and said, 'Something is happening'" (36)? Instead of providing readers with a stable viewpoint—and thus the possibility for identification—the confused narrative perspective calls attention to the sheer impossibility of (identifying with) a clear view of the event. During the disaster, as Karen and Marc come out of the building "into a world of ash and near night" (37), the event itself is impossible to apprehend and yet transforms those responding to—*seeing*—it: "There was no one else to be seen now on the street. Gray ash covering the cars and pavement, ash falling in large flakes [. . .]. The members of the group were masked and toweled, children in adults' arms, moving east

206 Don DeLillo's "In the Ruins of the Future"

and then north on Nassau Street, trying not to look around, only what's immediate, one step and then another, all closely focused, a pregnant woman, a newborn, a dog" (37). The circumstances demand this merging of perspective, not because it promises the possibility of democratic inclusiveness that will explain 9/11, but because the event induces a necessary incorporeal transformation of both itself and the responding subject. Neither event nor subject can be named other than with a date or indefinite articles and pronouns: *something* happened, *a* dog, and, finally, "*Someone* said, 'I don't want cheese on that.' *Someone* said, 'I like it better not so cooked'" (37, my emphases).

The first-person point of view eventually ensuing from this instantaneous transformation displays a remarkable descriptive insight into events it did not witness (the narrator was not in the apartment building when the towers crashed). By this means, the essay stylistically (neorealistically) marks the eventness of the event: it happens or happened and thus requires response, but it does not allow for preexisting subject positions to remain unaffected. Subjects respond because they are made to respond in a particular way, having been subjected to that which cannot be reduced to a preexisting position, a plot's limitations, the truthfulness of a subject's perception, or the ever-present demand for moral clarity.

Eventually, the section shifts back to a third person narration, but by then the narrator's aesthetic devices have induced a delirium that allows us no longer to respond to—or identify with—the essay's standpoint on the level of pure content. We are now trying to "catch up" (39) to what happened to us—to the rhetorical force relations inhering in the event of narrative, or language. If we thought that the narrative, or the multiple mini-narratives, meant to represent a truth about 9/11, then now we cannot have any faith in the veracity of these accounts. If we were tempted to believe that the fleeting counter-narratives would accrue a larger meaning, we are now affectively placed in a position—a becoming-other to one's self—that cuts across the experience the essay is attempting to provoke but not capture. But our experience reading DeLillo's essay is not "like" experiencing 9/11; nor is DeLillo's deployment of narrative mise-en-scène "like" that of the Italian neorealists. Nor is the experience of 9/11 "like" that of Auschwitz or Pearl Harbor, to name the two most unfortunate comparisons that have circulated through the media. Rather, De-Lillo's essay puts likeness at stake. The tower's implosion, so the narrator recounts,

> was so vast and terrible that it was outside imagining even as it happened. We could not catch up to it. But it was real, punishingly so, an expression of the physics of structural limits and a void in one's soul, and there was the huge antenna falling out of the sky, straight down, blunt end first, like an arrow moving backward in time.
>
> The event itself has no purchase on the mercies of analogy or simile. We have to take the shock and horror as it is. (39)[22]

Note the immediate erasure of the narrator's intuitive recourse to that which he asserts lies beyond the event's purview. The event is "like an arrow moving backward in time" only to be not "like" it at all precisely because the event is not reducible to representation: "We have to take the shock and horror *as it is*." This erasure is expressed with the force of an image event, one DeLillo produces by hitting the enter key on the keyboard to create a visual aporia marked by the white space between two paragraphs. So not only does the event have no grasp on the mercies of representational language, but, conversely, these very mercies have no purchase on the event because of its pure singularity. Or, as Deleuze and Guattari contend, an event is not *of* history (i.e., a narrative/plot), though it is born in and falls back into history through the inevitable appropriation of the event's becoming by narrative forces (*What Is Philosophy?* 110).

The point here is not to assert the impossibility of speaking, writing, or knowing; nor is it to suggest that ethics consists of an eternal erasing of the said by the saying. We do not adequately interrogate the event by wondering whether or not to write or speak about it. The movement of DeLillo's essay, its "aesthetic stance," rhetorically, indeed masocritically, images how to become receptive to the response-ability in the event: "Before politics, before history and religion, there is the primal terror. People falling from the towers hand in hand" (39). But there is also the primal force of language. DeLillo's essay tries to heed and render palpable this force or affect—the how, or sensation, of language. The form that response takes becomes the event's content (which is not to downplay or even deny the actual deaths themselves or the destruction of the cityscape), and so this particular mode of response immanently subsists within the event's necessary variability itself. Or, as the essay's narrator affirms, even though the language of representation has no purchase on the event's singularity, "living language is not diminished. [. . .] [L]anguage is inseparable from the world that provokes it. The writer begins in the towers, trying to imagine the moment, desperately" (39, my emphasis). The event has a discursive dimension, exists in and through discourse, even if it is not reducible to language.

Rather than a limitation, however, the event's discursive dimension is the writer's—as well as the director's or critic's—condition of possibility for response-ability. Within the event's virtual but real realm, the language of analogy or simile—representation and judgment—functions as a crucial territorializing force. It is a cliché (i.e., heroes versus villains) that reduces the irreducible to the familiar, or at least to that which we think we know—without ever marking that this knowledge has been cast in representational terms. In contrast, response begins *in* the event. Language immanently inheres and subsists in the event's variability or seriality, which provokes imaging. The problem with the logic of representation as resemblance is that it always positions the responding subject outside the event and so reduces the event to what subjects believe to be their point of view.

Yet, as Richard Powers's response to 9/11 insinuates, while there are no words that represent the event, "there are only words" (22).[23] And while "no comparison can say what happened to us[,] we can start with the ruins of our simile and let 'like' *move* us toward something larger, some understanding of what 'is'" (22, my emphasis). We might be unable to escape the language of similes, analogies, and thus meaning. The interesting aspect of an analogy, however, is not the points to be bridged but its modulation, its movement.[24] To be moved, to become affected—not so much in terms of feeling but in terms of thinking otherwise and being provoked to move elsewhere—constitutes the ethical responsibility of the writer, director, critic, teacher, or anyone else who engages images. This movement or moving proceeds elliptically, suspensefully. The process of *seeing* the event, as rhetorically inscribed in and by DeLillo's essay, leaps, to quote Bazin once more, "from one event to the other as one leaps from stone to stone in crossing a river" (2:35).

This elliptical process, however, does not work by judgment. According to Adorno, this is precisely what separates art from nonart, while always enabling the former to remain in relation to the latter. As he writes, "Artworks are, as synthesis, *analogous* to judgment; in artworks, however, synthesis does not *result* in judgment; of no artwork is it possible to determine its judgment or what its so-called message is. It is therefore questionable whether artworks can possibly be *engagé*, even when they emphasize their *engagement*. What works amount to, that in which they are unified, cannot be formulated as a judgment, not even as one that they state in words and sentences" (*Aesthetic Theory* 123, first two emphases mine). Art, and I suggest that DeLillo's essay is precisely an *artful* response to 9/11, can be regarded as being analogous to judgment without ever articulating, let alone *being*, a judgment. That is, analogy is not the same as a result: "how" is not the same as "what." Analogy *moves* intransitively rather than toward something. The distance effected by such analogical movement is not to be confused with what Marxist/psychoanalytic film theory of the 1970s (and to this day) associates with the so-called alienation effect that is supposed to turn the viewer into an active spectator rather than a passive consumer of escapist images. This latter kind of distance advocated by such film theorists is a distance to be created between images and reality so that viewers will engage the latter rather than identify with the former; in contrast, analogy as I am deploying it here creates a certain kind of a *distance from reality* and, conversely, a certain degree of *immediacy with the image*, with the imaged event, with the event that consists of points of view that give rise to the image of the event. As such, analogy allows the image, the event, to retain a measure of aesthetic (and thus ethical) autonomy, as Adorno argued in "Transparencies of Film," an essay in which he revised some of his earlier, flat-out negative views of the cinema.[25] From Adorno's perspective, such aesthetic autonomy slows down the movement toward a false identification of the particular and the universal, where the detailed image (the particular) ends up referring to (representing) something else (the universal). Suspending this referential logic (one driven by giving primacy to "reality" over images) in which the jackboots of the subject crush sensuous singularity, arepresentational analogous movement creates and maintains a distance between the particular and the universal, the image and reality, or to use the terms of masochism, between pleasure and pain.[26]

Yet, and this is key, through the intransitive character of analogy, analogical movement has a powerful purchase on the very world it simultaneously recedes from precisely because it *sets the world itself in motion*, thus necessarily affecting and transforming it. Through its descriptive-generative operation, art *sees* the world not as something to be beheld by a subject (as if the world existed *for* it, like a picture enframed for a subject's consuming pleasures) but as something to be seen by points of view that have yet to emerge from that which is to be seen: the object itself in its continual variation.[27] The need to see the object in its continual variation—encountering it qua becoming—is, it bears repeating, also what Bazin gets at when he approvingly describes Erich von Stroheim's rule for direction: "Take a close look at the world, *keep on doing so*, and in the end it will lay bare for you all its cruelty and its ugliness" (1:27, my emphasis). The imperative to "keep on doing so" is absolutely key to Bazin's theory of cinema and is also something that characterizes DeLillo's essay. Far from articulating a naïve form of realism, as many of Bazin's critics allege, Bazin crucially insists on the necessity of a cinematic act of repetition in form of an artificially induced intensification. Bazin's ethical faith in the cinema—the reason he thinks cinema is a superior art form—is precisely its ability to render visible the world's constitutive variability, its ongoing mutability, rather than an unchanging essence or truth. The power of cinema is, for Bazin, akin to the moment of staring at an object for such a long time that the object itself mutates in our eyes, thus making itself available to us in its constitutive variability or becoming. The problem, however, is that most of the time we are deprived of visible access to the world's becoming because of our institutionalized tendency to rely on entrenched, clichéd modes of perception—that is, judgment, which always proceeds at a speed not conducive to *seeing* the very processes of becoming that generate judgment's condition of articulation in the first place.

Literature and cinema thus provide rhetorical tools or strategies for responding to events that exceed their immediate realm of influence and concern, as well as go beyond subjects' ability to perceive them. Indeed, perception, *pace* the (neo)phenomenological tradition, appears to be unnecessary (though it might very well be useful at times) for response-ability. That is, understanding and meaning—indeed presence and Being (in the Heideggerian sense)—constitute problems only if one agrees with (neo)phenomenology that consciousness sits at the root of every response-ability. For Bazin, Deleuze, and DeLillo, however, presence or Being is no problem precisely because for them Being can be said only of becoming (see chapter 3, note 28). If Being is nothing but becoming—variation, differentiation—then perception or understanding at best serves as one among many lines of entry and flight. Rather than being dependent on perception in the phenomenological sense, then, learning to respond to the event requires heeding "the primacy of the object" (Adorno, *Aesthetic Theory* 145); it is learning how to deploy and respond to images without making them indebted to something that is not part of the event. One must follow the lines of incision or entry

somehow morally better and thus deserving of support) with one of his trenchant, chiasmic aphorisms: "glorification of splendid underdogs is nothing other than the glorification of the splendid system that makes them so" (*Minima Moralia* 28). Unlike the smug judgment of the underdog as "good" and the system as "bad" that accomplishes not much more than instilling self-satisfaction in the one passing the allegedly benign judgment, Adorno's negative dialectical intensification of this judgment suspends it and thus reveals in surprising fashion the violence inhering in the logic of judgment itself—a logic that is covered over and, in so doing, per-petuated and amplified by the very assumption of what appears to be at first a morally sound, if not superior, position to take vis-à-vis the option of rooting for the "underdog" or the "man."

Put differently, the careless deployment of representational language in the form of similes and analogies enforces a culture of judgment rather than prompting an investigation of how val-ues function. Of course, I am not suggesting that we can ever step outside the realm of representation and thus judgment, though I confess to sharing Foucault's dream "of a kind of criticism that would not try to judge" ("Masked Philosopher" 326). Rather, *because of* the impossibility of escaping this realm, it matters all the more how we deploy language, images, and forms of judg-ment. Or, as Fredric Jameson might say, the question whether representation is good or bad is irrelevant, as representation is indifferent to how it is judged; rather, the issue is how representa-tion *works*.[28] Given the contemporary prevalence of talking-head sound-bite pronouncements sold to us as "insights" into an event, I suggest that teachers of literature and film might try to heed DeLillo's encouragement to write counter-narratives. However, DeLillo's essay teaches that one deploys them productively not by pronouncing what "should" be thought but by asking again, with greater seriousness and rigor than ever before, how imaging events can render visible—*seeable*—an event such as 9/11, how the style of encounter matters at least as much as the ability to declare "what" happened. I have suggested throughout this book that what I call masocriticism is just such a style of encounter with violence whose response-ability inheres in and derives from the violence of an event itself.

DeLillo's essay's final section provides a subtle case in point. Recalling an image he witnessed one month before 9/11, the narrator describes the bustling scenery of Canal Street at sunset, with "the panethnic swarm of shoppers, merchants, residents and passersby, with a few tourists as well" (40). Amidst this hectic capitalist environment the narrator now recalls having seen a woman on a prayer rug, "young and slender, in a silk headscarf." Everyone is busy buying and selling, and "no one seemed much to notice her." This woman, "partly concealed by a couple of vendors' carts," was "kneeling, upper body pitched toward the edge of the rug" (40). While the narrator could have easily made the praying woman into an image akin to the media clichés of Islamic fundamentalism, he instead renders her visible as an invitation for readers to think of Islam as an intensification of the present rather than an archaic holdover from a distant past. Instead of having her practice represent the Eastern other to the Western self, he offers the woman's image as a line of flight directed at a future, a future that is infused with, not opposed to, the forces of the past. For while the woman practices her religion in ways seemingly recognizable to media images of fundamentalism, she does so by engaging—indeed mobilizing—the globalized present.

The narrator configures the woman as inhabiting a liminal—barely perceptible—space on the edge between her rug and "a storefront just a foot and a half from her tipped head." Traditionally, prayer rugs "include a *mirhab* in their design, an arched element representing the prayer niche in a mosque that indicates the direction of Mecca." Crucially, however, the "only locational guide the young woman needed was the Manhattan grid" (40). That is, in the praying woman's becoming-visible, global capitalism does not so much "represent" a force to be overcome as the terrorists appear to believe it does. Instead, the woman uses a constitutive organizing principle (the grid) of what is often considered the heart of globalization (Manhattan) to inhabit her tradition in the present environment. At this moment, then, she becomes visible as infusing her capitalist surroundings with a kind of spirituality that does not depend on representation in any form.

Inhabiting a liminal space in which globalization is shot through with spirituality, and spirituality with capitalist technology, the woman remains as unrecognizable to the busy citizen-shoppers as the woman pushing a stroller was to the terrorists. This liminal space's becoming-visible triggers in the narrator, in the post-9/11 present, the image of "the daily sweeping taken-for-granted greatness of New York," a city that "will accommodate every language, ritual, belief, and opinion" (40). But this image is characterized— indeed enabled—not so much by a liberal tolerance for difference as by the very absence of recognition. If it were merely a matter of tolerance, of open-mindedness, difference would be simply secondary to the logic of representation or identity (the self-other dialectic): difference exists then only because subjects recognize it. But DeLillo rhetorically images an ontological difference that persists prior to a pluralist politics of recognition. Not beholden to subjective recognition, this ontological difference necessarily subsists as an asubjective differentiating force relation (a "becoming" in the Deleuzean sense) rather than as an identity to be recognized and labeled as different. The ethical task, accordingly, is not to represent (i.e., recognize) difference but to respond to its always already present forces. Hence the essay's final image is "the fellowship with the dead" recalled in prayer at Mecca, a fellowship, a practice, resoundingly affirmed by the bilingual "*Allahu akbar*. God is great" (40). This fellowship with the dead is recalled through specific practices that treat the dead not as nonliving (representations of their former living selves) but as dead, as nonrepresentable, as nonrecognizable. But though the dead are treated as nonrecognizable, they become all the more *seeable* in their ongoing eventness.

Epilogue

As DeLillo's rhetorical actualization of a neorealist mode of seeing suggests, literature and film can respond to the contemporary moment—if they do not presume that response, or *seeing* the world, begins with the subject as a detached perceiver. The chance, rather, consists in their pausing in the space within which images are made to circulate, thus provoking a suspension of judgment without which, as a character in *City of Glass* says, "you'll never get anywhere" (Auster 29). Conversely, if we demand that literature or film speak to the world we live in, we cannot demand these media do so by (accurately or justly) "representing" 9/11, or any other event.

In contrast, as I have hoped to illustrate throughout this book, masocritically foregrounding the style—the ethical "how"—of response slows down the impetus to declare what an event is. This impetus supposes that an event such as 9/11 contains an essence, a representational truth that must be voiced—represented—by the perceiving subject. And since truth, as Nietzsche teaches, mainly operates on a moral register, the demand to say what's what is inevitably a demand for judgment, for affirming a "correct" morality—even in the absence of a language explicitly couched in the rhetoric of judgment. DeLillo's style of response, his aesthetic stance, refuses to hypothesize an essence of 9/11, toward which a subject must subsequently assume a clear position. Instead of constituting a correct standpoint to be defended, DeLillo's reconfiguration of response as an aesthetic stance—as response-ability—suggests that response is about a mood, a rhythm, or a capacity to give oneself over to the primacy of the event.

DeLillo's masocritical foregrounding of the event's how—its force relations rather than its meaning—temporarily defers the endless proliferation of judgments based on hasty answers to the question of what, interrupting a specific mode of position taking that, as DeLillo shows, might have partially produced the conditions for 9/11.[29] Deferring judgment, however, does *not* mean advocating moral relativism.[30] Deferral does not mean to "step outside," as if one ever could fully escape judgment's clutches. Rather, to defer, understood in the masocritical terms I have argued for throughout, is to *suspend*. Attending to the event's how suspends the event. Asking how the event works and what it does creates a suspenseful rhythm that might pedagogically function to slow down the rapid speed of judgment—not in order to escape judgment, but in order to examine the value of value itself.

But suspending the event in order to defer judgment is not avoiding taking a stance; rather, it is taking a stance that, paradoxically, is no stance at all. As opposed to position taking that necessarily presumes the speaking subject's perceptual mastery of the event, which is then affirmed as a generality—as the right way of seeing or representing it—a stance *as* suspension puts the very capacity to perceive at stake. Differently put, the "politically correct" demand for taking a position (preferably the correct, allegedly moral one) is expressive of the academic or critical project of enlightenment and demystification (i.e., ideology critique in whatever form) that, as Kriss Ravetto cogently writes, actually hides "the violence of the critic" precisely because such position taking (no matter how good the cause for which one takes this position is) inevitably reduces the sensation of the cinematic, literary, cultural, or *any* event (including so-called real-world events) "to a set of predetermined theoretical effects in order to secure for [the critic] the affirmative position of academic subjectivity" (254). Far from standing outside of and in opposition to such violence, such critical projects actually intensify that which they want to oppose by perpetuating the violence inherent to their own critical subjectivity. While it must be emphasized that the violence of a literary or cinematic event, let alone that of an event such as 9/11, is not the same as the violence perpetuated by critical positions grounded in representationalism, the latter nevertheless cannot but fail at accomplishing its goal of lessening violence precisely because it itself *adds* (however unintentionally) more violence to the specific environment within which it operates.

Of course, one of this book's central points has been to insist that violences are everywhere and that therefore the task for criticism can never be to get away from Violence; rather, the real questions to ask are always, what kind of violences are being effected in what manner, how do such violences work, and what do they end up doing? I have been contending throughout that such questions are absolutely necessary to ask (on ethical grounds) but that they are being blocked by representationalist assumptions. The effect of such blockage is that the violence at hand not only remains unaffected (because it does not care what kind of judgment one passes on it) but actually is capable of extending its effectivity when approached through a representationalist point of view. It manages to do so precisely because the latter serves as an intensifier for the very violence it claims to be morally opposed to. This is why I have been arguing throughout that the critical task for an engagement with violence in whatever form is to inhabit a style of response that is characteristic of masochism, namely, its logic of suspension. This is a logic that embraces such masochistic deferral (which is not the same as "close reading" or just good old fashioned "critical thinking," both of which presume the primacy of the subject) because it subjects itself to the force of Foucault's diagnostic insight that not "everything is bad but that everything is dangerous" ("Genealogy of Ethics" 231–32). This insight calls for a mode of encountering the world that intensively invests in the operation of *seeing* this danger, of taking an intense look at it and keep on doing so—not in order to judge this danger, but in the hope of relaying its forces, of transforming them through an immanent engagement with them. Such a transformation, of course, would necessarily consist of a double-becoming of both subject and object: *in* this intensive look at the danger the one who looks becomes-otherwise to himself just as the forces of this danger are reconfigured, redeployed, and thus made other to their prior territorialization.

Masocritical suspension constitutes an immanent mode of response that heeds the event's irreducible singularity, whereas representationalist judgment itself begins from outside the object or event to be judged, and the judging subject sits safely situated afar or above—unaffected and, allegedly, objective.[31] Put differently, judgment qua suspense constitutes an immanent mode of response. As such, the central question to ask of an event is not about what one's judgment of it should be but how response-ability itself is configured *by* the event—the answer to which is always singular in that it depends, precisely, on the event itself, as I demonstrated through the cases of Highsmith's fiction and DeNiro's acting, not to mention DeLillo's essay on 9/11. Suspension, in this sense, does not promise to result in a positive term, as does the suspense immanent to a dialectical sublation. Instead, this suspense works only *relationally*, akin to Deleuze's masochistic symptomatology as well as Adorno's negative dialectic. Recall that, against the Hegelian dialectics (the essence of which clearly continues to dominate critical practice today) that sublates a positive term from the opposition of two negative ones, Adorno casts negative dialectics as a critical operation that proceeds chiasmically with the result that it never arrives at the moment of resolution but instead prolifically produces new concepts, thoughts, and angles of entry for social diagnosis. As Adorno writes, to "change [the Hegelian] direction of conceptuality, to give it a turn toward nonidentity, is the hinge of negative dialectics. Insight into the constitutive character of the nonconceptual in the concept would end the compulsive identification which the concept brings unless halted by such reflection. Reflection upon its own meaning is the way out of the concept's seeming being-in-itself as a unit of meaning" (*Negative Dialectics* 12).

Of course, there are important differences between Adorno and Deleuze. For instance, one of the differences between their "methods" might lie in how they configure differently the question of "how does it work?" Whereas for Deleuze this question functions always already as linkage ("how does it work?" is always a question of doing and transformation in Deleuze's hands), in Adorno's case it is perhaps less clear whether the question of "work" actually transforms into a question of "doing" or "going elsewhere." But whatever the differences between Deleuze and Adorno's immanent diagnostics may be, both teach us that we cannot begin an encounter with an event assuming that the subject gets to choose what an object or event "is." Rather, both Adorno and Deleuze configure something like a "stance" only through a "contract": the contract governing the masochistic economy or the chiasmic rhythm characteristic of negative dialectics. Both carefully regulate the encounter with the other by giving primacy to the other, which is quite different from the representationalist project of inhabiting the space of the other through mediation or in mediated fashion. Consequently, Deleuze and Adorno's diagnostics emphasize the *production* of future events that are not pregiven by the terms of the contracts—or diagnostics—themselves. These future events manifest themselves only in and through their immanent relations, in their effects—affectively.[32]

Importantly, the masochist, "like" the negative dialectician, does not pretend to escape the force of judgment: a violation of the contract does not tend to be a "good" thing and can indeed be plain dangerous and thus undesirable. Yet, judgment is not the point of their modes of encounter. Instead, finding out *how* something works and what it does, as well as what transformational relays can be forged *through* the encounter, constitutes their diagnostic focus, one that by definition stresses the productive component of any encounter rather than the reproductive one. They both aim at the world without pretending to know what it is, rather than treating it as a knowable object. Precisely because neither Deleuze's symptomatology nor Adorno's negative dialectics is particularly interested in epistemology do they downplay (to different degrees) the role of consciousness and instead amplify the asignifying force of signaletic material.

The necessity of thinking of image processes as presenting a stance that aesthetically aims at the world rather than represents it (as does most public discourse as well as literary and film criticism, as I hope to have convincingly shown in this book) is, finally, what concerned us throughout this project, which, as I suggested in the preface, might best be considered an *experimental* encounter with the question of how to respond to violence. It is worth mentioning that in DeLillo's case, his essayistic response to 9/11, which occurs primarily on an aesthetic but therefore, as I argued, a profoundly ethical level, already affected the production of Ulrich Baer's *110 Stories*, which, to this date, strikes me as the most interesting collection of stories responding to 9/11. Baer in-process, reconfigure what it means for contemporary thought to respond ethically to whatever the event's violent content might be(come).

That such a mode of response cannot be taken for granted, however, becomes immediately obvious when considering, for instance, Žižek's "Welcome to the Desert of the Real." Žižek's extended essay on 9/11 predictably posits "the desert of the real" as the meaning of the event. That is, similar to what transpires in the contemporary Hollywood film *The Matrix* (dir. Andy and Larry Wachowski, 1999), according to the Lacanian cultural theorist, 9/11 has finally revealed the true "what-ness" underneath an America "corrupted by Hollywood" (Žižek, "Welcome"). Žižek, who has candidly admitted to often not reading or viewing what he is writing about ("Philosopher" 272), likens the event to a Hollywood film. In my view, Žižek's recourse to the representational language of resemblance not only constitutes a lazy way out of a more careful diagnostic of the event but also leads Žižek to relish in a certain tone of *Schadenfreude,* as when he suggests that the "unthinkable which happened was thus the object of fantasy: in a way, America got what it fantasized about, and this was the greatest surprise" ("Welcome"). It seems to me that one might want to take his admission that he has at times written about what he has not read or viewed more seriously than to chalk it up to the quirky admission of a famous intellectual, especially given his influence on academic studies of images. I wonder, for instance, whether there might not be a structural connection between the belief that one does not even have to "look" at what one engages and "reading" images as representational fantasies.

DeLillo, however, looks very carefully at this event. This is why I think that attending to DeLillo's remarkable response to 9/11 can teach much to those who engage images pedagogically in the classroom—perhaps currently the only real sphere of influence literature and film scholars have left in a social space dominated by attitudes displaying indifference and even hostility to the liberal arts. That is, carefully heeding *how* DeLillo responds to 9/11 might prove fruitful in that it forges an explicit connection between the realm of film/literature and nonimaginary, real-world violence, which is why I chose to end this book with my analysis of DeLillo's brief essay. That this analysis assumes an extent that seemingly stands in disproportionate relation to the length of DeLillo's text was intended as one final performative instantiation of the very mode of masocritical response-ability I have been theorizing throughout. A key point of my analysis of DeLillo's essay was precisely the logic of deferral (including that of my own analysis), of suspense—of inhabiting the interstices themselves as a means better to prolong the moment of encounter with the object and to keep at bay as long as possible the (inevitable) return to the secondary level of representation and thus judgment. Importantly, this intensification of DeLillo's essay itself came with an amount of violent affect produced by my very response to it. This affect is the effect of the violence I did to his text (as well as to the other texts I discussed throughout this book)—that is, it was intended as an example of the violence committed by the critic that, qua critical violence, never (so I hope) pretended to be anything but a critical deployment of violence as well as a violent deployment of critical force. What mattered to me was not to escape the violence of, or expressed by, an object but to forge immanent relations with it.

However, forging this connection between film or literature and nonimaginary, real-world violence does not so much ascribe a privileged space to film and literature as illustrate how the tools they offer can be used to encounter real-world violence in such a manner that the latter maintains its irreducible singularity. And it seems to me that heeding violence's singularities—expressed by the formula "violences, not Violence"—is a necessary requirement for any engagement with violent expressions, real or imaged (with images understood, in any case, not as reflections of reality but "the reality of a reflection," as one of the Leninist-Marxist revolutionaries in Godard's *La Chinoise* [1967] has it), that hopes to avoid some of the more obvious shortcomings of existing academic and popular treatments of violent texts and events.

Whatever future responses fiction and film will give to 9/11—

and to violence in general, in all its various guises—the difficult task at hand is to do so without reducing it to a moralistic lesson. DeLillo's essay, I believe, provides us with a potential pedagogical recipe for producing future responses (an encouraging example being *110 Stories*), just as Highsmith's fiction, DeNiro's screen acting, and the Coen Brothers' films do in perhaps slightly more implicit ways. What if, they all ask, we were to take seriously the (violent) event qua event, in its singularity, its unrepresentability in language because it is not of language? They all repeatedly wonder, "What if the event were like this, then what? Or if it were otherwise, then what?"

In short, the ruins of the future articulated by DeLillo's essay are the ruins of representational language. Throughout this book, I have been arguing for the importance of taking seriously this ruin, for masocritically encountering signaletic materials—violent in whatever form and shape—as arepresentational, rhetorical provocations rather than signifying vessels. Yet, since representational language is the (only?) one we have, asking again how to use it might not be a bad starting place for intervening in the world, for *seeing* it again, and, one hopes, for acting on it "for the benefit of a time to come" (Nietzsche, "Uses and Disadvantages" 60).

Notes

1. The Violence of Sensation

1. I should clarify that I consider (violent) images real as well. They have their own reality and therefore are not in opposition to "real violence": the reality of images and the reality of, say, murder, exist as different events on the same plane of immanence.

2. Of course, real acts of violence are controversial as well. Consider the controversy spawned by Reuters or the BBC, which at one time or another refused to use the term "terrorist" when talking about the people responsible for the attacks of 9/11 or the violence perpetrated against Israelis: clearly, someone's terrorist without any legitimate cause is a freedom fighter to someone else. Without intending to endorse one or the other label, I simply want to acknowledge the obvious: even real violence consistently receives different responses. However, I am primarily going to focus on violent *images* taken from American literature and cinema, which is why, from here on, I will not continue to refer to "real violence" unless the context obviously demands it.

3. Quite obviously, the Coens playfully engage genre conventions throughout their work. In addition to their neo-noirlike reworking of film noir and pulp fiction genre conventions, consider also *Intolerable Cruelty* (2003), which is their attempt to reactivate the classical Hollywood "comedy of remarriage" subgenre for the postmodern age, as well as their remake of one of the best-known Ealing comedies, *The Ladykillers* (2004; original dir. Alexander Mackendrick, 1955). See Foster Hirsh's *Detours and Lost Highways* for a comprehensive discussion of neo-noir; Stanley Cavell's *Pursuits of Happiness* for more on comedies of remarriage in Hollywood films of the 1930s; and R. Barton Palmer's *Joel and Ethan Coen* for an extended discussion of the Coen Brothers as postmodern filmmakers.

4. For Deleuze and Guattari's most extensive discussion of the body without organs, see *A Thousand Plateaus* 149–66.

5. We might also frame this distinction in terms analogous to the difference between the time-image and the movement-image, respectively, that Deleuze maps out in his two cinema books. Given the omnipresence of "sensational" violence in contemporary media culture, Bacon's strategy for engaging violence appears to be one of "slowing down" rather than "speeding up" violence. If today we indeed face an excess of kinetic violence then perhaps the best way to confront violence is by making violent sensations move *intensively* rather than *extensively*. Bacon's particular strategy might be thought of as paralleling the cinematic aesthetic of directors such as Vittorio DeSica (*The Bicycle Thief*, 1948), Alain Resnais (*Hiroshima Mon Amour*, 1959), or Chris Marker (*La Jetée*, 1962), who all prefer to slow down their respective narratives in order to render visible the *sensation* of violence.

6. The function of color in the Coen Brothers' work deserves a longer study in its own right. Just recall the dominant color schemes of their films such as the red in *Blood Simple* (1984) and *Barton Fink* (1990), the white in *Fargo* (1996), the yellow in *O Brother, Where Art Thou* (1998), or the luminous, impeccable black and white in *The Man Who Wasn't There* (2001) that visually renders this film as more noir than "original" film noir ever was.

7. For the best recent studies of violence in film see Barker and Petley; Scharrett; Prince, *Screening Violence*; Slocum, *Violence in American Cinema*; Schneider; and Gormley. For studies of violence in American literature, see Kowalewski, Slotkin, and Giles. It should be pointed out that film studies tends to expend considerably more energy on studying violent images than literary studies, possibly because of the commonly held perception that violence in the media (including cinema) has more immediate (negative) effects on an audience than violent literary images. The work of Stephen Prince, with its strong appeal to the "findings" of the social sciences as well as cognitivism, is particularly noteworthy. Opposing the merely "interpretative frameworks that have literary currency" ("Film Scholars" B18), Prince's work is at the forefront of the larger "post-theory" attack on so-called Grand Theory in film studies initiated by David Bordwell and Noël Carroll's landmark volume *Post-Theory*. Bordwell was one of the first film scholars to turn to cognitivism as a paradigm for film studies (see his "Case for Cognitivism").

8. Criminal characters struggle with chance in many of the Coens' films. Think, for instance, of *Fargo* or *The Ladykillers*.

9. Caspar's sense of morality is unconventional only to the degree

that conventional morality does not tend to argue in favor of cheating. Yet, even this is questionable in an age of globalized corporate fraud that constitutes not so much a "bad apple" exception to the rule of morally good capitalism than its most intensified instantiation. After all, at the height of the internet boom in the mid to late 1990s, all share holders wanted was for the companies' CEOs to drive up the stock prices, thus increasing share holders' personal profits. No one really bothered to tell those CEOs not to use illegal methods, which became a problem *only* once these companies—and consequently their share holders—incurred massive financial losses.

10. Caspar's ethics are thoroughly capitalist. As he clearly believes, there are people who have ethics, and there are those (including Bernie) who do not. Not only does this static, possessive, conception of ethics starkly contrast with the performative ethics theorized by Jeffrey T. Nealon and cinematically mobilized by the Coens, but it also would seem that it provokes us to consider the inherent violence of capitalism as such.

11. "A whole category that could be termed clichés already fills the canvas, before the beginning" (Deleuze, *Francis Bacon* 72).

12. In fact, the overall impact of Deleuze's relatively early work *Masochism* on his entire oeuvre has yet to be articulated in systematic ways and surely demands a longer study in its own right.

13. In Deleuze's *Masochism*, the masochist is always male. However, see the work of Gaylyn Studlar for a feminist appropriation of Deleuze's sense of masochism. Studlar allows for a female masochism that does not necessarily stand in a dialectical relationship to a male sadist (i.e., sadomasochism), as is the case in both Freudian psychoanalysis and its appropriation in canonical film studies by feminists such as Laura Mulvey (see "Visual Pleasure and Narrative Cinema") or Kaja Silverman (see, for instance, her essays "Masochism and Subjectivity" and "Masochism and Male Subjectivity"). Slavoj Žižek ("An Ethical Plea") recently addressed masochism in ethical terms, but despite his reference to Deleuze's book on the subject he remains thoroughly faithful to psychoanalysis. For my money, however, the best articulation of cinema as a masochistic economy can be found in Steven Shaviro's remarkable *Cinematic Body*.

14. For more on this, see my essay on the film from which I have adapted the current discussion.

15. Keep in mind, though, that any proper scientific experiment is based on, and works with, rules. Neither the scientist nor the masochist is interested in either creating chaos or blowing up things.

16. I will elaborate on the concept of symptomatology in the next chapter.

17. Or, as the rhetorician Richard Doyle is fond of saying, "you have to run the computer program to know whether it works."

2. Judgment Is Not an Exit

1. Dennis Harvey calls Ellis's novel "arguably one of the most-loathed and least-read novels in recent memory"; likewise, Kristen Baldwin describes Ellis's text as "one of the most shockingly violent novels ever published [. . .] the most reviled book of the decade" (36). These two popular press assessments merely recall the brutality of the tone that had been levied against Ellis's novel throughout the 1990s—not only in popular publications but also in academic articles, most notably in Tara Baxter and Nikki Craft's essay with the telling title, "There Are Better Ways of Taking Care of Bret Easton Ellis Than Just Censoring Him." As for the novel's publishing history, when Knopf, which had paid Ellis a $300,000 advance on the novel, eventually declined to publish *American Psycho*, Random House immediately jumped on the opportunity to publish it in its well-received and influential Vintage Contemporaries series.

2. All of these images are taken from Ellis's novel.

3. Discussing the relationship between comedy and violence in New Hollywood cinema, Geoff King discusses films such as Oliver Stone's *Natural Born Killers* (1994), Quentin Tarantino's *Pulp Fiction* (1994), and *American Psycho* (2000), examining their use of comedy and satirical function. Crucially, as he points out, the very concept of "satire—comedy with a critical-social edge—is sometimes used as a legitimating framework, making a claim to 'seriousness' that seeks to absolve the text from accusations that its violence is merely 'gratuitous'" (126). The essay goes on to show how the judgment of violence in such films hinges on whether critics use or reject a claim to satire made by the filmmaker or other critics. In my view, however, these critical positions are six of one, half dozen of the other: whether or not the claim to satire is accepted, framing a debate about (film) violence in terms of satire automatically territorializes the question of violence onto the level of signification.

4. For other critical assessments that favor the movie over the novel, see Smith, Holden, Gleiberman, and Lane.

5. See David Slocum's essay "The 'Film Violence' Trope" for an excellent

discussion of the historical origins of this "wisdom," which he attributes to the function the 1960s play in the discourse of cinematic violence.

6. For examples, see Kowalewski, Frohock, and Stein, as well as Kinder. Genre criticism, of course, is yet another well-known example of the comparative spirit of criticism.

7. My argument relies on Deleuze's important, yet often overlooked, essay "The Simulacrum and Ancient Philosophy," in which he diagnoses Platonism's denigration of the simulacrum and its effectuation of a history of representation and judgment based on a metaphysical foundation. Whereas Deleuze affirms Nietzsche's call for the overturning of Platonism as the quintessential task of modern philosophy, my project might be thought of as working toward an overturning of representationalism in modern criticism. See chapter 3 for a more extended rendering of this crucial point.

8. Even in criticism on decidedly nonrealist texts such as science fiction we can observe this tendency, for much of the criticism responding to these texts concentrates on its allegorical status—that is, how science fiction is, in the final analysis, about reality.

9. This is as good a moment as any to point out that Deleuze and Guattari's writing on linguistics in *A Thousand Plateaus* (see especially chapters 4 and 5) underlies much of my argument. The upshot of their analysis of the asignifying force of signs is not to deny the existence of representations but to foreground that representations are, at best, merely one among many ways by which language affects the social.

10. Both Jacques Derrida (in, e.g., *Of Grammatology*) and Maurice Blanchot (in, e.g., *The Infinite Conversation*) show how language—writing and speaking, respectively—is an act of violence. And Deleuze adds that "thought is primarily trespass and violence" (*Difference and Repetition* 139). The act of criticism, in this sense, has no choice but to be violent.

11. At its limits, this argument suggests that judgment perpetuates the primacy of identity/Same in relation to which difference exists merely as a secondary category. For the most compelling refutation of this ontological assumption, see especially the introduction to and chapter 1 of Deleuze's *Difference and Repetition*, the central point of which is to "think difference in itself independently of the forms of representation which reduce it to the Same" (xix).

12. One of Deleuze's earliest attempts at comparing and classifying is his brief 1966 essay on hardboiled detective fiction, "Philosophy of the *Série Noire*."

13. It is hardly surprising, then, that Žižek—perhaps Lacan's greatest reader—is in effect incapable of reading Deleuze as anything other than a poor man's Lacan (see Žižek, *Organs without Bodies*).

14. The debate originated in popular reviews of the novel. For one of the few examples arguing that Ellis succeeds at satirizing the 1980s, see Weldon. For some of the many examples arguing Ellis's satire fails due to his lack of talent, see Stiles, Rosenblatt, Lehmann-Haupt, Archer, Plagens, Teachout, and, most ingeniously, Mailer and Udovitch. For the best account of the public response to Ellis's novel, see Eberly 103–31. Academic discourse, with the usual time lapse, continued this discussion. For instance, Elizabeth Young asserts that the novel is indeed a satire but reads it ultimately as an affirmation of conservative moral values (85–122). Likewise, James Annesley claims that Ellis's failure to consider that his representation of American capitalism might be inaccurate undermines the success of his satire (11–22). For a more positive take on Ellis's endeavor, see Giles 160–74; Kauffman 243–60; Price; Hume, *American Dream* 190–94; and feminist critic Carla Freccero, who warrants the most interesting defense of the novel.

15. For the best accounts of this response, see Kauffman 243–60, and Price. The latter symptomatically begins his essay on the novel by stating that he is in accord with those critics who contend that Ellis's novel has to be understood as a "type of satirical novel that condemns the dominant American culture of the 1980s" (322).

16. For an example of the former attitude, see Udovitch who recognizes the satirical intent of the novel but deems it "profoundly conservative" (65), largely because Ellis "remains an amateurish formalist and a downright lousy stylist" (66) so that he remains incapable of transcending the gore in which his novel dwells. Norman Mailer infamously concurs with this assessment, finding that he "cannot forgive" (221) Ellis for lacking the writerly skills necessary for following through with his satirical intent.

17. Considering that filmmaking, independent or not, is an enterprise perhaps more closely tied to the culture industry than any other art form, the very location of the discourse surrounding Ellis's book—major and minor newspapers, magazines, TV shows, etc., all of which are owned by larger corporations that also have stakes in Hollywood's production, distribution, and exhibition machinery—it is hard to see how it could have been otherwise

18. Harron's own promotional statements about her motives for

tackling Ellis's novel consistently reveal that her intention was indeed to wrestle away the text from its most vitriolic critics and foreground the progressive satirical quality instead of the more sensationalist aspects of the novel. As she writes in the *New York Times*, she sees the novel as "a surreal satire and although many scenes were excruciatingly violent, it was clearly intended as a critique of male misogyny, not an endorsement of it" (AR 13). Authorial intention is, of course, yet another critical concept that relies on and is expressive of a representational logic in which "meaning" (either located in the text as expressive, however unconsciously, of authorial intentions, or in the author's intentions that we can access through letters, biographical material, etc.) is the ne plus ultra of the textual encounter.

19. For examples of the former, see Baldwin, Holden, Rothkopf, or Smith; for examples of the latter, see Harvey or James, "Sick City Boy."

20. These views are held by, among others, Roger Rosenblatt and Terry Teachout.

21. A number of critics have discussed the question of whether the film insinuates that most, if not all, of the events merely happened in Bateman's sick imagination. See Harvey; Holden; James, "Sick City Boy"; King; Rayns; and Travers. Likewise, in their Lacanian reading of both novel and film, Jaap Kooijman and Tarja Laine argue that the serial killer identity of Patrick Bateman is merely his own, imaginary construction.

22. Given that Ellis's novel quite obviously alludes to Batman (just as it refers to many other pop culture artifacts), I find it intriguing that Christian Bale's performance of the protagonist in Christopher Nolan's *Batman Begins* (2005) relies on many of the same acting mannerisms that he has already displayed in his performance of Patrick Bateman in Harron's film. It is as if Nolan and Bale wanted to foreground the psychotic core at the heart of Batman that Ellis's brutal text implicitly hinted at fifteen years earlier. The fact that both Bateman and Batman are rich, snobbish, narcissistic, buff, attractive males inhabiting Gotham/New York City goes a long way to substantiate that this connection may not be coincidental.

23. David Robinson discusses further differences between film and novel—changes that, according to Robinson, help clarify the film's basic premise of suggesting that the "American consumer mindset, taken to its logical extreme, will expose itself as inherently violent" (35). In this reading, Bateman commits his atrocities because of his "deep dissatisfaction and [his] failure to attain a primal need" (35). That is, his violence

points to, indeed represents, the existence of a lack of stable subjectivity/ identity that is endemic to consumer culture—a culture that, therefore, is deemed morally corrupt by the film (and the essay's point of view).

24. As I will argue in chapter 3, undecidability is in the end not all that different from arriving at a specific decision about a text's meaning.

25. This project's masocritical gambit is, of course, to develop a few of these tools by showing how some practitioners of imaged violence have mobilized them all along.

26. See note 11.

27. Perhaps it is better to say that these texts are particularly good at showing us something about language and images in general, namely, that *all* signaletic material works based on levels of intensity. That is, affect is not a scarce occurrence but a constitutive attribute. Perhaps one should show how representational criticism that does not attend to affect is itself always already shot through with affect.

28. I should point out, however, that during the period in which I wrote this book, the question of affect has begun to solicit more attention in the humanities and even sciences. See Clare Hemmings's essay "Invoking Affect" for a critique of the "contemporary emergence of affect as critical object and perspective through which to understand the social world and our place within it" (548). Still, in my view the Deleuzean sense of affect that Massumi has in mind (i.e., as something that is preindividual, presubjective, and thus not reducible to or describable in terms of mere "feelings") has yet to be developed as a critical concept and tool, especially with regard to literary and film studies. I hope to contribute with this book to this task.

29. Kathryn Hume recently addressed the issue of narrative speed— "in the sense of the narrative being accelerated beyond some safe comprehension-limit" ("Narrative Speed" 106)—in contemporary fiction. Hume diagnoses in how far narrative speed "serves both escape and control functions" (107)—that is, how it assists "the purposes either of hegemonic powers or of revolution" (107).

30. Another way of putting this: unlike the film, the novel does not preach to the liberal choir. It instead shows how bourgeois liberalism— embodied in the logic of representationalism—is itself complicit with the very violence it allegedly opposes. See my discussion of Hardt and Negri's *Empire* in chapter 4 for more on this.

31. See Colebrook for an excellent discussion of Deleuze's take on voice and point of view, as well as chapter 6.

32. The enormity of this task will be illustrated in chapter 4.

33. Chapter 5 will return to this seeming paradox, suggesting that it is precisely this alleged phenomenological obviousness of violence that tends to obfuscate its effectivity.

34. See the opening section of chapter 6 for more on this particular issue.

35. The subsequent chapters on Highsmith, DeNiro, and DeLillo attempt to do just that, however tentatively.

36. Differentiating his thought from Foucault's, Deleuze writes: "I have therefore no need for the status of phenomena of resistance; if the first given of a society is that everything takes flight, then everything in it is deterritorialized" ("Desire and Pleasure" 189).

37. I investigate most fully how one might affectively respond to the medium of film in chapter 5.

3. Are We All Arnoldians?

1. Film criticism too remains fettered by the desire to judge images. See, e.g., Frus and Goldberg, who both are clearly invested in condemning what the writers perceive to be immoral violent images. Not unimportantly, these images are deemed immoral because they allegedly misrepresent—falsify—reality. Noteworthy is also the work of Noël Carroll, who explicitly advocates a mode of film criticism, which, based on Kantian categories, is capable of arriving at clear value judgments about film productions. See, e.g., his essay "Introducing Film Evaluation," which, ironically, is included in *Reinventing Film Studies*. How, exactly, an emphasis on film evaluation based on Kantian concepts can be considered "reinventing" anything is beyond me. In general, of course, film criticism has inherited many of its critical operations from literary studies due to its institutional history that emerged out of English departments.

2. This collection, we may recall, features a number of essays that almost single-handedly institutionalized a critical practice we now remember as American deconstruction.

3. Although this is not the time and place to elaborate on this, I should point out that to me American deconstruction is a far cry from the actual provocation of Derrida's work. For whereas the former remains wedded to an understanding of language as representation, Derrida views language as "force." See, for instance, his seminal essay "Différance," specifi-

cally footnote 20, which approvingly points to Deleuze's *Nietzsche and Philosophy*, a book that insists that, for Nietzsche, language is force, not representation.

4. Film studies too moved toward reception studies (see, e.g., Bordwell, Prince, or Staiger). This change of emphasis occurred as an explicit reaction against Lacanian film theory, which dominated the 1970s and 1980s. Anti-Lacanians such as Stephen Prince began to accuse Lacanian film theory for having "constructed theories of spectatorship from which [real] spectators are missing" ("Psychoanalytic Film Theory" 83); in contrast, reception oriented film studies foregrounds the meaning making capacity of the actual viewer. Whereas for Lacanians "meaning" tends to be a matter of the relation between the Imaginary and Symbolic (and how these realms governed spectators' responses), reception theorists examine how the spectator plays a much more active role in making meaning. Both David Bordwell and especially Prince give this turn to the viewer a particularly scientific twist, with their advocacy of cognitivism as a means to study film. For instance, in "True Lies," a challenging essay on the problematic dominance of "indexically based notions of film realism" (31) in film theory, Prince points out that traditional film theory has failed to attend to consider how "realism" functions from a viewer's perspective and instead obsessed about the "codes" of realism. To Prince, realism is based on spectators' cognitive experiences. Hence, a digital film can be as realist as an analog film. What matters is what the spectator has cognitively available (much of which is hardwired, according to Prince), since she uses this experience in watching a film to compare the images to her real experience. If images reasonably correspond to the cognitive library, she will perceive the images as realistic, regardless of whether the image is a dinosaur that never existed in the real world or a man with a bicycle trying to make a living in war-ravaged Rome. Note, however, that what both approaches have in common is the emphasis on meaning.

5. Even writers who are otherwise sympathetic to post-structuralist thought charge Derrida with this criticism. E.g., Constantin Boundas complains that Derridean deconstruction conceives of texts as "labyrinths where one can err forever and fishnets in which one could become caught. [. . .] As for the referent, it is not only bracketed [. . .] but it loses its pertinence: one can always find a referent, but it is going to be another text" (165). See, however, Baucom for an essay that explains why the countless eulogies written about deconstruction might have been premature.

6. Once more, film studies follows a parallel trajectory. Today, as Todd McGowan and Sheila Kunkle correctly point out in their introduction to *Lacan and Contemporary Film*, "theory as such has given way almost completely to historicism and empirical research" (xii n. 1). An excellent example supporting this point is, e.g., J. D. Slocum's recent *Cinema Journal* essay on World War II combat films. Slocum offers "an alternative model for understanding film violence" (58) whose targets are the universalizing claims of psychoanalytic as well as more behaviorist-based theories. Slocum's approach, so he argues, is rigorously "grounded in history" (57), as it is guided by "the idea of a 'civilizing process' that attends both to specific representations in war films and to the institutional role of cinema in socializing and regulating individual behavior" (37).

7. See, however, Jeffrey T. Nealon's *Double Reading,* in which he makes a forceful case for a reading of deconstruction that clearly requires this systemic displacement, as this is precisely what the second deconstructive move offered by Derrida demands as a necessary compound of deconstructive practice. As Derrida writes, "Deconstruction cannot limit itself or proceed immediately to a neutralization [of the binary]; it must, by means of a double gesture, a double science, a double writing, practice an *overturning* of the classical opposition *and* a general *displacement* of the system" ("Signatures Event Context" 329).

8. The point here is that cultural studies—generally speaking a left-liberal academic niche—is not so far removed from Arnold's enterprise. It is, of course, no surprise that more conservative leaning critics make no bones about continuing to work in an Arnoldian tradition. See Michael Bérubé's critique of conservative writers such as Allan Bloom or Dinesh D'Souza in *The Village Voice,* where he makes a similar point.

9. I realize that in hindsight it might seem absurd that literary culture once embraced Bret Easton Ellis. Indeed, even at the height of his fame (achieved overnight as an undergraduate student when he published his first novel), not everyone embraced this supposed literary wunderkind. Yet, the fact remains that for a brief moment he was *the* celebrated enfant terrible of U.S. literature. The point here is not to endorse or oppose this view of him but to show the discursive operation of which he was part.

10. While similar distinctions exist outside the United States, it seems true that in other countries "controversial" writers often acquire a certain status of respect precisely because of their work's provocation. The controversy surrounding the work of French author Michel Houellebecq is but one recent case in point.

11. See also Hardt and Negri, *Empire*, for support of this argument.

12. Massumi praises Grossberg for paying attention to affect in his work but points out that "Grossberg slips into an equation between affect and emotion at many points" (260n3).

13. Of course, the surge of interest in the 1990s in Deleuze's work must be acknowledged, but this interest was mainly of philosophical nature (with the occasional essay concerning literature). Cultural studies has remained rather hostile to Deleuze, despite a few special issues devoted to his thought, such as, e.g., *Cultural Studies* 14.2 (2000) and *South Atlantic Quarterly* 96.3 (1997), as well as excellent studies such as *Animating (Deleuze and Guattari)*, a volume edited by Jennifer Daryl Slack; J. Macgregor Wise's *Exploring Technology and Social Space*; and Charles Stivale's *Disenchanting Les Bons Temps*. And despite recent book publications such as Gregg Lambert's *The Non-Philosophy of Gilles Deleuze*, Ian Buchanan and John Marks's *Deleuze and Literature*, and Ronald Bogue's *Deleuze on Literature*, it seems to me that Deleuze's position in literary studies remains marginal. In film studies too Deleuze's work occupies at best an in-between position: most film studies do not know what to do with his two books on cinema, and those who engage him by and large do so on the margins of the field. (See, however, D. N. Rodowick's and Steven Shaviro's powerful works on Deleuze and cinema, as well as Flaxman's edited volume.) In other words, to this day, no "Deleuzean school" has formed, as has been the case with Derrida (American deconstruction), Foucault (New Historicism), or Lacan (Lacanian psychoanalysis), not to mention Marx and Freud. Foucault's famous (and undoubtedly somewhat jesting) claim that "perhaps one day, this [twentieth] century will be known as Deleuzian" ("Theatrum Philosophicum" 165) has yet to register institutionally—and if it ever did, this (future) institutionalization would prove Foucault wrong, as Deleuze's entire work is characterized by a hostility to schools (generalities) and instead favors singularities, events, and the untimely or yet to come (which never ceases to be just that).

14. An almost inevitable outcome of this interest in (political) representation was cultural studies' founding rejection of Theodor Adorno's thought, since the latter makes it exceedingly difficult to have any faith in a politics based on the (representational) recognition of difference. It therefore comes as no surprise that Max Horkheimer and Adorno's landmark essay "The Culture Industry" was included in Simon During's seminal *Cultural Studies Reader* only as a shortened version, with the

Frankfurt School theorists' central aphoristic salvo against "difference"—"Anyone who resists can survive only by being incorporated. Once registered as diverging from the culture industry, they belong to it as the land reformer to capitalism. Realistic indignation is the trademark of those with a new idea to sell" (*Dialectic of Enlightenment* 104)—completely omitted.

15. For excellent essays on the problematic reception of Deleuze in the United States, see Elie During and Lotringer.

16. See also my essay on Deleuze's interest in Jack Kerouac for a discussion of literary studies questionable appropriation of Deleuze and Guattari's concept of "minor literature." Whereas for the latter this concept has nothing to do with representation (it is not a numerical concept), literary studies has generally applied this concept as a means to advocate one or the other underrepresented minority writer.

17. For an excellent recent essay that takes seriously the notion of "tracking down" in Plato's engagement with the Sophists, see Muckelbauer.

18. See Baudrilliard, *Simulations*, and Jameson, *Postmodernism*.

19. Deleuze points out that Plato seems to have recognized this ("Was it not Plato himself who pointed out the direction for the reversal of Platonism?" ["Simulacrum" 256]), though he then shied away from its implications. Thus, Deleuze suggests that Plato can be said to have begun the overturning of Platonism himself. That Plato "failed" to affirm his own insight merely indicates the degree of difficulty of thinking without judgment. Chapter 4 will elaborate on the difficulty of "overturning" Platonism.

20. Patricia Dunker's novel *Hallucinating Foucault* (1996) provocatively plays with this distinction. I want to thank Gina Ercolini for having called my attention to it.

21. In chapter 6, I will differentiate between "seeing" and "perception"; whereas the latter is governed by the logic of authenticity (and thus representation), the former is a mode of production that does not originate with and in a subject and his or her ability to perceive correctly.

22. Even—or, better, most importantly—Kant argues in his *Critique of Judgment* for the aesthetic (and aesthetic judgment) as a middle ground mediating the relationship between the perceiving subject and the object of perception. He thus elevates reason as the final arbiter of aesthetic taste, allocating affect a place to be governed by "state-ly" rationality and its attending institutions: jurisprudence and aesthetic criticism.

23. Distinguishing "antiquarian history" from both "monumental" and "critical" history, Nietzsche claims that the first "knows only how to *preserve* life, not how to engender it; it always undervalues that which is becoming because it has no instinct for divining it—as monumental history, for example, has. Thus, it hinders any firm resolve to attempt something new, thus it paralyses the man of action who, as one who acts, will and must offend some piety or other" ("Uses and Disadvantages" 75).

24. Patton argues that "the importance of the concept of simulacra is limited to the predominantly negative phase of Deleuze's project" (35), citing a comment Deleuze made in a letter to another critic. Yet, I suggest that precisely because Platonism still works through and thus affects contemporary practices we cannot overestimate the importance of Deleuze's encounter with Plato(nism). Rather, in this short essay on Plato, Deleuze provides us with a crucial "tool" that can be deployed as a means to encounter or move *through* the dominance of representational criticism.

25. This is part of the reason why I do not think that film studies ought to privilege so-called empirical methodologies, as Prince urges. In my view, the concept of the subject that currently is at work in, say, cognitivist film studies strikes me as problematically undertheorized. In an odd way, one might say that current versions of film studies are not yet empirical enough.

26. In contemporary film studies, David Bordwell is the best-known proponent of this approach to moving images. See, e.g., his aptly titled *Making Meaning*.

27. This is not to deny that we are frequently exposed to just this actualization of violence: violence is done to us all the time, in different ways and with different effects, just as, perhaps less obviously, all of us also cannot but do violence to others, to different degrees and with different results.

28. It should be noted that Deleuze's notion of simulacrum does not introduce a new foundation. Contrary to Alain Badiou's provocative reading of Deleuze, the simulacrum is an "un-founding" (Deleuze, "Simulacrum" 263). Badiou insists that Deleuze is the thinker of the One, of foundationalism, which is true only to the degree (one *not* acknowledged by Badiou) that the One for Deleuze is always just one part of an assemblage, an effect. While it is true that Deleuze makes much of Duns Scotus's thesis of the univocity of being, Deleuze clarifies that he understands this thesis as articulating the Being of becoming: "the essential in

univocity is not that Being is said in a single and same sense, but that it is said, in a single and same sense, *of* all its individuating differences or intrinsic modalities. Being is the same for all these modalities, but these modalities are not the same" (*Difference and Repetition* 36). That is, Being can be considered univocal (one, foundational) only to the extent that it is constituted by processes of becoming, of "different/ciation" (*Difference and Repetition*, 209).

29. I return to the question of pedagogy throughout the following chapters but will place particular emphasis on it in the concluding chapter.

30. Deleuze is not the only one who leads us to think this. In addition to Derrida's and Blanchot's claims that, respectively, writing and speech are violence (see chapter 2, note 10), Foucault argues that history is violence: it "is not made for understanding; it is made for *cutting*" ("Nietzsche, Genealogy, History" 154, my emphasis). Marx, of course, teaches us about the violence of the market. It seems that very little is left that might constitute a nonviolent space once we add these theories together.

4. Serializing Violence

1. The film was eventually nominated for five Academy Awards, though it did not win any. See also Michael Bronski's review of what he calls Minghella's "Masterpiece Theaterized *The Talented Mr. Ripley*" (42) for a cogent explanation of the film's instantaneous acclaim and success.

2. In addition to *The Talented Mr. Ripley*, the Everyman's edition also includes *Ripley Under Ground* (originally published 1970) and *Ripley's Game* (1974). The two Ripley novels not included are *The Boy Who Followed Ripley* (1980) and *Ripley Under Water* (1991).

3. I take the term "new violence" from Michael Stein's two-part essay "The New Violence, or Twenty Years of Violence in Films: An Appreciation." See also Schneider for an extended engagement with new Hollywood violence.

4. See Kakutani, Cox, Rafferty, or Maerker.

5. In addition to countless made-for-TV productions (especially for German and French TV), Highsmith's work has thus far given rise to more than a dozen films, the majority of which were produced and

released in European countries. The most famous film adaptations include Hitchcock's *Strangers on a Train* (1951), René Clément's *Plein Soleil* (Purple Noon; 1959, based on *The Talented Mr. Ripley*), Wim Wenders's *Der amerikanische Freund* (The American Friend) (1977, based on *Ripley's Game*), Claude Miller's *Dites-lui que je l'aime* (1977, based on *This Sweet Sickness*), Claude Chabrol's *Le Cri du Hibou* (1987, based on *The Cry of the Owl*), and Liliana Cavani's *Ripley's Game* (2002). Tom Cox reports that further adaptations of Highsmith's work are currently under way.

6. Deleuze, in his last book with Félix Guattari, famously proposes that the most fundamental task of philosophy is to form, invent, and fabricate concepts (*What Is Philosophy?* 2). If philosophy encounters a problem, then the task of solving it is to invent a concept proper to the problem: "All concepts are connected to problems without which they would have no meaning and which can themselves only be isolated or understood as their solution emerges" (16). Solutions, in other words, emerge in the task of inventing concepts, but this task is intricately, inevitably, immanently related to the problem at hand: the solution (the concept) cannot be found outside of the problem and thus cannot be located anywhere else but in the space defined and delineated by the problem.

7. *Strangers on a Train*, Highsmith's first novel, was published in 1950; *Small g: a Summer Idyll* found posthumous publication just after her death in 1995. Highsmith published a few short stories in the 1940s. The importance of the concept of seriality will become clearer, as my discussion of Highsmith's work will focus on the function of her only serialized character, Tom Ripley, in conjunction with, and as interruption of, the rest of her prolific writing career.

8. I would caution against reducing Highsmith's work to this Oedipal drama, as Wilson's otherwise illuminating biography tends to do.

9. For a brilliant analysis of Melville's story, see Deleuze's "Bartleby; or, The Formula." Hardt and Negri also make interesting use of this famous line of refusal in *Empire* (203–4).

10. According to Deleuze, Nietzsche "compares the thinker to an arrow shot by Nature that another thinker picks up where it has fallen so that he can shoot it somewhere else" (*Nietzsche and Philosophy* ix).

11. Deleuze makes this point also in his television interview with Claire Parnet, *L'Abécédaire de Gilles Deleuze*, in section "E comme 'Enfance.'"

12. In many ways, the same can be said of Bret Easton Ellis's work,

which obsessively returns to a limited set of concerns as well. His latest novel, *Lunar Park* (2005), provides a remarkable faux-biographical, retrospective metacommentary on Ellis's oeuvre and its central themes. Likewise, Don DeLillo, to whom I will turn in the last chapter, clearly obsesses about issues such as consumer culture and the force of images. Yet, oddly enough, the scholarship on all three of these writers has paid scant attention to this obsessive quality and how it might affect not only the writing itself but also the *style* of engagement with a given subject matter at hand. The acting work of Robert DeNiro, the subject of chapter 5, is also characterized by such an obsessive rhythm.

13. As Deleuze shows in his reading of Plato (see chapter 3), the act of judgment, dependent on its purchase on truth, is an effect of the prior force of difference, of the simulacrum, of the power of the false.

14. We cannot entirely ignore the force of labels. As has been argued by genre theorists, genres can function as an "aesthetic and social contract between audiences and [artistic producers]" (Matthew Bernstein qtd. in Slocum, "Film Violence" 664). And notwithstanding Rick Altman's powerful critique of genre studies that view genres in contractual terms (see, e.g., *Film/Genre*), it seems clear that Highsmith would have had a rough time publishing her work without at least minimally heeding genre expectations. In fact, in *Plotting and Writing Suspense Fiction*, Highsmith tells her readers of her occasional difficulties in finding a publisher for works that seemed to be too un-Highsmithean. Thus, writing within certain genre expectations—and finding lines of flight within them—became one of her greatest artistic and commercial challenges, as evidenced by her work's reception, which shows frequently more admiration for commercially less successful novels such as *Edith's Diary* (1977) than for her more obvious suspense efforts such as the Ripley series. (According to Highsmith herself, critics considered *Edith's Diary* her "best [novel] to date" (*Plotting and Writing* 135), an opinion Russell Harrison concurs with, calling it "Highsmith's most ambitious novel" [81].)

15. Deleuze and Guattari first developed the concept of "minor literature" in *Kafka: Toward a Minor Literature*.

16. Clapp writes that her "books were always more successful in Europe than in the United States" and that even as late as 1986 a new novel by Highsmith, *Found in the Street*, "sold scarcely four thousand copies in the States; in Germany, it sold forty thousand" (96). Joan Dupont speculates that Highsmith's lack of recognition in the United States might have resulted from "her amoral explorations of perverse behavior [that]

have confused American readers of crime fiction" (60). And Rich reports that "just as her first novel, *Strangers on a Train*, had been rejected by six publishers at the start, so her final novel, *Small g: a Summer Idyll*, was rejected by Knopf (though published in Europe) the year she died."

17. In addition to Hubly, see Hilfer, Cochran, and Rich for this sort of reading of Ripley.

18. The next chapter addresses the question of acting and what it suggests vis-à-vis our central problematic in greater detail.

19. Of course, Nietzsche, as early as "On Truth and Lying in the Extra-Moral Sense," shows that imitation does not rely on recollection in the first place. Instead, the force of *forgetting* produces the world: we desire and deploy "truth" only as an effect of having forgotten that language itself does never really "represent" the world, that truth as articulated in language is merely a convention, an eradication of difference.

20. Minghella, among others, makes much of this suggestion—one that one can, but by no means has to, take as an accurate description of Ripley's character. The cost of doing so, however, is to suggest that Ripley's violence occurs because he wants—but cannot have—Dickie, something that is patently not the case. Violence is not the outcome of an experience of lack, at least not in Highsmith's work. The first adaptation of this novel, *Plein Soleil*, does a better job at showing this, for in the French film Ripley is not shown to desire Dickie but his lifestyle. As if to confirm this reading of her first Ripley novel, Highsmith writes in her second novel, published ten years after *Plein Soleil*, that Tom "had longed for leisure and a bit of luxury when he had met Dickie Greenleaf, and now that he had attained it, the charm had not palled" (*Ripley Underground* 100).

21. I will elaborate on this argument in the next chapter.

22. For more on the order-word, see Deleuze and Guattari, *Thousand Plateaus* 75–85.

23. As long as we keep in mind Deleuze's suggestion that the virtual is real, we can also think about this event as an instance where we witness the virtual being actualized. It is because of the virtuality of violence—Ripley's already having become-Dickie—that he can now actualize it, become-violent, so smoothly, so instantaneously. For Deleuze's discussion of the relationship between the virtual and the actual, see, e.g., *Bergsonism* 91–106 and *Difference and Repetition* 208–14.

24. Kakutani's negative judgment of the later Ripley novels is, in fact, rooted in her rather traditional moralistic assumption that representa-

tions of violence are acceptable only if they are rendered realistically. The media's glorification of Spielberg's World War II drama *Saving Private Ryan* merely brings this tendency to a peak: the incredible violence of the film's opening sequence is celebrated precisely because it pretends to have a purchase on the real—that it truly represents the hell American soldiers had to go through to overcome the German forces at Omaha Beach. Compare the assessment of a show such as *South Park*: its violence is frequently condemned (as the movie version of the TV show mockingly depicts) because it does not hold a claim to realism, thus foregoing any purchase on the allegedly pedagogical possibilities of realistic representations.

25. The allusions here are of course to Aristotle's theory of tragedy, elaborated in his *Poetics*, and to Richard Slotkin's "regeneration through violence" thesis, respectively. Slotkin famously shows in *Regeneration through Violence* how the use of violence has been integral to the construction of a uniquely American mythogenesis. Arguing that the "founding fathers were not those eighteen-century gentlemen who composed a nation at Philadelphia [but] those who [. . .] tore violently a nation from implacable and opulent wilderness," Slotkin proposes that "regeneration ultimately became the means of violence, and the myth of regeneration through violence became the structuring metaphor of the American experience" (5). This neo-Aristotelian argument has been widely applied to American literature and fiction, especially to frontier literature and Western films.

26. Highsmith's work, of course, is not the only one that bears this characteristic. It might be interesting to compare, e.g., her work to that of two other crime writers roughly contemporary to her: Jim Thompson and Chester Himes. The former is ultimately more interested in a psychopathic version of violence, and the latter in a more social one (with an emphasis on race). Yet, all three deploy seriality as means to intensify the mood of their work. They heighten the *affective* quality of violence to such a degree that the singularity of the violences rendered remains irreducible to any attempt at accounting for them through recourse to mere individual psychologizing or allegory. For an excellent essay on the affective quality of Himes's fiction, see Eburne.

27. *American Psycho* (366–70) also features a scene in which an apparent crime is covered over for the sake of business.

28. Avery Gordon also cautions of an all too quick embrace of "difference" as the *nom du jour*. In his analysis of contemporary corporations, he convincingly shows how companies themselves have coopted difference

as "a mode of governance responsive to late capitalism" (6): "Corporate culture links a vision of racial and gender *diversity* to its existing relations of ruling to produce something that might be called multicultural corporatism" (3). In this analysis, diversity becomes a "management problematic" (13), just like for Max Horkheimer and Theodor Adorno difference is what is being sold to eager consumers. Hence, we see Nike advertising its product with the slogan "Just do it!" (be different) and Sprite proclaiming "Obey your thirst" (which will make you different from those losers who look to commercials with sports stars for what they should drink). Also consider that today corporate America is quite interested in upholding some sort of affirmative action policy pertaining to higher education. It has long recognized that its survival in the global marketplace depends on its ability to draw upon an applicant pool that is sufficiently comfortable with racial and cultural others.

29. Foucault describes Maurice Blanchot, the thinker most often attributed with having theorized the "outside," and his work in these terms: "Blanchot is perhaps more than just another witness to [the thought of the outside]. So far as he has withdrawn into the manifestations of his work, so completely is he, not hidden by his texts, but absent from their existence, that for us he is that thought itself—its real, absolutely distant, shimmering, invisible presence, its inevitable law, its calm, infinite, measured strength" ("Maurice Blanchot" 19). See also Deleuze's *Foucault* (esp. 70–123) for a pertinent articulation of how Foucault himself is another thinker for whom the outside was nothing but a fold. This folded-in outside, of course, is precisely the image Deleuze gives his plane of immanence: like a folded piece of paper, the inside that ensues from the folding process is nothing but the folded-in outside, the surface area. Depth, in other words, is merely an effect of this folding operation and thus a secondary principle to that of pure immanence.

30. The abolishment of the gold standard in 1971 at Bretton Woods plays a crucial role in Hardt and Negri's narrative. This transformative, or intensifying, moment in capitalist history almost perfectly coincides with the publication of Highsmith's second Ripley novel. Just as Empire intensified its logic to such a degree that, according to Hardt and Negri, any forces of transcendence gave way to pure immanence, so Highsmith's encounter with violence now shifts into full immanent gear. From this moment on, both her novels and her short fiction never stop affirming the solution to the *problématique* of violence that Highsmith already offered in her first Ripley novel.

31. Critics who see her influenced by existentialism include Kakutani, Klein, and Shore. Highsmith herself, however, did not seem to harbor much sympathy for existentialism: "The word existentialist has become fuzzy. It's existentialist if you cut a finger with a kitchen knife—because it has happened. Existentialism is self-indulgent, and they try to gloss over this by calling it a philosophy" (Cooper-Clark 314).

32. My discussion of Robert DeNiro in the next chapter will continue this argument.

33. Jean-Paul Sartre is, of course, the main thinker we associate with that philosophy. His play *Les Jeux Sont Faits* is but one example of his in which he plays out the necessity of *amor fati* in light of the fact that you can never change your actions, that even when given the hypothetical opportunity you will not be able to change the initial outcome: the eternal return is always and necessarily one of sameness.

34. The story is about E. Taylor Cheever who "wrote books in his head, never on paper. By the time he died aged sixty-two, he had written fourteen novels and created hundred and twenty-seven characters, all of whom he, at least, remembered distinctly" (1). Cheever, whose dying wish is to be buried next to Tennyson in Westminster Abbey's Poet's Corner, engages in this peculiar "writerly" practice in direct response to a rejection he received for his first, and only, novel he actually put on paper. In other words, notwithstanding the absence of violence in this story, Highsmith's central concern is once again the violence of judgment.

35. Here too Highsmith stands in remarkable kinship to the experimental ethics of Foucault and Deleuze. Dissecting Hegel's widely influential philosophy of difference and recognition—one that makes difference an effect of a prior sameness or identity—Deleuze argues that the "misfortune in speaking is not speaking, but speaking *for others* or representing something" (*Difference and Repetition* 52).

36. Lest it be thought that only the political right would make these distinctions, turn to the writings of Henry Giroux, one of the most respected American left-leaning cultural critics. He derides Tarantino's hyperreal violence because he views it as essentially immoral (for it is sexist, racist, and oppressive of the working class) and lauds the "symbolic violence" of Spielberg because it "serves to reference a broader logic and set of insights" (62).

37. Incidentally, Ellis's fiction is shot through with the notion of acting, for both Bateman in *American Psycho* and Ward in *Glamorama* see themselves as actors in films, though it is more clearly the case with the latter.

5. Becoming-Violent, Becoming-DeNiro

1. The poster's image is a still taken from the film's climactic scene when Travis enters a brothel finally to follow through with his obsession to "clean up" New York City. The image does not indicate whether he has already shot someone in the hallway, but his manic expression leaves no doubt that at the very least he enjoys the anticipation of doing so.

2. In fact, perhaps with the exception of James Cagney in the 1930s and 1940s, or possibly Robert Mitchum in the 1950s and 1960s, no actor has more singularly embodied violence than DeNiro.

3. For two recent essays on the role of the face in Deleuze's work, see Rushton and Sotirin.

4. According to the *Internet Movie Database*, *Meet the Parents* grossed more than $166 million in its U.S. theatrical release alone. The film's sequel, *Meet the Fockers* (dir. Jay Roach, 2004), was even more successful, grossing close to $280 million, thus making it one of the most successful film sequels of all time. *Analyze This* raked in a respectable $107 million.

5. In "Trauma, Absence, Loss," LaCapra extends his discussion of mourning and melancholia in response to the question of traumatic experience in general. For another interesting study dealing with trauma, see Landsberg.

6. See also Ellis's first two novels, *Less Than Zero* (1985) and *Rules of Attraction* (1987). It seems no coincidence that in addition to *American Psycho* both of these novels were adapted for the big screen as well. And with an adaptation of *Glamorama* currently in production (directed, like *Rules of Attraction* (2002), by Roger Avary), *The Informers* (1994) and *Lunar Park* now remain the only Ellis novels not yet adapted for the big screen.

7. Just like Ellis's *American Psycho*, so Oliver Stone's film was accused of having caused disturbed minds to kill people in real life.

8. For their most extensive critique of psychoanalysis, see *Anti-Oedipus*.

9. See Naremore, *Acting*, and Hirsch, *Method*, for excellent discussions of, respectively, the history of acting and the famous Actors Studio, an acting school that is single-handedly responsible for the enormous popularity of the Method.

10. I will return to the issue of "realism" in the final chapter, especially in the first section. For an excellent recent anthology on cinematic realism, see Ivone Margulies's *Rites of Realism: Essays on Corporeal Cinema*.

11. This film is often considered ground zero for the Method in American film history. For an excellent discussion of the film and its relation to the Method, see Naremore, esp. 193–212.

12. In other words, Strasberg's "affect" is unlike the one I theorize throughout this book. Strasberg equates affect with emotion and thus reduces the former to the horizon of the subject; the affect I have in mind is reducible neither to a subject's emotion nor human beings' bodies. Affect, in the Deleuzean sense, is properly thought as presubjective and nonanthropomorphic.

13. To name but two films influenced by *Mean Streets*, consider the first feature-length efforts by Wong Kar-Wai, *As Tears Go By* (1988), and Fatih Akin, *Kurz und Schmerzlos* (Short Sharp Shock, 1998). Both films, despite the vastly different sociocultural context of their settings, repeat *Mean Streets*' narrative drama featuring a wild, upstart, small-time criminal running head-on into ruin while a slightly older mentor finds himself unable to prevent his protégé from destroying himself. Stylistically, all three films could be considered as expressionistic realism: that is, while they make great use of street locations and a number of other devices that mark their style as street realism, this slice of life atmosphere is intensified by various cinematic devices (such as the use of color and slow motion, e.g.) that are decidedly expressionistic.

14. In the documentary on the making of Spike Lee's *Do the Right Thing* (1989), actor Bill Nunn, who played Radio Raheem, the character who is brutally strangled to death by a cop with his stick, puts this point in plain terms when explaining how he decided to play that scene: "I felt sorry for the kid. Just the sympathy I evoked within myself for the character helped me to be the character. It wasn't like a deep process. I mean, I'm not deep. I'm not one of them Johnny Carson cats who get on Johnny and say 'well, when I was preparing for Raheem, you know, I went and lived with gang members and you know had 'em whoop my ass a couple of times so I could really see how it felt.' No, I don't have to get my ass kicked to play like him."

15. Given that *Taxi Driver* so carefully delineates Travis's becoming-violent, it seems to me fundamentally misguided to read the film's famous mirror scene in terms of "fetish" and "castration anxiety," as, e.g., Amy Taubin does (56). In that scene, Travis does not misrecognize his own powers; he does not "disavow what is known and replace it with belief and suspension of disbelief" (56). Instead, the mirror scene dramatizes working through as a process immanent to acting out; it consti-

tutes a continuation—an intensification—of Travis's becoming-violent that DeNiro describes as a becoming-crab.

16. Perhaps it is the very discipline necessary for accomplishing this that explains why one is hard-pressed to find testimonies (including those of the most outspoken critics of violence in movies) that bemoan the violence of, say, the *Star Wars*, *Rambo*, or *Terminator* franchises. Although these movies feature a great number of casualties, it seems that images of violence that affect viewers are remarkably absent in them. That is, I do not think that these films have proven virtually immune to the wrath of campaigning politicians merely because of their ideologically conservative content.

17. In "Math Anxiety," an excellent essay that mobilizes some of Deleuze's key concepts, Aden Evens makes remarkably similar claims about the function of problems and solutions in mathematics.

18. Incidentally, the film itself leads Menand to arrive at this claim because it refuses to provide the viewers with any sustained analysis of LaMotta's behavior—despite the fact that *Raging Bull* is a biopic of a real person, meaning the generic expectations would lead audiences to expect much biographical material that could help us understand LaMotta's violence. Interestingly enough, LaMotta himself does provide information about his rough childhood in his autobiography, *Raging Bull: My Story*, but Scorsese's film elects not to make use of that kind of information at all.

19. That imitation is all about action is perhaps best expressed by contemporary advertising, especially the successful Gatorade and Nike commercials in which viewers are encouraged to "Be like Mike" or "Just do it!"—the latter being a command in which the exclamation point most concisely expresses that the process of imitation requires (unproblematized) action.

20. I say "occasionally" because DeNiro's career has its share of cliché performances. Think *The Fan* (dir. Tony Scott, 1996), e.g.

21. According to the *Internet Movie Database*, *Cape Fear* grossed $79.1 million in U.S. theatrical release. It was Scorsese's biggest all-time box office hit until *The Aviator* (2004), which grossed $102.61 million. The grosses for Scorsese's other collaborations with DeNiro, in order of commercial success in U.S. theatrical releases are *GoodFellas* ($46.84 million), *Casino* ($42.44 million), *Raging Bull* ($30 million), *Taxi Driver* ($21.1 million), *New York, New York* ($13.8 million), *King of Comedy* ($2.5 million). No data is available for their first collaboration, *Mean Streets*, but I think

it is unlikely to have exceeded the million-dollar mark. I list these numbers to call attention to the fact that their collaboration is one of the most celebrated in movie history despite their films' relatively mediocre or even poor box office performance.

22. The great French film *La Haine* (Hate; dir. Mathieu Kassovitz, 1996) probably most effectively used an homage to the mirror scene for its own purposes. But see also *Down in the Valley* (dir. David Jacobson, 2005) in which Harlan, played by Edward Norton, who is often considered the legitimate heir to DeNiro, stands in front of a mirror, gun in hand, producing what Stephanie Zacharek nicely describes as a "stuttering stream of crazy talk: Harlan's like Travis Bickle crossed with Andy Warhol's silkscreen portrait of a gun-slinging Elvis, a man out of time."

Will Smith's acclaimed performance in Michael Mann's *Ali* (2001) at once comes to mind as an example of the lasting impact of DeNiro's tour de force in *Raging Bull*. Likewise, consider Christian Bale's performance in *The Machinist* (dir. Brad Anderson, 2004). The thinness of Bale's body—most reviewers liken it to images of concentration camp inmates—is deeply disturbing, not least because it juxtaposes so starkly to his buff body in *American Psycho* (as well as in *Batman Begins*).

23. Before *Heat*, DeNiro and Pacino worked together on the second Godfather film, but they never shared a scene.

24. Pacino, e.g., has never really learned to express intensity through calmness and has been criticized for over acting in this and other films, particularly because he appears to rely too much on the (voluminous) strength of his vocal chords. In contrast, DeNiro has received great praise for his performance in *Heat* that is well summarized by Rob Fraser, who characterizes DeNiro's performance, especially in the coffee store scene with Pacino, as amounting "to a master class in non-verbal acting: it's as though his thoughts and conflicting emotions are written in bold type across his face" ("Mann's World" 171).

25. I lift this explanation from my review essay of Andrea Landsberg's book *Prosthetic Memory*.

26. Incidentally, this function has nothing to do with criteria of "quality." It seems to me therefore misguided to assert, as one critic does, that DeNiro's "prime associative value [is] with what we might call mainstream 'cinema of quality'" (Jackson 113).

27. See, e.g., Godard, *Historie(s) du Cinéma* (1998) as well as Richard Brody's profile of Godard.

6. Don DeLillo's "In the Ruins of the Future"

1. V. S. Naipaul, recipient of the Nobel prize in literature in October 2001, is one of the more prominent writers who has recently made such arguments, maintaining that "only nonfiction could capture the complexities of today's world" (Donadio, "Irascible Prophet"). As Rachel Donadio reports in the *New York Times*, today's magazine editors share this unease about the relevance of fiction. As a result, many magazines such as *The Atlantic Monthly, Paris Review, Esquire*, or GQ have drastically cut, or totally eliminated, the space they traditionally used to allocate for the publication of fiction ("Stronger Than Fiction").

2. For more on this relationship, see Baker, Simmons. In an oddly prescient manner, Bret Easton Ellis's *Glamorama* also foregrounded the relationship between consumerism, the society of the spectacle, and terrorism as a last-minute attempt to stop, and even undo, this development.

3. Eisenstein postulates that "absolute realism is by no means the correct form of perception. It is simply the function of a certain form of social structure" (35). Dialectical montage supposedly reveals to viewers their true conditions of life and inspires them to act accordingly.

4. That Bazin carefully distinguishes between perception and seeing—that he suspends perception as an event—essentially disqualifies him from being considered a phenomenologist, even though he is frequently labeled as just that (see Sobchack, Rosen, and Jay). Further, Bazin's considerable influence on the cinema thought of Deleuze, who, as John Protevi compellingly argues in *Political Physics*, is not a phenomenologist but a materialist, should also trouble any assessment of Bazin's writings as phenomenological. Likewise, Daniel W. Smith, one of Deleuze's most brilliant exegetes, persuasively argues in his translator's introduction to Deleuze's study of Francis Bacon's paintings that "Deleuze is not a phenomenologist" (xv), notwithstanding the surface similarities between some of Deleuze's concepts and those of phenomenologists such as Erwin Straus or Maurice Merleau-Ponty.

5. Addressing a different kind of screen—the painter's canvas—Deleuze argues in *Francis Bacon*, "it would be a mistake to think that the painter works on a white and virgin surface. The entire surface is already invested virtually with all kinds of clichés, which it will be necessary to break with" (12). Also remember that Deleuze considers the virtual real.

6. In *Cinema 2*, Deleuze writes, "If the world has become a bad cinema,

in which we no longer believe, surely a true cinema can contribute to giving us back reasons to believe in this world and in vanished bodies" (201).

7. Deleuze argues that the fetish so crucial to the masochistic economy functions not as a symbol, as psychoanalysis claims, but as a "frozen, arrested, two-dimensional image" (*Masochism* 31) that ultimately opens up a path for novelty to emerge.

8. That DeLillo's mode of narration functions neorealistically might not be a coincidence considering that, as Deleuze argues, the neorealist mode of seeing emerged from the destruction permeating Europe at the end of World War II (*Cinema 2* xi). DeLillo's narrative begins within and responds to another, albeit different, ruin.

9. Throughout DeLillo's career, moving images have strongly infused his narratives. See, e.g., *Americana* (1971), *White Noise* (1985), or *Underworld* (1997).

10. Nicholas Spencer provides an excellent analysis of the resonances between Virilio's theory of perception and DeLillo's *Underworld*. He concludes that "it is tempting to read DeLillo's novel as a nostalgic appeal to humanist subjectivity. However, both DeLillo's and Virilio's interest in the movement of the human body in social space disposes with phenomenology and humanism" (217). The terms and sentiment of Spencer's conclusion strongly resonate with the present analysis.

11. I will return to this thought.

12. For an excellent essay on DeLillo and seriality, see Karnicky, "Wallpaper Mao."

13. According to his introduction to his *In the Shadow of No Towers*, Spiegelman's firsthand experience of 9/11 compelled him to return to comix after having "spent much of the decade before the millennium trying to avoid making [them]." During his hiatus from comix, he created many of the best-known cover art for the *New Yorker*—the most famous one being, of course, his black-on-black afterimage that appeared on the magazine's cover six days after the attacks.

14. For the best and most comprehensive articulation of Deleuze's theory of language, see LeCercle.

15. For an excellent examination of Adorno's chiasmic style, see Nealon, "Maxima Immoralia?"

16. See also Romuald Karmakar's film *Hamburger Lektionen* (Hamburg Lectures, 2006) for a powerful cinematic example that brings across this very point. Restaging word for word two actual lectures given by Imam Mohammed Fazazi at the Al Quds mosque in Hamburg that

might have been attended by various members of the so-called Hamburg Cell, including three of the four pilots used in the attacks of 9/11, this exercise in radical cinematic minimalism affectively enables its intended, presumably "enlightened" audience to sense the fundamentally different logic within which the Imam and his listening interlocutors operate—a logic that simply sidesteps any appeals to the notion of recognition as configured by Enlightenment discourses. For a brief discussion of the film, see Abel, "Post-Wall Reality."

17. *Empire* analyzes fundamentalism as something that is "not backward-looking at all, but rather a new invention that is part of a political project [Empire] against the contemporary social order" (148)—an "empirical" project that relentlessly intensifies capitalism's processes.

18. On paranoia in DeLillo's work, see Allen, Hantke, and Knight.

19. This novel is the first part of Grossman's American Letter Trilogy, which also includes *The Book of Lazarus* (1998) and *Breeze Avenue* (unpublished). The trilogy itself is loosely patterned on Dante's "Divine Comedy," with *The Alphabet Man* being an articulation of hell, *The Book of Lazarus* a working through of purgatory, and *Breeze Avenue* an expression of salvation. Ironically, it appears that Grossman offers his readers salvation in form of a novel that, when finished, is going to be three million pages in length and, according to the author's own book description on his Web site, "will be permanently installed in a reading room in Los Angeles in 2007." Speaking of violent affect . . .

20. This is indeed one of the key provocations of Deleuze and Guattari's work. As Shaviro glosses this point, "Deleuze and Guattari insist that social formations be defined not by their hegemonic institutions and ideologies but by their potentials for change, not by their norms but by 'lines of flight'" (23).

21. We can observe this sudden zooming in on a particular story in many neorealist films. The narrative strategy is common to many cinema aesthetics, but the choice of focus tends to be more random and less inevitable in neorealism than in, say, classical Hollywood cinema. For instance, De Sica's *The Bicycle Thief* focuses on the father-son relationship, but the film's overall aesthetic suggests that it could have been otherwise, that there is no intrinsic importance to the telling of the specific story. That DeLillo's narrator quickly abandons the focus on his nephew merely intensifies this neorealist device: what seems to be most personal—and almost by definition most important—is provided as merely one non-privileged link in a series of images.

22. Here, one might also recall the opening lines from Thomas Pynchon's *Gravity's Rainbow*: "A screaming comes across the sky. It has happened before but there is nothing to compare it to now" (3).

23. In his perceptive analysis of DeLillo's early novel, *End Zone* (1972), James R. Giles attributes this insight to DeLillo, concluding that the author "ultimately recognizes that words are all he has" (108).

24. Deleuze makes a similar argument in chapter 13 of *Francis Bacon*.

25. See, e.g., Horkheimer and Adorno, "Culture Industry," for such negative views.

26. See part 2 of Adorno's essay for his discussion of the *ethical* need to maintain a distance between the (cinematic) image and reality.

27. For more on the notion of enframing see, e.g., Heidegger.

28. See, e.g., his *Postmodernism*, esp. 46.

29. Any cursory look at the discourse surrounding the burgeoning conflict between the United States and Islamic fundamentalism before 9/11 immediately reveals judgment as a strategic force both sides relentlessly mobilized to the detriment of almost any other mode of encounter. While this rhetoric of judgment did not cause 9/11, it played a significant role in the event's genealogy.

30. The U.S. Embassy in Seoul, South Korea, seems to disagree. Commenting on a shorter version of this chapter published in PMLA, the embassy's Website abstracts my article by claiming that my argument is "advocacy of moral relativism," as if to warn potential readers to be leery of my argument lest they get sucked into un-American ways of thinking.

31. If anything, a rushed affirmation of judgment constitutes moral relativism, as Nietzsche argues in *The Genealogy of Morals*, asking, what if "morality was the danger of dangers" (20)?

32. Given their different realms of influence over contemporary thought, an extended analysis of Deleuze's and Adorno's work in conjunction with each other might very well prove to be enormously fruitful for disciplines such as film and literary studies, cultural studies, as well as philosophy. To date, though, surprisingly few critical analyses of the relationship between these two thinkers have been produced. For the most interesting, see Toole; Nesbitt, "Musical Multiplicity" and "Expulsion of the Negative"; and chapters 5 and 6 in Stuhr.

33. See Žižek, *Sublime Object of Ideology*, esp. 201–7. In Silverman's *World Spectators*, which merges Lacan and Heidegger in order to show that "visual perception [rather than linguistic expression] comes first" (128), the sublime, though not named as such, percolates as the Laca-

nian "impossible non-object of desire" inflected by Heideggerian "Dasein." Kant discusses the sublime in his *Critique of Judgment.*

34. Jean-François Lyotard aphoristically expresses this when he asserts, "*that* there is [precedes] *what* there is" (*Inhuman* 82). For Lyotard, this "there is" articulates the sublime as a relation of force or "a matter of intensification" (100). Although he successfully wrestles the sublime away from theories that configure it in terms of lack, I hesitate to turn to Lyotard simply because I fear that theories of lack have too much of a stronghold over the discourse of the sublime for the discourse of the sublime to be useful to this project's purposes. Paul Virilio discusses in depth the issue of speed in, e.g., *Aesthetics of Disappearance* and *Ground Zero*, his essay on 9/11.

Bibliography

9/11. Dir. Jules and Gédéon Naudet. 2002. DVD. Paramount Home Video, 2002.

Abel, Marco. "*Fargo*: The Violent Production of the Masochistic Contract as a Cinematic Concept." *Critical Studies in Mass Communication* 16.3 (1999): 308–28.

———. "The State of Things Part Two: More Images for a Post-Wall German Reality." *Senses of Cinema: An Online Film Journal Devoted to the Serious and Eclectic Discussion of Cinema* 39 (April–June 2006). http://www.sensesofcinema.com/contents/festivals/06/39/berlin2006.html.

———. Rev. of *Prosthetic Memory: The Transformation of American Remembrance in the Age of Mass Culture*, by Alison Landsberg. *Quarterly Review of Film and Video* 23.4 (2006): 377–88.

———. "Speeding across the Rhizome: Deleuze Meets Kerouac *On the Road*." *Modern Fiction Studies* 48.2 (2002): 227–56.

Acker, Kathy. "Writing, Identity, and Copyright in the Net Age." Accessed April 9, 2002. http://www.calarts.edu/~acker/ackademy/copyright.html.

Adorno, Theodor. *Aesthetic Theory*. Trans. Robert Hullot-Kentor. Minneapolis: University of Minnesota Press, 1999.

———. *Minima Moralia: Reflections from a Damaged Life*. Trans. E. F. N. Jephcott. London: New Left Books, 1974.

———. *Negative Dialectics*. Trans. E. B. Ashton. New York: Continuum, 1973.

———. *Prisms*. Trans. Samuel and Sherry Weber. Cambridge: MIT Press, 1994.

———. "Transparencies on Film." *New German Critique* 24/25 (Fall 1981–Winter 1982): 199–205.

Allen, Glen Scott. "Raids on the Conscious: Pynchon's Legacy of Paranoia and the Terrorism of Uncertainty in Don DeLillo's *Ratner's Star*." *Post-*

modern Culture 4.2 (1994). Accessed July 26, 2002. http://muse.jhu
.edu/journals/postmodern_culture/voo4/4.2allen.html.

Altman, Rick. *Film/Genre*. London: BFI, 1999.

American Psycho. Dir. Mary Harron. 2000. DVD. Universal Studios,
2000.

Analyze This. Dir. Harold Ramis. 1999. VHS. Warner Bros., 2000.

Annesley, James. *Blank Fictions: Consumerism, Culture, and the Contemporary American Novel*. New York: St. Martin's Press, 1998.

Archer, Mark. "The Funeral Baked Meats." Rev. of *American Psycho*, by
Bret Easton Ellis. *The Spectator* April 27, 1991:31.

Auster, Paul. *City of Glass*. In *The New York Trilogy*. New York: Penguin,
1986.

Badiou, Alain. *Deleuze: The Clamor of Being*. Trans. Louis Burchill. Minneapolis: University of Minnesota Press, 2000.

Baer, Ulrich, ed. *110 Stories*. New York: NYU Press, 2002.

Baker, Peter. "The Terrorist as Interpreter: *Mao II* in Postmodern Context." *Postmodern Culture* 4.2 (1994). Accessed July 26, 2002. http://
muse.jhu.edu/journals/postmodern_culture/voo4/4.2allen.html.

Baldwin, Kristen. "Psychodrama." *Entertainment Weekly* 14 April 2000:
34–38.

Barker, Martin, and Julian Petley, eds. *Ill Effects: The Media/Violence Debate*. New York: Routledge, 1997.

Baucom, Ian. "Globalit, Inc.; or, The Cultural Logic of Global Literary
Studies." *PMLA* 116.1 (2001): 158–72.

Baudrillard, Jean. *Simulations*. Trans. Paul Foss, Paul Patton, and Philip
Beitchman. New York: Semiotext[e], 1983.

———. "The Spirit of Terrorism." Trans. Rachel Bloul. November 14,
2001. Accessed March 5, 2002. http://cryptome.org/baud-terr.htm.

Baxter, Tara, and Nikki Craft. "There Are Better Ways of Taking Care of
Bret Easton Ellis Than Just Censoring Him." *Making Violence Sexy:
Feminist Views on Pornography*. Ed. Diana E. H. Russell. New York:
Teacher's College Press, 1993. 245–53.

Bazin, André. *What Is Cinema?* Vols. 1–2. Trans. Hugh Gray. Berkeley:
University of California Press, 1967, 1972.

Bérubé, Michael. "Public Image Limited: Political Correctness and the
Media's Big Lie." *Village Voice* June 12–18, 1991. Accessed July 23,
2005. http://villagevoice.com/news/9125,berube,22585,1.html.

Blanchot, Maurice. *The Infinite Conversation*. Trans. Susan Hanson. Minneapolis: University of Minnesota Press, 1993.

———. *The Space of Literature*. Trans. Ann Smock. Lincoln: University of Nebraska Press, 1989.

Bogue, Ronald. *Deleuze on Literature*. New York: Routledge, 2003.

Bordwell, David. "A Case for Cognitivism." *Iris* 9 (Spring 1989): 11–40.

———. *Making Meaning: Inference and Rhetoric in the Interpretation of Cinema*. Cambridge: Harvard University Press, 1989.

Bordwell, David, and Noël Carroll. *Post-Theory: Reconstructing Film Studies*. Madison: University of Wisconsin Press, 1996.

Bordwell, David, Janet Staiger, and Kristin Thompson. *The Classical Hollywood Cinema: Film Style and Mode of Production to 1960*. New York: Columbia University Press, 1985.

Bouchard, Donald F., ed. and trans. *Language, Counter-Memory, Practice: Selected Essays and Interviews by Michel Foucault*. Ithaca: Cornell University Press, 1977.

Boundas, Constantin. "On Tendencies and Signs: Major and Minor Deconstruction." *Angelaki* 5.2 (2000): 163–76.

Brody, Richard. "An Exile in Paradise." *New Yorker* November 20, 2000:62–76.

Bronski, Michael. "The Talented Mr. Ripley." Rev. of *The Talented Mr. Ripley*, by Patricia Highsmith. *Cineaste* 25.3 (2000): 41–43.

Browne, Nick, Theresa Webb, et al. "American Film Violence: An Analytic Portrait." *Journal of Interpersonal Violence* 17.4 (2002): 351–67.

Buchanan, Ian, and John Marks, eds. *Deleuze and Literature*. Edinburgh: Edinburgh Press, 2000.

Carroll, Noël. "Introducing Film Evaluation." *Reinventing Film Studies*. Ed. Christine Gledhill and Linda Williams. New York: Arnold, 2000. 265–78.

Cavell, Stanley. *Pursuits of Happiness: The Hollywood Comedy of Remarriage*. Cambridge: Harvard University Press, 1981.

Cavigelli, Franz, Fritz Senn, and Anna von Planta, eds. *Patricia Highsmith: Leben und Werk*. 5th ed. Zürich: Diogenes, 1996.

La Chinoise. Dir. Jean-Luc Godard. 1968. DVD. Optimum Releasing, 2005.

Clapp, Susannah. "The Simple Art of Murder." *New Yorker* December 20, 1999:94–97.

Cochran, David. "Some Torture That Perversely Eased: Patricia Highsmith and the Everyday Schizophrenia of American Life." *American Noir: Underground Writers and Filmmakers of the Postwar Era*. Washington: Smithsonian Institute Press, 2000. 114–30.

Colebrook, Claire. "Inhuman Irony: The Event of the Postmodern." *Deleuze and Literature*. Ed. Ian Buchanan and John Marks. Edinburgh: Edinburgh University Press, 2000. 100–134.

Cooper-Clark, Diana. "Patricia Highsmith: Interview." *Armchair Detective* 14.4 (1981): 313–20.

Cox, Tom. "Will the Real Mr. Ripley Please Step Forward?" *ZA@Play* March 16, 2000. Accessed August 28, 2005. http://www.chico.mweb .co.za/mg/art/film/0003/000316–ripley.html.

Cunningham, Valentine. *Reading after Theory*. New York: Blackwell, 2001.

Deleuze, Gilles. "Bartleby; or, The Formula." *Essays Critical and Clinical*. Trans. Daniel W. Smith and Michael A. Greco. Minneapolis: University of Minnesota Press, 1997. 68–90.

———. *Bergsonism*. Trans. Hugh Tomlinson and Barbara Habberjam. New York: Zone Books, 1991.

———. "The Brain Is the Screen: An Interview with Gilles Deleuze." Flaxman 365–73.

———. *Cinema 2: The Time-Image*. Trans. Hugh Tomlinson and Robert Galeta. Minneapolis: University of Minnesota Press, 1989.

———. "Desire and Pleasure." *Foucault and His Interlocutors*. Ed. Arnold I. Davidson. Chicago: University of Chicago Press, 1997. 183–94.

———. *Difference and Repetition*. Trans. Paul Patton. New York: Columbia University Press, 1994.

———. *Foucault*. Trans. Seán Hand. Minneapolis: University of Minnesota Press, 1988.

———. "On Four Poetic Formulas That Might Summarize the Kantian Philosophy." *Essays Critical and Clinical*. Trans. Daniel W. Smith and Michael A. Greco. Minneapolis: University of Minnesota Press, 1997. 27–35.

———. *Francis Bacon: The Logic of Sensation*. Trans. Daniel W. Smith. Minneapolis: University of Minnesota Press, 2004.

———. *Kant's Critical Philosophy: The Doctrine of the Faculties*. Trans. Hugh Tomlinson and Barbara Habberjam. Minneapolis: University of Minnesota Press, 1999.

———. "Literature and Life." *Essays Critical and Clinical*. Trans. Daniel W. Smith and Michael A. Greco. Minneapolis: University of Minnesota Press, 1997. 1–6.

———. *Masochism*. Trans. Jean McNeil. New York: Zone Books, 1994.

———. *Negotiations*. Trans. Martin Joughin. New York: Columbia University Press, 1995.

————. *Nietzsche and Philosophy*. Trans. Hugh Tomlinson. New York: Columbia University Press, 1983.

————. "One Less Manifesto." *Mimesis, Masochism, and Mime: The Politics of Theatricality in Contemporary French Thought*. Ed. Timothy Murray. Ann Arbor: University of Michigan Press, 1997. 239–58.

————. "Philosophy of the Série Noire." Trans. Timothy S. Murphy. *Genre* 34 (Spring–Summer 2001): 5–10.

————. "The Simulacrum and Ancient Philosophy." *The Logic of Sense*. Trans. Mark Lester with Charles Stivale. New York: Columbia University Press, 1990. 253–79.

————. "To Have Done with Judgment." *Essays Critical and Clinical*. Trans. Daniel W. Smith and Michael A. Greco. Minneapolis: University of Minnesota Press, 1997. 126–35.

Deleuze, Gilles, and Félix Guattari. *Anti-Oedipus: Capitalism and Schizophrenia*. Trans. Robert Hurley, Mark Seem, and Helen R. Lane. Minneapolis: University of Minnesota Press, 1983.

————. *Kafka: Toward a Minor Literature*. Trans. Dana Polan. Minneapolis: University Minnesota Press, 1986.

————. *A Thousand Plateaus: Capitalism and Schizophrenia*. Trans. Brian Massumi. Minneapolis: University of Minnesota Press, 1987.

————. *What Is Philosophy?* Trans. Hugh Tomlinson and Graham Burchell. New York: Columbia University Press, 1994.

Deleuze, Gilles, and Claire Parnet. *L'Abécédaire de Gilles Deleuze*. Arte November 1994–Spring 1995. Transcript available at http://www.langlab.wayne.edu/Cstivale/D-G/ABCs.html. Trans. Charles Stivale. Accessed July 4, 2006.

————. *Dialogues*. Trans. Hugh Tomlinson and Barbara Habberjam. New York: Columbia University Press, 1987.

DeLillo, Don. "In the Ruins of the Future: Reflections on Terror and Loss in the Shadow of September." *Harper's Magazine* December 2001:33–40. Reprinted in *The Guardian*. Online access at http://guardian.o.uk/Archive/Article/0,4273,4324579,00.html.

————. *Libra*. New York: Penguin, 1991.

————. *White Noise*. New York: Penguin, 1986.

De Man, Paul. *Allegories of Reading*. New Haven: Yale University Press, 1979.

Denby, David. "Brute Force." *Perspectives on Raging Bull*. Ed. Steven G. Kellman. New York: G. K. Hall, 1994. 43–45.

DeNiro, Robert. Interview with James Lipton. *Inside the Actors Studio*. Bravo. January 31, 1999.

Derrida, Jacques. "Différance." *Margins of Philosophy*. Trans. Alan Bass. Chicago: University of Chicago Press, 1982. 1–27.

———. *Of Grammatology*. Trans. Gayatri Chakravorty Spivak. Baltimore: Johns Hopkins University Press, 1976.

———. "Signatures Event Context." *Margins of Philosophy*. Trans. Alan Bass. Chicago: University of Chicago Press, 1982. 309–30.

Dickstein, Morris. "Stations of the Cross: *Raging Bull* Revisited." *Perspectives on Raging Bull*. Ed. Steven G. Kellman. New York: G. K. Hall, 1994. 77–83.

Donadio, Rachel. "The Irascible Prophet: V. S. Naipaul at Home." *New York Times Book Review* August 7, 2005. Accessed August 30, 2005. http://www.nytimes.com/2005/08/07/books/review/07DONADIO .html?ex=1162616400&en=b1984d879ccac25c&ei=5070.

———. "Truth Is Stronger than Fiction." *New York Times Book Review* August 7, 2005. Accessed August 30, 2005. http://www.nytimes .com/2005/08/07/books/review/07DONA2.html?ex=1162616400 &en=66b66b82a18fd37c&ei=5070.

Do the Right Thing. Dir. Spike Lee. 1989. DVD. Criterion, 2001.

Dougan, Andy. *Untouchable: A Biography of Robert DeNiro*. New York: Thunder's Mouth Press, 1996.

Dupont, Joan. "Criminal Pursuits." *New York Times* June 12, 1988, Magazine Desk:60–63.

During, Elie. "Blackboxing in Theory: Deleuze versus Deleuze." *French Theory in America*. Ed. Sylvère Lotringer and Sande Cohen. New York: Routledge, 2001. 163–90.

During, Simon, ed. *The Cultural Studies Reader*. New York: Routledge, 1993.

Eberly, Rosa A. *Citizen Critics: Literary Public Spheres*. Urbana: University of Illinois Press, 2000.

Eburne, Jonathan P. "The Transatlantic Mysteries of Paris: Chester Himes, Surrealism, and the Série Noir." PMLA 120.3 (2005): 806–21.

Eisenstein, Sergei. *Film Form: Essays in Film Theory*. Ed. and trans. Jay Leyda. New York: Harcourt Brace, 1977.

Ellis, Bret Easton. *American Psycho*. New York: Vintage, 1991.

Ellroy, James. *American Tabloid*. New York: Fawcett Columbine, 1997.

Evans, Aden. "Math Anxiety." *Angelaki* 5.3 (2000): 105–16.

Evenson, Brian. *The Brotherhood of Mutilation*. Shrewsbury MA: Earthling Publications, 2003.

———. "The Polygamy of Language." *Contagion and Other Stories*. La Grande: Wordcraft of Oregon, 2000. 9–24.

Fargo. Dir. Joel Coen. 1996. DVD. MGM, 2000.

Flaxman, Gregory, ed. *The Brain Is the Screen: Deleuze and the Philosophy of Cinema*. Minneapolis: University of Minnesota Press, 2000.

Foucault, Michel. *The Foucault Reader*. Ed. Paul Rabinow. New York: Pantheon Books, 1984.

———. "The Masked Philosopher." *Politics, Philosophy, Culture: Interviews and Other Writings 1977–1984*. Ed. Lawrence D. Kritzman. New York: Routledge, 1990. 323–30.

———. "Maurice Blanchot: The Thought from Outside." Trans. Brian Massumi. *Foucault / Blanchot*. New York: Zone Books, 1990. 7–60.

———. "Nietzsche, Genealogy, History." Bouchard 139–64.

———. "On the Genealogy of Ethics: Overview of Work in Progress." *Michel Foucault: Beyond Structuralism and Hermeneutics*. 2nd ed. Ed. Hubert L. Dreyfus and Paul Rabinow. Chicago: University of Chicago Press, 1983. 229–52.

———. *The Order of Things: An Archeology of the Human Sciences*. Trans. Alan Sheridan. New York: Vintage Books, 1994.

———. "Theatrum Philosophicum." Bouchard 165–96.

Foucault, Michel, and Gilles Deleuze. "Intellectuals and Power." Bouchard 205–17.

Frank, Thomas. *The Conquest of Cool: Business Culture, Counterculture, and the Rise of Hip Consumerism*. Chicago: University of Chicago Press, 1998.

Fraser, Rob. "Mann's World: How DeNiro and Pacino Generated 'Heat.'" Hunter 167–78.

———. "'Performing Miracles': Notes on a Life in Screen Acting." Hunter 5–22.

Freccero, Carla. "Historical Violence, Censorship, and the Serial Killer: The Case of *American Psycho*." *Diacritics* 27.2 (1997): 44–58.

Freud, Sigmund. "Mourning and Melancholia." *Collected Papers*. Trans. Joan Riviere. Vol. 4. New York: Basic Books, 1962. 152–70.

Frohock, W. M. *The Novel of Violence in America*. 2nd ed. Dallas: Southern Methodist University Press, 1957.

Frus, Phyllis. "Documenting Domestic Violence in American Films." Slocum, *Violence in American Cinema* 226–44.

Giles, James R. *The Spaces of Violence*. Tuscaloosa: The University of Alabama Press, 2006.

Giroux, Henry. *Fugitive Cultures: Race, Violence, and Youth*. New York: Routledge, 1996.

Gleiberman, Owen. "Chopping Spree." Rev. of *American Psycho*, dir. Mary Harron. *Entertainment Weekly* April 14, 2000:46–47.

Godard, Jean-Luc. "Let's Talk about Pierrot." *Godard on Godard*. Ed. and trans. Tom Milne. New York: Da Capo Press, 1986. 215–34.

Goldberg, Elisabeth Swanson. "Splitting the Difference: Global Identity Politics and the Representation of Torture in the Counterhistorical Dramatic Films." Slocum, *Violence in American Cinema* 245–70.

GoodFellas. Dir. Martin Scorsese. 1990. DVD. Warner Bros., 1997.

Gordon, Avery. "The Work of Corporate Culture: Diversity Management." *Social Text* 44.3 (1995): 3–29.

Gormley, Paul. *The New-Brutality Film: Race and Affect in Contemporary Hollywood*. Bristol: Intellect, 2005.

Grist, Leighton. *The Films of Martin Scorsese, 1963–77: Authorship and Context*. London: Macmillan Press, 2000.

Grossberg, Lawrence. "The Victory of Culture." *Angelaki* 3.3 (1998): 3–29.

———. *We Gotta Get Out of This Place: Popular Conservatism and Postmodern Culture*. New York: Routledge, 1992.

Grossman, Richard. *The Alphabet Man*. Boulder: Fiction Collective Two, 1993.

———. Home page. Accessed July 5, 2006. http://richardgrossman.com.

Hamburger Lektionen. Dir. Romuald Karmakar. Pantera Film, 2006.

Handke, Peter. "Die privaten Weltkriege der Patricia Highsmith." Cavigelli, Senn, and von Planta 169–82.

Hantke, Steffen. "'God Save Us from Bourgeois Adventure': The Figure of the Terrorist in Contemporary American Conspiracy Fiction." *Studies in the Novel* 28.2 (1996): 219–43.

Hardt, Michael, and Antonio Negri. *Empire*. Cambridge: Harvard University Press, 2000.

Harrison, Russell. *Patricia Highsmith*. New York: Twayne, 1997.

Harron, Mary. "The Risky Territory of 'American Psycho.'" *New York Times* April 9, 2000: AR13, 16.

Harron, Mary, Bret Easton Ellis, and Christian Bale. Interview with Charlie Rose. *Charlie Rose* (Show No. 2660) PBS. April 13, 2000.

Harvey, Dennis. "Flesh Flies in Dubious 'American Psycho.'" Rev. of *American Psycho*, dir. Mary Harron. *Variety Online* January 24, 2000. Accessed January 26, 2000. http://dailynews.yahoo.com/h/nm/20000124/en/review-filmpsycho_1.html.

Hayward, Susan. *Key Concepts in Cinema Studies*. New York: Routledge, 1996.

Heat. Dir. Michael Mann. 1995. DVD. Warner Bros., 1999.

Heidegger, Martin. "The Question Concerning Technology." *The Question Concerning Technology and Other Essays*. Trans. William Lovitt. New York: Harper and Row, 1977. 3–35.

Hemmings, Clare. "Invoking Affect: Cultural Theory and the Ontological Turn." *Cultural Studies* 19.5 (2005): 548–67.

Highsmith, Patricia. *The Blunderer*. New York: Penzler Books, 1985.

———. *Carol*. London: Bloomsbury, 1990.

———. *Edith's Diary*. London: Heinemann, 1977.

———. *The Glass Cell*. Garden City NY: Doubleday, Crime Club, 1964.

———. "The Man Who Wrote Books in His Head." *Slowly, Slowly in the Wind*. New York: The Mysterious Press, 1979. 1–6.

———. *Plotting and Writing of Suspense Fiction*. New York: St. Martin's Press, 1983.

———. *Ripley Underground*. New York: Vintage, 1992.

———. *The Story-Teller*. New York: Manor Books, 1976.

———. *The Talented Mr. Ripley*. New York: Vintage, 1992.

———. *This Sweet Sickness*. London: Penguin, 1987.

———. *The Tremor of Forgery*. New York: Atlantic Monthly Press, 1988.

———. *The Two Faces of January*. New York: Atlantic Monthly Press, 1988.

Hilfer, Anthony Channell. "'Not Really Such a Monster': Highsmith's Ripley as Thriller Protagonist and Protean Man." *Midwest Quarterly* 25 (1984): 361–74.

Hirsch, Foster. *Detours and Lost Highways: A Map of Neo-Noir*. New York: Limelight Editions, 1999.

———. *A Method to Their Madness: The History of the Actors Studio*. New York: Da Capo Press, 1984.

Historie(s) du Cinéma. Dir. Jean-Luc Godard. TV. Le Studio Canal+, 1998.

Hochkeppel, Willy. Interview with Patricia Highsmith. Cavigelli, Senn, and von Planta 183–86.

Holden, Stephen. "Murder! Fiend! (But Well Dressed)." Rev. of *American Psycho*, dir. Mary Harron. *New York Times* April 14, 2000:B1, 28.

Holman, C. Hugh, and William Harmon. *A Handbook to Literature*. 6th ed. New York: Macmillan, 1992.

Horkheimer, Max, and Theodor Adorno. "The Culture Industry." *Dialectic of Enlightenment*. Trans. Edmund Jephcott. Stanford: Stanford University Press, 2002. 94–136.

Hubly, Erlene. "A Portrait of the Artist: The Novels of Patricia Highsmith." *Clues* 5 (1984): 115–30.

Hume, Kathryn. *American Dream American Nightmare: Fiction Since 1960.* Urbana: University of Illinois Press, 2000.

———. "Narrative Speed in Contemporary Fiction." *Narrative* 13.2 (2005): 105–24.

Hunter, Jack, ed. *Robert DeNiro: Movie Top Ten.* Creation Books, 1999.

Internet Movie Database. http://www.imdb.com.

Jackson, Neil. "Robert DeNiro, the Gangster Film and 'Once Upon a Time in America.'" Hunter 111–30.

James, Nick. "My Bloody Valentine." *Sight and Sound* February 2000:14–17.

———. "Sick City Boy." *Sight and Sound* May 2000:22–24.

Jameson, Fredric. *Postmodernism; or, The Cultural Logic of Late Capitalism.* Durham: Duke University Press, 1995.

Jay, Martin. *The Downcast Eye: The Denigration of Vision in Twentieth-Century French Thought.* Berkeley: University of California Press, 1994.

JFK. Dir. Oliver Stone. 1991. DVD. Warner Bros., 2000.

Kakutani, Michiko. "The Kinship of Macabre and Banal." Rev. of *The Talented Mr. Ripley, Ripley Underground,* and *Ripley's Game,* by Patricia Highsmith. *New York Times* November 19, 1999, Leisure/Weekend Desk. Accessed November 1, 2000. http://query.nytimes.com/gst/fullpage.html?res=9C0DE7DA163CF93AA25752C1A96F958260.

Kant, Immanuel. *Critique of Judgment.* Trans. J. H. Bernard. New York: Hafner Press, 1951.

———. *Foundations of the Metaphysics of Morals.* Trans. Lewis White Back. Indianapolis: Bobbs-Merrill, 1969.

Karnicky, Jeffrey. *Contemporary Fiction and the Ethics of Modern Culture.* New York: Palgrave Macmillan, 2007.

———. "Wallpaper Mao: Don DeLillo, Andy Warhol, and Seriality." *Critique* 42.4 (2001): 339–58.

Kauffman, Linda S. *Bad Boys and Sick Girls: Fantasies in Contemporary Art and Culture.* Berkeley: University of California Press, 1998.

Kinder, Marsha. "Violence American Style: The Narrative Orchestration of Violent Attractions." Slocum, *Violence in American Cinema* 63–102.

King, Geoff. "'Killing Funny': Mixing Modalities in New Hollywood's Comedy-with-Violence." Schneider 126–43.

Kings of the Road. Dir. Wim Wenders. 1976. VHS. Pacific Arts Video, 1987.

The Kinks. "Celluloid Heroes." *The Ultimate Collection*. Sanctuary Records, 2002.

Klein, Kathleen Gregory. "Patricia Highsmith." *And Then There Were Nine—More Women of Mystery*. Bowling Green: Bowling Green State University Popular Press, 1985. 170–97.

Knight, Peter. "Everything Is Connected: *Underworld*'s Secret History of Paranoia." *Modern Fiction Studies* 45.3 (1999): 811–36.

Knox, Sara L. "The Productive Power of Confessions of Cruelty." *Postmodern Culture* 11.3 (2001). Accessed July 27, 2001. http://muse.jhu.edu/journals/postmodern_culture/v011/11.3knox.html.

Kooijman, Jaap, and Tarja Laine. "*American Psycho*: A Double Portrait of Serial Yuppie Patrick Bateman." *Post Script* 22.3 (2003): 46–56.

Kolker, Robert Philip. *A Cinema of Loneliness*. 3rd ed. New York: Oxford University Press, 2000.

Kowalewski, Michael. *Deadly Musings: Violence and Verbal Form in American Fiction*. Princeton: Princeton University Press, 1993.

LaCapra, Dominick. *History and Memory after Auschwitz*. Ithaca: Cornell University Press, 1998.

———. "Trauma, Absence, Loss." *Critical Inquiry* 25 (Summer 1999): 696–724.

Lambert, Gregg. *The Non-Philosophy of Gilles Deleuze*. New York: Continuum, 2002.

LaMotta, Jake. *Raging Bull: My Story*. With Joseph Carter and Peter Savage. New York: Da Capo Press, 1997.

Landsberg, Alison. *Prosthetic Memory: The Transformation of American Remembrance in the Age of Mass Culture*. New York: Columbia University Press, 2004.

Lane, Anthony. "To the Limit." Rev. of *American Psycho*, dir. Mary Harron. *New Yorker* April 17, 2000:124–25.

Lebeau, Vicky. *Lost Angeles: Psychoanalysis and Cinema*. New York: Routledge, 1995.

Lecercle, Jean-Jacques. *Deleuze and Language*. Houndmills: Palgrave Macmillan, 2002.

Lehmann-Haupt, Christopher. "'Psycho': Whither Death without Life" Rev. of *American Psycho*, by Bret Easton Ellis. *New York Times* March 11, 1991:C18.

Levinas, Emanuel. *Otherwise Than Being, or Beyond Essence*. Trans. Alphonso Lingis. The Hague: Martinus Nijhoff, 1981.

———. *Totality and Infinity*. Trans. Alphonso Lingis. Pittsburgh: Duquesne University Press, 1969.

Lotringer, Sylvère. "Doing Theory." *French Theory in America*. Ed. Sylvère Lotringer. New York: Routledge, 2001. 125–62.

Lyotard, Jean-François. *The Inhuman*. Stanford: Stanford University Press, 1991.

Maerker, Christa. "Ich liebe Klarheit: Über Patricia Highsmith." *Horen* 38.4 (1993): 146–53.

Mailer, Norman. "Children of the Pied Piper." *Vanity Fair* March 1991:154–59.

Mann, Paul. *Masocriticism*. Albany: SUNY Press, 1999.

Margulies, Ivone, ed. *Rites of Realism: Essays on Corporeal Cinema*. Durham: Duke University Press, 2003.

Maslin, Janet. "Stealing a New Life: Carnal, Glamorous, and Worth the Price." Rev. of *The Talented Mr. Ripley*, dir. Anthony Minghella. *New York Times* December 24, 1999:E1.

Massumi, Brian. *Parables for the Virtual: Movement, Affect, Sensation*. Durham: Duke University Press, 2002.

McGowan, Todd, and Sheila Kunkle, eds. *Lacan and Contemporary Film*. New York: Other Press, 2004.

Mean Streets. Dir. Martin Scorsese. 1973. DVD. Warner Bros., 1998.

Meet the Fockers. Dir. Jay Roach. 2004. DVD. Universal, 2005.

Meet the Parents. Dir. Jay Roach. 2000. VHS. Universal, 2001.

Menand, Louis. "Methods and Madness." *Perspectives on Raging Bull*. Ed. Steven G. Kellman. New York: G. K. Hall, 1994. 60–68.

Miller's Crossing. Dir. Joel Coen. 1990. VHS. 20th Century Fox, 1991.

Muckelbauer, John. "Sophistic Travel: Inheriting the Simulacrum through Plato's 'The Sophist.'" *Philosophy and Rhetoric* 34.3 (2001): 225–44.

Mulvey, Laura. "Visual Pleasure and Narrative Cinema." *Movies and Methods*. Ed. Bill Nichols. Vol. 2. Berkeley: University of California Press, 1985. 303–14.

Naremore, James. *Acting in the Cinema*. Berkeley: University of California Press, 1990.

Nealon, Jeffrey T. *Alterity Politics: Ethics and Performative Subjectivity*. Durham: Duke University Press, 1998.

———. *Double Reading: Postmodernism after Deconstruction*. Ithaca: Cornell University Press, 1993.

———. "Maxima Immoralia? Speed and Slowness in Adorno's *Minima Moralia*." *Theory and Event* 4.3 (2000). Accessed September 13, 2000. http://muse.jhu.edu/journals/theory_&_event/v004/4.3nealon.html.

Nesbitt, Nick. "Deleuze, Adorno, and the Composition of Musical Multiplicity." *Deleuze and Music*. Ed. Ian Buchanan and Marcel Swiboda. Edinburgh: Edinburgh University Press, 2004. 54–75.

———. "The Expulsion of the Negative: Deleuze, Adorno, and the Ethics of Internal Difference." *Substance* 34.2 (2005): 75–97.

Ngai, Sianne. "Stuplimity: Shock and Boredom in Twentieth-Century Aesthetics." *Postmodern Culture* 10.2 (2000). Accessed April 13, 2000. http://muse.jhu.edu/journals/postmodern_culture/v010/10.2ngai.html.

Nietzsche, Friedrich. *The Genealogy of Morals and Ecce Homo*. Trans. Walter Kaufmann and R. J. Hollingdale. New York: Vintage, 1989.

———. "On the Uses and Disadvantages of History for Life." *Untimely Meditations*. Ed. Daniel Braezale. Oxford: Cambridge University Press, 1997. 59–123.

———. "On Truth and Lying in the Extra-Moral Sense." *Friedrich Nietzsche on Rhetoric and Language*. Ed. Sander Gilman. Oxford: Oxford University Press, 1989. 246–57.

The Norton Anthology of English Literature. 6th ed. Vol. 2. New York: W. W. Norton, 1993.

Palmer, R. Barton. *Joel and Ethan Coen*. Urbana: University of Illinois Press, 2004.

Patton, Paul. *Deleuze and the Political*. New York: Routledge, 2000.

Plagens, Peter. "Confessions of a Serial Killer." Rev. of *American Psycho*, by Bret Easton Ellis. *Newsweek* March 4, 1991: 58–59.

Powers, Richard. "The Image." *New York Times Magazine* September 23, 2001: 21–22.

Price, David W. "Bakhtinian Prosaics, Grotesque Realism, and the Question of the Carnivalesque in Bret Easton Ellis's *American Psycho*." *Southern Humanities Review* 32.4 (1998): 321–46.

Prince, Stephen. "Psychoanalytic Film Theory and the Problem of the Missing Spectator." Bordwell and Carroll 71–86.

———. *Savage Cinema: Sam Peckinpah and the Rise of Ultraviolent Movies*. Austin: University of Texas, 1998.

———, ed. *Screening Violence*. New Brunswick: Rutgers University Press, 2000.

———. "True Lies: Perceptual Realism, Digital Images, and Film Theory." *Film Quarterly* 49.3 (1996): 27–37.

———. "Why Do Film Scholars Ignore Movie Violence?" *Chronicle of Higher Education* August 10, 2001:B18, 19.

Protevi, John. *Political Physics*. New York: The Athlone Press, 2001.

Pynchon, Thomas. *Gravity's Rainbow*. New York: Penguin, 1987.

Rafferty, Terrence. "Fear and Trembling." *New Yorker* January 4, 1988:74–76.

Raging Bull. Dir. Martin Scorsese. 1980. DVD. MGM, 2000.

Rajchman, John. *The Deleuze Connection*. Cambridge: MIT Press, 2000.

Ravetto, Kriss. "Frenchifying Film Studies." *French Theory in America*. Ed. Sylvère Lotringer and Sande Cohen. New York: Routledge, 2001. 237–58.

Rayns, Tony. Rev. of *American Psycho*, dir. Mary Harron. *Sight and Sound* May 2000:42.

Rich, Frank. "American Pseudo." *New York Times* December 12, 1999: Magazine Desk.

Robinson, David. "The Unattainable Narrative: Identity, Consumerism, and the Slasher Film in Mary Harron's *American Psycho*." *CineAction* 68 (2006): 26–35.

Rodowick, D. N. *Gilles Deleuze's Time Machine*. Durham: Duke University Press, 1997.

Rosen, Philip. *Change Mummified: Cinema, Historicity, Theory*. Minneapolis: University of Minnesota Press, 2001.

Rosenblatt, Roger. "Snuff This Book! Will Bret Easton Ellis Get Away with Murder?" Rev. of *American Psycho*, by Bret Easton Ellis. *New York Times Book Review* December 16, 1990:7, 3.

Rothkopf, Joshua. "No Jacket Required." Rev. of *American Psycho*, dir. Mary Harron. *In These Times* May 15, 2000:24–25.

Rothman, William. "Violence and Film." Slocum, *Violence in American Cinema* 37–46.

Rushton, Richard. "What Can a Face Do? On Deleuze and Faces." *Cultural Critique* 51 (2002): 219–37.

Sartre, Jean-Paul. *Les Jeux Sont Faits*. Paris: Nagel, 1966.

Saturday Night Live. "Weekend Update." NBC, October 14, 2000.

———. "Weekend Update." NBC, October 21, 2000.

Scanlan, Margaret. "Writers among Terrorists: Don DeLillo's *Mao II* and the Rushdie Affair." *Modern Fiction Studies* 40.2 (1994): 229–52.

Scharrett, Christopher, ed. *Mythologies of Violence in Postmodern Media*. Detroit: Wayne State University Press, 1999.

Schatz, Thomas. Introduction. Schneider 1–10.

Schneider, Steven Jay, ed. *New Hollywood Violence*. Manchester: Manchester University Press, 2004.

Schomp, Caroline. "Denver: Ground Zero in Gun Debate." *Denver Post* April 22, 1999:B11.

Shaviro, Steven. *The Cinematic Body*. Minneapolis: University of Minnesota Press, 1991.

Shore, Robert. "Screen: The Talented Ms. Highsmith." *The Guardian* January 28, 2000. Accessed August 10, 2002. http://film.guardian.co.uk/Feature_Story/feature_story/0,4120,129496,00.htm.

Silverman, Kaja. "Masochism and Male Subjectivity." *Camera Obscura* 17 (May 1988): 31–66.

———. "Masochism and Subjectivity." *Framework* 12 (1980): 2–9.

———. *World Spectators*. Stanford: Stanford University Press, 2000.

Simmons, Ryan. "What Is a Terrorist? Contemporary Authorship, the Unabomber, and *Mao II*." *Modern Fiction Studies* 45.3 (1999): 675–95.

Slack, Jennifer Daryl, ed. *Animations (of Deleuze and Guattari)*. New York: Peter Lang, 2003.

Slocum, David. "Cinema and the Civilizing Process: Rethinking Violence in the World War II Combat Film." *Cinema Journal* 44.3 (2005): 35–63.

———. "Film Violence and the Institutionalization of Cinema." *Social Research* 67.3 (2000): 649–82.

———. "The 'Film Violence' Trope: New Hollywood, 'the Sixties,' and the Politics of History." Schneider 13–33.

———, ed. *Violence in American Cinema*. New York: Routledge, 2001.

Slotkin, Richard. *Regeneration through Violence: The Mythology of the American Frontier, 1600–1860*. Middletown: Wesleyan University Press, 1973.

Smith, Gavin. Rev. of *American Psycho*, dir. Mary Harron. *Film Comment* 36.2 (2000): 72.

Sobchack, Vivian. *The Address of the Eye: A Phenomenology of Film Experience*. Princeton: Princeton University Press, 1992.

Sotirin, Patty. "Suckling Up to the BWO." Slack 59–74.

Spencer, Nicholas. *After Utopia: The Rise of Critical Space in Twentieth-Century American Fiction*. Lincoln: University of Nebraska Press, 2006.

Spiegelman, Art. *In the Shadow of No Towers*. New York: Pantheon Books, 2004.

Staiger, Janet. *Perverse Spectators: The Practice of Film Reception*. New York: NYU Press, 2000.

Stein, Michael Eric. "The New Violence, or Twenty Years of Violence in Films: An Appreciation." *Films in Review* 46.1 (1995): 40–48.

———. "The New Violence, or Twenty Years of Violence in Films: An Appreciation (Part Two)." *Films in Review* 46.2 (1995): 14–21.

Stiles, Todd. "How Bret Ellis Turned Michael Korda into Larry Flint." Rev. of *American Psycho*, by Bret Eaton Ellis. *Spy* December 1990:43.

Stivale, Charles. *Disenchanting Les Bons Temps: Identity and Authenticity in Cajun Music and Dance.* Durham: Duke University Press, 2002.

Studlar, Gaylyn. "Masochism and the Perverse Pleasures of the Cinema." *Movies and Methods.* Ed. Bill Nichols. Vol. 2. Berkeley: University of California Press, 1985. 602–21.

Stuhr, John J. *Pragmatism, Postmodernism, and the Future of Philosophy.* New York: Routledge, 2002.

Symons, Julian. "Verbrecher in der Gesellschaft." Cavigelli, Senn, and von Planta 142–54.

The Talented Mr. Ripley. Dir. Anthony Minghella. 1999. DVD. Paramount Pictures, 2000.

Taubin, Amy. *Taxi Driver.* London: BFI, 2000.

Taxi Driver. Dir. Martin Scorsese. 1976. DVD. Columbia Pictures, 2000.

Taylor, Ella. "The 5,000-Pound Maus." *LA Weekly* November 13–19, 1998. Accessed February 6, 2002. http://www.laweekly.com/artbooks/art/the-5000-maus/7508.

Teachout, Terry. "Applied Deconstruction." Rev. of *American Psycho*, by Bret Easton Ellis. *National Review* June 24, 1991:45–46.

Thomson, David. "Without Them, Mr. Ripley Would Be a Nobody." *New York Times* December 19, 1999, Arts and Leisure, sect. 2:17.

Toole, David. "Of Lingering Eyes and Talking Things: Adorno and Deleuze on Philosophy Since Auschwitz." *Philosophy Today* 37.3 (1993): 227–46.

Travers, Peter. Rev. of *American Psycho*, dir. Mary Harron. *Rolling Stone* April 27, 2000:79–80.

Two or Three Things I Know about Her. Dir. Jean-Luc Godard. 1966. DVD. Nouveaux Pictures, 2005.

Udovitch, Mim. "Intentional Phalluses." Rev. of *American Psycho*, by Bret Easton Ellis. *Village Voice* March 19, 1991:65–66.

Ulmer, Gregory. *Heuristics: The Logic of Invention.* Baltimore: John Hopkins University Press, 1994.

U.S. Department of State. Embassy of the United States, Seoul, Republic of South Korea. Accessed July 25, 2005. http://seoul.usembassy.gov/.

Virilio, Paul. *The Aesthetics of Disappearance.* Trans. Philip Beitchman. New York: Semiotext(e), 1991.

———. *Ground Zero*. Trans. Chris Turner. New York: Verso, 2002.

———. *War and Cinema: The Logistics of Perception*. Trans. Patrick Camiller. New York: Verso, 1999.

Weldon, Fay. "Now You're Squeamish?" Rev. of *American Psycho*, by Bret Easton Ellis. *Washington Post* April 28, 1991: C1, 4.

Wilson, Andrews. *Beautiful Shadow: A Life of Patricia Highsmith*. New York: Bloomsbury, 2003.

Wise, J. Macgregor. *Exploring Technology and Social Space*. New York: Sage, 1997.

Young, Elizabeth. "The Beast in the Jungle, the Figure in the Carpet: Bret Easton Ellis, *American Psycho*." *Shopping in Space: Essays on America's Blank Generation Fiction*. By Elizabeth Young and Graham Caveney. New York: Atlantic Monthly Press, 1993. 85–122.

Zacharek, Stephanie. Rev. of *Down in the Valley* by David Jacobson. *Salon* May 5, 2006. Accessed July 3, 2006. http://www.salon.com/ent/movies/review/2006/05/05/down/index.html.

Žižek, Slavoj. "An Ethical Plea for Lies and Masochism." McGowan and Kunkle 173–86.

———. *Organs without Bodies: On Deleuze and Consequences*. New York: Routledge, 2004.

———. "Philosopher, Cultural Critic, and Cyber-Communist." Interview with Gary A. Olson and Lynn Worsham. *JAC* 21.2 (2001): 255–86.

———. *The Sublime Object of Ideology*. New York: Verso, 1994.

———. "Welcome to the Desert of the Real." *Re:constructions: Reflections on Humanity and Media after Tragedy*. September 15, 2001. Accessed March 1, 2002. http://web.mit.edu/cms/reconstructions/interpretations/desertreal.html.

Index

Abel, Marco, 253n16

acting: language of, 140–41; as mimetic procedure, 144; as a practice of imagining, 111; technique of, 161

Acting in the Cinema (Naremore), 135

acting out, 140, 142, 144–45, 157–63, 166; Method mode of, 171; mirror scene shows, 249n15; moral quality of, 167; and repetition, 169, 170; as violence, 143; and working through, 179

Actors Studio, 148, 150, 248n9

adaptations, cinematic, 31

Adler, Stella, 147, 148, 151, 152, 154; conception of acting of, 158; and influence on DeNiro, 166

Adorno, Theodor, xiv, 198, 209, 210, 238n14, 245n28; chiasmic style of, 253n15; and negative dialectic, 220–21; and poetry after Auschwitz, 212–13

"aesthetic realism," 146

Aesthetics of Disappearance (Virilio), 256n34

affect, 6, 7, 224; as cliché, 54; as constitutive attribute, 234n27; as crucial force, 93;

definition of, 11, 57; and emotion, 238n12; as force of difference, 85; and intensity, 41; as main force, 74; as means of articulation, 47; as nonanthropomorphic, 249n12; as response to traumatic events, 141; violence as, 119, 173; vocabulary of, 48; waning of, 50

"affective memory," 147, 148, 149

Akin, Fatih, 249n13

algorithm: methodological, 19; pedagogical, 19

Ali (Mann), 251n22

Allegories of Reading (de Man), 64

The Alphabet Man (Grossman), 203, 254n19

al-Quaeda, plotting of, 202

alterity, 26

Altman, Rick, 243n14

Amateur (Hartley), 151

America, violence in, 133–34

Americana (DeLillo), 253n9

American Psycho (book) (Ellis), xvi, xvii, 29, 230n1, 248n7; critical discourse about, 31, 33, 57; forces of violence in, 71; hatred of, 38, 87; immorality of, 39; and representation, 27; satire of, 40; as sequence of masks, 83; shock of, 72